Savor the Moment

Entertaining Without Reservations

The Junior League of Boca Raton

Guest of Honor: E. M. Lynn Foundation

Savor the Moment

Entertaining Without Reservations

The Junior League of Boca Raton

Photography by Dan Forer

Savor the Moment

Copyright © 2000
by the Junior League of Boca Raton, Inc.

Photographs Copyright ©1999
by the Junior League of Boca Raton, Inc.

To obtain additional copies of
Savor the Moment
in printed or CD-ROM format, use the order form
at the back of this book or contact:

Junior League of Boca Raton
261 N.W. 13th Street
Boca Raton, Florida 33432
Telephone: (561) 620-2553
Facsimile: (561) 620-2554
Toll free: 1-866-574-9229
E-Mail: cookbook@jlbr.org
Website: www.jlbr.org

Edited, Designed, and Manufactured by
Favorite Recipes Press
An imprint of FRP
P. O. Box 305142, Nashville, Tennessee 37230
First Printing: 2000   20,000 copies
Second Printing: 2000   20,000 copies
Third Printing: 2005   10,000 copies

Book Design: Steve Newman

Library of Congress Catalog Number: 99-095381
Cookbook ISBN: 0-9670944-0-2
Cookbook/CD-ROM ISBN: 0-9670944-2-9
Cookbook UPC: 693056-00001

The Junior League of Boca Raton, Inc. is an organization
of women committed to promoting voluntarism, developing
the potential of women, and improving the community through
effective action and leadership of trained volunteers. Its purpose is
exclusively educational and charitable.

The Junior League of Boca Raton reaches out to women of
all races, religions, and national origins who demonstrate
an interest in and commitment to voluntarism.

All proceeds from the sale of **Savor the Moment** will
benefit the community and the charitable activities of the Junior
League of Boca Raton.

PHOTOGRAPHY: DAN FORER
FOOD STYLING: PATTY FORRESTEL, ASSISTED BY JOESY MISSIMER
NON-RECIPE TEXT: MARY DOYLE KIMBALL
FLORAL DESIGNS: BOCA BY DESIGN
GRAPHICS CONSULTING: TINSLEY ADVERTISING
MULTI-MEDIA PRODUCTION: CENTRAL DYNAMICS CORPORATION
CD-ROM FOOD PHOTOGRAPHY: DARCY PLIMPTON-SIMS
CD-ROM VOICE OVER: ROXANNE STEIN

Cover Photograph: Barefoot Elegance at Boca Raton's beachfront South Inlet Park. (See pages 210 and 211)
Title Page Photograph: East Meets West at Delray Beach's Morikami Park. (See pages 232 and 233)

Printed in China

Invited Guests

We would like to raise our glasses and thank the Special People and Companies that came to the table and generously supported the Junior League of Boca Raton in our cookbook endeavor to help the community.

Guest of Honor
E. M. Lynn Foundation

Premier Guest
Boca Raton Resort & Club

Regal Guests
Sun-Sentinel
Premier Beverage Company
Boca Raton Community Hospital

Titled Guest
Boca Raton Magazine

Majestic Guests
Boca by Design
Tyco International (USA), Inc.

Noble Guests
Northern Trust Bank
Allied Domecq Spirits USA

Distinguished Guests
Aim Riverside Press
Aldrich Party Rental
Arvida Realty Services
Bombay Sapphire by Bacardi
Carls Furniture
Digital City South Florida
Korbel Champagne Cellars
Office Depot
The Perfect Setting of Boca Raton
Mr. and Mrs. William S. Reiling
Mr. and Mrs. David W. Roberts
Rutherford, Mulhall & Wargo, P. A.
Robert Sheetz

Table of Contents

Celebration Classics
As Time Goes By

Celebration Classics
Wedding in a Secret Garden

Celebration Classics
A Yankee Doodle Dandy Day

Appetizers Beverages
Casting Off the Day

Breads Breakfasts
French Country Charm

Thank You for Coming

Dear Reader:

Thank you for supporting the community projects of the Junior League of Boca Raton by buying this book.

The Junior League of Boca Raton's unwavering commitment to the community has elevated our volunteer organization to new heights. Based on focus areas determined by our membership, we address needs in our community from start to finish. Following meticulous research, we use grant-writing skills, corporate and private underwriting solicitations, and membership-based fund-raisers to provide the funding to open the doors of our projects. We oversee start-up operations and select board members from our community and membership. We use volunteer hours to launch and maintain our projects. The Junior League of Boca Raton finds long-term solutions to community needs.

We are committed to making our community a better place to live, work, and play. By purchasing this cookbook, you have assisted us in providing daycare for one more farmworker family while they are working in the fields; diapers, hugs, medicine, and shelter for one more abused child; or staples, canned goods, and basic groceries for one more family who can't make ends meet.

We are grateful for your participation in our projects through your purchase of *Savor the Moment*. We thoroughly enjoyed creating it, and we hope it brings you many moments to savor as well.

Bon Appetit!

The Membership of the Junior League of Boca Raton, Inc.

Celebrating Every Day

There's an art to celebrating the everyday things—to gathering special friends and family, to creating a memorable setting, and to transforming a collection of recipes into a special occasion. *Savor the Moment* illustrates the art of entertaining without reservations by putting all of the ingredients for your next special moment right at your fingertips while bringing you a taste of Florida and a cuisine from the world over.

Boca Raton á la carte

Once a sleepy little town midway between Palm Beach and Fort Lauderdale, Boca Raton is now a sea of entertaining activity 70,000 people strong. Here, the air is clear, the sky is sapphire blue, and the sand glows like crystal in the sun. Palm trees sway in the breeze, pine and ficus tree canopies cover waterfront parks and old front yards, and the ocean surf is a constant, both invigorating the body and calming the mind.

People here bring something unique to the table when entertaining friends, giving of themselves to create a sterling moment. South Floridians pull from northern traditions and southern hospitality with equal grace. The cultures of three continents and a myriad of countries meet at our crossroads along the ocean.

Boca Raton is a place dotted with pink birthday-cake buildings, Mediterranean style á la mode, mixed with Bermuda and California. There's a taste of the sea in the air, and colors are lighter and happier all year round. Antiques are more likely to be covered in cotton than velvet and mixed with world-class contemporary art.

While visitors will say this is a land with no seasons, residents have a rhythm that moves with the changes of a tropical beat. Thanksgiving begins the social season. People step up their desire to entertain in grand style as they partake of a full cultural schedule of events that come to the area.

Sometime in Spring the beach beckons. The water temperature quickly rises to 80 degrees and will go beyond soon. This is the time for picnics and casual cocktail parties, a time to savor the weather we are so fortunate to enjoy and are about to wave on.

Summer arrives and lasts all the way through Halloween. It's a time to get up very early to play golf and tennis, ride bikes, or jog. When having a party at this time of year, we just add water to the menu of activities. This is the time to watch the sunrise at the beach and never get chilled. This is a season to live in the pool.

Around September, people talk of the tiniest breeze in the evening. They are sure it was cooler when they got up in the morning, even if it was only by one degree. Light bites rather than five courses still suit.

Welcome to Boca Raton.

Show Your Style

In *Savor the Moment* we designed and photographed a series of parties at some of our most eye-catching landmarks. We'll tell you about the inspiration for the party, the mood, accessories, table settings, and menu. We cover the invitation and any afterglow ideas, as well.

And most importantly, we'll tell you how to adapt the party to your lifestyle, or where else you can hold a moveable feast like it and still keep the spirit.

Each chapter opener is a place to dream, designed to herald you on to new heights in entertaining. We take you into the minds of our hostesses, really a composite of dozens of the best party givers we've interviewed.

The excitement of this endeavor is about inspiring you to look at everything you own with a new eye and do the unexpected with it. Chapter openers cover simple ideas, such as using edible flowers on a cake, putting a veil of organdy over a tablecloth for a special occasion, and bringing out a collection of antique silver or crystal to fill up the white space between the centerpiece and the candelabra. Some ideas need more planning, like dipping silver spoons in chocolate and giving them as party favors, or sending a message in a bottle as your invitation to a treasure hunt buffet on the beach.

We'll take you on location: aboard a yacht, by a waterfall, playing croquet and watching the fireworks, overlooking a secret garden pool, on the polo fields, inside a tiled courtyard, under a beachside gazebo, downtown, out to breakfast, and through the massive doors of the ultimate dining room.

Sidebars are sprinkled throughout the chapters, and spotlight tidbits of fun information from detailed party planning tips to a slice of life in the history of our landmarks and traditions, all sunny side up.

The more than 300 recipes in the book have been tested multiple times for ease of execution, reliability of results, and aesthetic presentation. More than 400 great cooks, including dozens of professional chefs and caterers, have opened their kitchen doors to tell their secrets.

In our Resource section, you'll find wonderful sources for goods and services to help your entertaining reach new heights. We hope you'll call on them whenever you can. They have been a tremendous help to the Junior League of Boca Raton.

More At Your Fingertips

Savor the Moment is also available in a special CD-ROM version that includes everything in this book, plus photographs of every single recipe, and more! Take it with you to the office and print out that night's dinner recipe, before you head to the market on your way home! It's a great addition to your computer library.

Our hope with *Savor the Moment* is that you will be tempted to cook something new and use something old in a novel way. Perhaps you'll serve Firecracker Chile Cheese Pie (page 42) or Persian Chicken Sandwich (page 141) at your picnics, fill the crystal vase with French bread instead of flowers, decorate with leaves and fruit as coasters when you barbecue, buy some Italian music and Chianti bottles when serving lasagne, or grow your own miniature "lawn" for a picnic on the balcony.

In the end, the emphasis is on having a great time picking a theme, finding a focal point, and reinforcing it wherever you can—at the entry, in the serving areas, and on the dining tables; with fabric, great finds, flowers, candles, and, of course, a fabulous array of delicious food. Look around and use what you have. Go for the maximum effect. Just one idea magnified over and over can make the difference.

From our homes to yours, *Savor the Moment* by celebrating every day and experience the joy of entertaining without reservations; it's all worth the effort.

Celebration Classics

As Time Goes By

Ten, nine, eight, seven, six—stop the clocks—all of them! Listen as your friends count down the seconds to midnight. Noise makers in hand and champagne flutes poised to toast in the New Year; the band is ready to play "Auld Lang Syne." Laughter echoes in the trees.

The night is young, some people are still arriving from other parties. But you've made this "the" place to be just before the clock strikes twelve. The center of town—here, it's Boca Raton's historic Old Town Hall at Sanborne Square—finds your favorite friends under the stars, and dancing in the night air. It doesn't get any better. A new tradition, spawned from years of watching Guy Lombardo and Dick Clark as the ball dropped in New York's Times Square. Why not be out and about in your own town?

Let's turn the clock back to the beginning of this party. The jewel in this collection is the sterling silver cooler designed to hold two bottles of champagne in the center and eight bottles of wine around the perimeter. Not only is this the entry focal point of the party—every memorable occasion has one—but it's also the ice breaker. The hostess has arranged a wine and champagne tasting for her guests. Cleanse the palate with a little caviar on diamond toast points and taste some more.

Since time won't tell, go see the soothsayer and her crystal ball. She has tarot cards and can read your palm. A smoke machine billows into the open air while "Smoke Gets in Your Eyes" is played. That's the one everyone dances to; it's a moment for romance, a touch of nostalgia.

Guests feel the excitement in the air the moment they arrive at this very special New Year's Eve Celebration. The clocks count down to midnight all around them, against a backdrop of Boca Raton's historic Old Town Hall.

Mix it up with Bette Midler's "Boogie Woogie Bugle Boy" and "In the Mood." What are your favorites? Write them down in the order you'll want them played. Make the most of live music. Ask people for their requests in the invitation, and let the band leader announce, "This one's for our friend, Cindy."

Now the chimes are letting you know dinner is being served exactly on time—ten o'clock according to the Ralph Lauren chargers which add to the timely theme. Next to the plates are the clever tuxedo napkins arranged in a regular tie shape with three black dots and a black bow tie at the "neck" for an easy way to dress up the linens.

The top hat and chilled champagne-shaped salt and pepper shakers are an excellent party favor for each guest. Or like this hostess, you could give away the elegant crystal bottle stoppers used to hold the place cards at each table.

Exploring Subtle Differences

Notice that each centerpiece is different. There's a sparkling gold top hat and candle at one table, and a mask or two along with the hurricane candle holders at another. While it's important to carry out the theme by repeating choices, each item does not have to match, just coordinate.

Distinguish the champagne table with six squares of gold fabric, folded into triangles. Masking tape will hold each in place, as well as the gold and black tassels.

The topper for the serving table is an amber-colored mirror with hand-stamped gold diamonds. In this case, the hostess hand stamped diamonds all around the perimeter of the table and then filled them in with more gold paint because the surface was so slick. She used acrylic paint, which a good window cleaner can remove in no time, readying the mirror for the next occasion's creative theme.

Details on the serving table enhance the theme of the party. The hostess found a clever way to display the menu using a picture frame that blends with her design theme. Here she chose mother of pearl and onyx. To dress it further, she glued ribbon around the edges.

This hostess did not miss a beat when it came to entertainment. In addition to the live dance music, as dessert was being served, a magician appeared for a few magical moments. Soon it was time for more dancing, and the clocks began ticking again toward midnight...

A Change of Heart

Keep the colors and the clock theme for an elegant 40th or 50th birthday party. A little gilding and black silk is much more fun than black crepe! The diamonds work well for a 50th wedding anniversary. Exchange gold for silver for a 25th anniversary.

Switch the colors to red and white with a splash of pink, change the diamonds to hearts, and this party is ready for Valentine's Day. What about the pitter-patter of little feet for a baby shower or the leaves of Fall?

Think of the symbols you associate with the occasion to be celebrated. You'll have a good list in five minutes if you brainstorm with a friend. Invest in a glass tabletop to store on its side in the garage to provide a changeable canvas for a variety of designs.

Setting the Scene

The invitation is the calling card for the mood of the party. While it is always nice to receive the traditional cream and gold stock with black calligraphy, some parties naturally lend themselves to a touch of whimsy.

For this timely theme consider sending everyone a watch stopped at the exact date and time of the party, along with your note to save the date. The watches could be housed in elegant gold and black boxes with a scroll invitation beside them. You'll never get another chance to make a good first impression about your party again. So seize the moment!

The entrée is an elegant Lattice Salmon with Tomato Coulis and Spinach Sauce (page 22) on a glass plate atop a Ralph Lauren clock charger. Top hat and champagne salt and pepper shakers, and tuxedo napkins, also dress the dining tables for New Year's Eve.

Menu

*Pictured recipes

A New Year's Wish

*"What better wish can be given
you than that in the coming year
you may never lose an old friend,
but gain many new; that you
may never do an unkindness, for
which you may be sorry; that while
God's sunshine is upon you, then
will not be forgotten the blessing
of it. That when clouds arrive, you
will think with joy of the possibility
of sunshine; and that on the gay
opening day of the year, you will
remember 'If all the year were
playing holidays, To sport
would be as tedious as work.'"*
The Delineator, 1882.

Spicy Oysters with Mango Dip

A delectable pearl from the sea.

Oysters
2 cups bread crumbs
2 cups flour
2 teaspoons curry powder
1 tablespoon paprika
1 teaspoon white pepper
1 quart Florida oysters
3 cups vegetable oil

Mango Dip
1 cup puréed mango
1 cup sour cream
$^1/_2$ cup honey
$1^1/_2$ teaspoons salt

For the oysters, combine the bread crumbs, flour, curry powder, paprika and pepper in a bowl. Drain the oysters and coat with the bread crumb mixture. Heat the oil in a skillet to 350 degrees. Add the oysters and fry until golden brown.

For the dip, combine the mango, sour cream, honey and salt in a bowl and mix well. Chill until serving time. Serve with the oysters.

Serves eight to ten

Ginger Chicken Rumaki

Be prepared to double this recipe.

12 ounces boneless skinless
   chicken breasts
$^1/_4$ cup orange marmalade
2 teaspoons soy sauce
1 garlic clove, minced

$^1/_2$ teaspoon ground ginger
12 slices bacon
1 (8-ounce) can whole water
   chestnuts, cut into halves

Cut the chicken into 24 bite-size pieces. Combine the marmalade, soy sauce, garlic and ginger in a bowl and mix well. Add the chicken and stir to coat well. Marinate, covered, in the refrigerator for 30 minutes; drain.

Broil the bacon for 1 to 2 minutes or until partially cooked but not crisp; drain and cut into halves crosswise. Wrap 1 piece of bacon around each chicken piece and a water chestnut half; secure with wooden picks.

Broil 4 to 5 inches from the heat source for 3 to 5 minutes or until the chicken is cooked through.

Serves eight

This silver nautilus cooler by Cazenovia adds a new twist to classic Korbel Champagne at this toasting table. Swirls of wire ribbon complement the airy designs of the candelabra, as well as the nautilus shape of the cooler and the graceful champagne flutes. Notice that the roses do not have to stand on end to be dramatic. This Baccarat diva vase is the easiest path to an elegant arrangement. Between sets, guests are encouraged to come up and toast a friend at the party. Cheers! And, Bon Appetit!

When in Rome

In ancient Rome, the first day of the year honored Janus, the god of gates and doors–endings and beginnings. Revelers in every country have added their own festive customs to this celebration. The English and the Swiss make merry with masks and costumes. Some cultures believe that the New Year should be given physical help, and beat out the old year with sticks and bells. The Chinese celebrate with fireworks. The Austrians and Germans toot in the New Year with trumpets and fanfare. The Dutch invite everybody for an open house. The Scots ring out the old year with strains of Robert Burns' "Auld Lang Syne."

Lemon Grass Turkey Bites

One bite is never enough!

1 pound ground turkey
1 cup fine fresh bread crumbs
3 tablespoons minced tender inner portion of lemon grass,
    about 1 stalk
3 tablespoons minced fresh mint
3 tablespoons minced fresh basil
2 tablespoons grated onion
1 large garlic clove, minced
1$\frac{1}{2}$ teaspoons olive oil
1 large egg, lightly beaten
$\frac{1}{2}$ teaspoon salt
vegetable oil

Combine the turkey, bread crumbs, lemon grass, mint, basil, onion, garlic, olive oil, egg and salt in a bowl and mix well. Shape into 1$\frac{1}{4}$-inch balls; place on a tray.

Heat $\frac{1}{2}$ inch vegetable oil in a large skillet over medium heat until hot but not smoking. Add the turkey bites in batches and fry for 3 to 5 minutes or until cooked through, shaking the skillet gently to brown evenly.

Remove to paper towels with a slotted spoon to drain. Place in a baking dish and keep warm in a 250-degree oven. Transfer to a serving dish and serve warm with Sweet and Hot Sauce (page 19).

Note: Lemon grass is available at Southeast Asian markets.
Serves eight

Sweet and Hot Sauce

Serve with Lemon Grass Turkey Bites or other appetizers.

2 tablespoons sesame oil
1 tablespoon minced gingerroot
1 tablespoon minced garlic
6 tablespoons cider vinegar
2 tablespoons rice wine vinegar
$^1/_4$ cup packed brown sugar
$^1/_2$ cup dark molasses

1 tablespoon dry sherry
$^1/_2$ cup soy sauce
2 tablespoons minced fresh red or green chiles
2 tablespoons cornstarch
$2^1/_2$ tablespoons cold water

Heat the sesame oil in a sauté pan over medium-high heat until hot but not smoking. Add the ginger and garlic and sauté for 2 to 3 minutes or until golden brown.

Add the cider vinegar, rice wine vinegar, brown sugar, molasses, sherry, soy sauce and chiles. Bring to a boil and reduce the heat. Simmer for 3 minutes, stirring frequently.

Whisk the cornstarch and cold water in a small bowl. Whisk into the simmering sauce and bring to a boil, whisking constantly. Simmer for 5 minutes longer, stirring frequently. Cool to room temperature.

Makes three cups

Caramelized Onion and Cheese Canapés

Satisfy your favorite onion lovers with this elegant addition to your cocktail party.

2 large red onions, thinly sliced
2 tablespoons olive oil
2 tablespoons brown sugar

2 tablespoons balsamic vinegar
24 ($^1/_4$-inch) round slices bread
12 ounces chèvre

Sauté the onions in the olive oil in a skillet over medium heat for 15 to 20 minutes or until light brown. Add the brown sugar. Sauté for 3 minutes. Add the vinegar and cook for 1 minute longer.

Arrange the bread slices on a baking sheet. Toast lightly in the oven. Spread the cheese on the bread and top each with the onion mixture.

Serves eight

Mark the Family Calendar

Unwrapping the new year's calendar just after a New Year's morning family breakfast is a tradition worth establishing. Mark special events of the year in red crayon or marker. Highlight birthdays, vacations, and holidays. This tradition will symbolize a fresh start for each family member and unite everyone in looking forward to special occasions together.

Keeping Strawberries Fresh

To keep strawberries fresh, arrange them in a single layer on a paper towel-lined plate and place them in the refrigerator. Wash and trim them just before serving.

Town and Country Salad

Add sliced grilled chicken for a main course luncheon.

Poppy Seed Dressing
^{1}/4 onion, grated
^{1}/2 cup sugar
^{1}/2 cup salad oil
^{1}/3 cup apple cider vinegar
1 teaspoon dry mustard
1^1/2 teaspoons poppy seeds

Caramelized Almonds
^{1}/2 cup slivered almonds
^{1}/4 cup sugar

Salad
romaine, Bibb or red leaf
lettuce, torn
strawberries, sliced
Brie cheese, cubed

For the dressing, combine the onion, sugar, half the oil and a small amount of the vinegar in a bowl and mix well. Add the remaining oil and vinegar gradually, mixing well. Stir in the dry mustard and poppy seeds. Chill until serving time.

For the almonds, combine the almonds with the sugar in a skillet. Cook over medium heat until the sugar melts and browns, stirring constantly. Spread on foil to cool.

For the salad, combine the lettuce, strawberries and cheese in a serving bowl. Add the dressing and toss to coat. Top with the almonds.

Note: Do not use double-cream Brie for this recipe.

Serves eight

Sahara Dates

Your guests will cross 100 miles of sand for these.

^{1}/2 cup finely chopped walnuts or
almonds
1 tablespoon unsalted butter
^{1}/2 cup bleu cheese, at room
temperature

^{1}/4 cup whipped cream cheese,
softened
coarse salt to taste
16 large dates

Sauté the walnuts in the butter in a skillet until light brown. Drain on a paper towel and set aside. Combine the bleu cheese, cream cheese and salt in a bowl and mix well. Cut the dates into halves, discarding the pits. Spoon the cheese mixture into the date halves. Sprinkle with the walnuts. Serve at room temperature.

Note: You may substitute whole pitted small dates for the large ones.

Serves eight

Corn Terrine with Red Bell Pepper Sauce

A very special vegetable with a creamy custard and vibrant color.

Terrine
2 large red bell peppers, seeded,
    coarsely chopped
1 tablespoon melted butter
kernels of 6 ears fresh corn, or
    2 (10-ounce) packages
    frozen corn, thawed
1 tablespoon butter
2 medium leeks, coarsely
    chopped
6 tablespoons (^{3}/$_4$ stick) butter
^{1}/$_4$ cup flour
1^1/$_2$ cups half-and-half, scalded
2^1/$_2$ teaspoons salt, or to taste
freshly ground pepper to taste
1 cup shredded very sharp
    Swiss cheese
6 eggs, beaten

^{1}/$_4$ cup dry bread crumbs

Red Bell Pepper Sauce
3 medium red bell peppers, cut
    into 1-inch pieces
1 tablespoon butter
2^3/$_4$ pounds tomatoes, peeled,
    seeded, chopped
6 extra-large fresh basil leaves
1 tablespoon butter
salt and pepper to taste

Garnish
fresh basil leaves

For the terrine, sauté the bell peppers in 1 tablespoon melted butter in a skillet over medium-low heat for 10 minutes or until tender. Combine with the corn in a large mixing bowl. Add 1 tablespoon butter and the leeks to the skillet and sauté for 6 minutes or until tender. Add to the corn mixture.

Melt 6 tablespoons butter in a heavy medium saucepan over medium-low heat. Add the flour and cook for 2 minutes, stirring constantly. Cool for 2 minutes. Whisk in the heated half-and-half. Simmer over medium heat for 3 minutes or until thickened, stirring constantly. Cool slightly. Add to the corn mixture. Stir in the salt, pepper, cheese and eggs.

Sprinkle the bread crumbs into a buttered 5x9-inch loaf pan, coating well. Spoon in the corn mixture. Place in a larger baking pan and add boiling water halfway up the sides of the loaf pan.

Bake at 325 degrees for 1^3/$_4$ hours or until the terrine is firm to the touch. Cool for 20 minutes.

For the sauce, sauté the bell peppers in 1 tablespoon butter in a heavy large skillet over medium-low heat for 10 minutes or until tender. Process in the food processor until smooth. Return to the skillet and add the tomatoes, basil and 1 tablespoon butter. Cook over medium heat for 45 minutes or until the liquid evaporates, stirring frequently. Season with salt and pepper.

Invert the terrine onto a serving platter. Spoon the sauce around the terrine. Garnish with basil.

Serves eight to ten

Popping the Cork

The best way to pop a cork on a bottle of champagne is to first make sure the bottle has been stationary for at least a couple of hours. This reduces the volatility of the carbonation, lessening the likelihood of the cork flying out when the bottle is opened. Hold the cork in place with one hand and, with the other hand, untwist the wire cage that secures the cork in the bottle. Rest the bottle on your hip, and twist the bottle slowly, while continuing to hold the cork in place. Ease the cork upward, applying gentle pressure to keep it from popping out and making sure that the bottle is not pointed toward anyone. To prevent accidents, wrap the top of the bottle in a towel.

A champagne bottle contains 750 milliliters. A split is ^{1}/$_4$ of a bottle. A magnum is 1^1/$_2$ bottles; a Jeroboam is 4 bottles; a Rehoboam is 6 bottles; a Methuselah or Imperial is 8 bottles; a Salmanazar is 12 bottles; a Balthazar is 16 bottles; and a Nebuchadnezzar is 20 bottles.

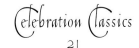

From their ancient Greek origins, toasts have long enjoyed an important place in international diplomacy. Herald the New Year with the ancient custom of drinking to "Your Good Health" in languages reflecting the heritage of family and friends:

American–Cheers
Russian–Na zdorovia
Chinese–Kan bei
French–A Votre Santé
Swedish–Sköal
German–Prosit
Spanish–Salud
Irish & Scottish–Slainte
Japanese–Kampai
Israeli–L'Chaim

Lattice Salmon with Tomato Coulis and Spinach Sauce

A beautiful salmon presentation.

Tomato Coulis
1 tablespoon unsalted butter
1/4 cup olive oil
2 large shallots, finely chopped
2 teaspoons tomato paste
1 1/2 pounds ripe tomatoes, peeled, seeded, chopped
1/2 teaspoon sugar
2 garlic cloves
1 bay leaf
salt and pepper to taste

Spinach Sauce
2 cups heavy cream
1 (10-ounce) package fresh spinach
2 garlic cloves, coarsely chopped
salt and pepper to taste

Salmon
4 pounds salmon fillets
salt and pepper to taste
1/4 cup (1/2 stick) melted butter

For the coulis, melt the butter with the olive oil in a heavy medium saucepan. Add the shallots and sauté for 3 minutes or until they begin to brown. Stir in the tomato paste. Reserve 2 tablespoons of the tomatoes for garnish. Add the remaining tomatoes and coulis ingredients to the saucepan. Simmer, covered, for 30 minutes, stirring frequently. Discard the garlic and bay leaf. Process the mixture in a blender until smooth. Return to the saucepan and heat over medium heat until thickened to the desired consistency. Adjust the seasoning.

For the spinach, cook the cream in a heavy medium saucepan over medium-high heat until slightly thickened and reduced. Reserve several small spinach leaves for garnish. Add the remaining spinach and garlic to the cream. Cook for 3 minutes or until the spinach is wilted and the cream coats the back of the spoon. Process the mixture in a blender until smooth. Return to the saucepan and season with salt and pepper. Keep warm.

For the salmon, cut the fillets into forty-eight 1/2x4-inch strips. Season with salt and pepper. Line a broiler pan with foil and grease the foil.

Weave 6 strips at a time into a lattice on the foil, using 3 strips horizontally and 3 strips vertically. Trim the ends even and secure the intersections with wooden picks that have been soaked in water. Brush with the melted butter. Broil without turning for 6 to 8 minutes or until cooked through.

To serve, spoon 2 tablespoons of the coulis on 1 side of each serving plate and 2 tablespoons of the spinach sauce on the other. Tip the plates to coat half with green, half with red. Lift each salmon lattice carefully with a wide spatula, blot on a paper towel and place in the center of each plate, discarding the wooden picks. Garnish with the reserved spinach leaves and chopped tomatoes.

Serves eight

White Chocolate Martini

A favorite nightcap with a lingering kiss of chocolate at Delray's Dakotah 624 Restaurant.

2 ounces orange-flavored vodka
3/4 ounce amaretto
1 ounce white chocolate liqueur
chocolate hard shell

baking cocoa
confectioners' sugar
1 chocolate kiss

Fill a shaker with cubed ice. Add the vodka, amaretto and white chocolate liqueur. Shake to mix well.

Dip the rim of a chilled martini glass into the chocolate shell. Dip into baking cocoa and confectioners' sugar. Place a candy kiss in the glass. Strain the vodka mixture into the prepared glass.

Serves one

Brandied Irish Creme

The toasts have been made and the dancing is over. It's time to kick off your shoes and pour a nightcap!

3 eggs
1 tablespoon chocolate syrup
1 cup sweetened condensed milk

1 1/4 cups brandy
1 teaspoon vanilla extract

Beat the eggs in a mixing bowl. Add the chocolate syrup, condensed milk , brandy and vanilla and beat until smooth. Pour into sealable bottles. Store in the refrigerator for 4 weeks or longer before serving.

Makes three cups

Open Me First

Never underestimate the importance of an envelope! Do you remember which pieces you opened first when you last sifted through your mail? You can be sure that a beautifully lettered envelope with an interesting stamp will catch the eye of its recipient. The intrigue of a message starts long before the message is ever read. Whether it is a carefully crafted invitation, a thoughtful thank-you note, or a funny birthday card, your message is worth the extra effort of a thoroughly beautiful presentation.

Black and White Torta

Quite simply . . . elegant.

Torta Crust
2 cups graham cracker crumbs
$1/2$ cup baking cocoa, sifted
1 cup sugar
$1/2$ cup (1 stick) unsalted butter,
    melted

Dark Chocolate Filling
16 ounces bittersweet chocolate,
    coarsely chopped
$1^1/2$ cups heavy cream

White Chocolate Filling
16 ounces white chocolate,
    coarsely chopped
3 cups heavy cream
2 teaspoons unflavored gelatin
2 tablespoons cold water
$1^1/2$ teaspoons vanilla extract

Garnish
white and dark chocolate
    shavings or curls

For the crust, mix the graham cracker crumbs, baking cocoa, sugar and melted butter in a bowl. Press evenly over the bottom and side of a 10-inch springform pan. Bake at 350 degrees on the center oven rack for 5 minutes. Cool on a wire rack.

For the dark chocolate filling, melt the bittersweet chocolate with the cream in a double boiler over hot but not simmering water, stirring to blend well. Pour into the prepared pan and chill for 30 minutes.

For the white chocolate filling, melt the white chocolate with 1 cup of the cream in a double boiler over hot but not simmering water, stirring to blend well. Set aside.

Soften the gelatin in the cold water in a small heatproof bowl for 5 minutes. Place in a saucepan with water halfway up the side of the bowl. Heat for 3 to 4 minutes or just until the gelatin dissolves, stirring constantly; do not simmer.

Beat the remaining 2 cups cream with the vanilla in a large chilled mixing bowl until soft peaks form. Beat in the white chocolate mixture and the gelatin mixture gradually. Spread evenly over the chilled dark chocolate layer.

Chill for 8 hours or longer. Run a thin knife around the side of the pan to loosen the torta. Place on a serving plate and remove the side of the pan. Garnish with grated chocolate or chocolate curls.

Serves twelve

Dessert is a Black and White Torta (page 24) decorated with the hands of a clock.
Instead of painstakingly forming the hands with fondant, the hostess chose to pluck the hands off an inexpensive wall clock.
Tiny chocolates or any other edible jewels could also be used to mark the time.

Celebration Classics

Wedding in a Secret Garden

Romance is in full bloom at this gorgeous garden wedding set around an alluring aqua pool in late Spring. Nature is engaged to refresh the eye and to soothe the soul as sacred vows are exchanged and friends celebrate the joy of the day.

Flowers are everywhere, from the front walkway, with a lavish wreath of roses on the door, to a wonderful arbor of roses at the garden entrance.

A rented trellis, a grouping of urns with potted palms or topiaries, or garland embellished columns also could have been chosen. Consider architectural elements that transport guests from reality to a dream-like setting.

At the entry table, lilies of the valley symbolize happiness and ivy underscores fidelity. A series of sepia photos of family weddings for the last three generations is also displayed in silver frames.

Everywhere you look, the bride has mixed something old and something new to create her own set of traditions. The antique German silver bridal cup, for example, is fashioned so both bride and groom can drink from it at the same time. A lace-like sterling cake basket lined with moss holds the favors. The Victorian sterling silver ring box for the engagement ring not only adds a nostalgic touch for today, but it can also grace the bride's dressing table forever.

The beauty and repose of a garden wedding is carried in the heart of your guests forever. A slice of heaven for all in attendance, this secret garden is in Boca Raton's Old Floresta neighborhood, part of the National Register of Historic Places.

The cake is decorated with fresh flowers, in keeping with the garden theme. This bride chose her favorite soft pink roses, with the traditional white. Notice the pink roses in the cone-shaped silver nosegay holders for the bridal party. They, too, are a beautiful keepsake.

While this fanciful garden and historic home set the mood for a wonderful afternoon nuptial, a lovely museum sculpture garden or arbor by the sea could do the same. Any place harboring a special place in the bride's heart should find itself on the wish list.

Great Expectations

Once this bride decided on the setting, the season and time of day, she took a careful look at logistics before she chose the food. Lists of everything she wanted to use or needed to rent or to hire were part of the meticulous planning important for the smooth fulfillment of great expectations.

Small round tables were chosen because of limited poolside space. Their size led to the choice of a delicate, antique English china with a fluted edge by Royal Crown Derby. This Lombardie pattern has hand-painted turquoise flowers, which echo the color of the water in the pool. Silver chargers were chosen to coordinate. A fresh leaf charger would also have worked well in this setting. Adding another layer of detail enhances the elegance of any special occasion.

These dining tables were set with Waterford stemware and Strasbourg sterling. Early 19th century mother-of-pearl fish forks and knives add a natural shimmer and are perfect for the Shrimp-Filled Won Ton Baskets (page 30) appetizers.

Instead of traditional ivory or white linen for the tables, the bride chose a lavender fabric and covered it with a veil of white organdy to soften the tone. Each ballroom chair is graced with French ribbon enhanced with pearls and tiny flowers. The look is reminiscent of the bridesmaids' gowns of years gone by.

Very special antique place card holders that double as tiny mint dishes are part of the bride's trousseau. The mother of the bride has also been collecting sterling napkin rings for 20 years. Each is different. Matching napkins tie the look together.

Follow Your Heart

Even though this is an afternoon wedding, the couple is not rushing off to catch a plane. They party with guests into the night. Today's bride is free to make her own traditions; she doesn't have to adhere to strict rules. One mandate: follow your heart on your wedding day, choose details that flow and make your guests feel the joie de vivre of your radiant day.

Throughout the reception, the bride and groom plan to have their picture taken with guests at each table. Those photos, in tiny frames, will accompany thank you notes.

The groom has brought along a tradition of his own. He will pass his silver toasting stein to his three lifelong friends, and each will salute the bride.

The couple walk through the trio of arbors as guests make a wish for them and release envelopes of live butterflies. Legend says that butterflies will carry those wishes to the heavens.

The Honour of Your Presence

Plan as far in advance as you can. Engraved invitations are a timeless classic for formal occasions. Invitations for a small, but formal gathering, like this one, may be calligraphied by hand. Seal with wax stamped with your own crest or initials.

Write your own wedding program. It will help guests know what's coming. Printed calligraphy on parchment with a tassel makes a nice keepsake. Include a poem, information on the ceremony, and music inside. Note the marriage details on the front cover with a garland, dove or other symbol of the upcoming nuptials.

Mixing acquired treasures and family heirlooms personalizes any occasion. Here, the mother of the bride sets the tables with her collection of antique silver napkin rings. Each place setting is also graced with antique mint dishes passed down to the bride from her grandmother. The footed antique porcelain butter dishes also have been in the family for generations. All coordinate with the new hand-made baskets covered in iron for the centerpieces.

Menu

A Promise Fulfilled

A wedding is many things. It is a rite of passage, an end and a beginning, a fulfillment and a promise. It is one of three major milestones in life and, in the company of death and birth, the only one that is voluntary, premeditated, and undertaken in full consciousness. The wedding is anchored at the very heart of civilization. Its components, regardless of nationality and religion, are legacies from primitive times: the veil is an emblem of chastity; the wedding ring goes on a finger with a vein that was thought to go directly to the heart; the bridesmaids and groomsmen are reinforcements from the days of marriage by capture; the flowers symbolize fertility; and the food is a feast of celebration. A wedding is also a proclamation or public announcement of a new relationship between two members of society. In light of all of this, a wedding is a ritual and celebration of the highest order.

Shrimp-Filled Won Ton Baskets with Basil Cream

As delicate and lovely as a China doll; the basil cream sauce completes the picture.

Shrimp Filling
12 ounces medium shrimp, peeled with tails intact, deveined
1 medium shallot, finely chopped
2 garlic cloves, minced
1 tablespoon unsalted butter
3 ounces mushrooms, chopped
1 tablespoon chicken stock
1 teaspoon white wine vinegar
$\frac{1}{2}$ teaspoon salt
$\frac{1}{3}$ cup drained ricotta cheese
$\frac{1}{3}$ cup (or more) grated Parmesan cheese
2 tablespoons lime juice
2 tablespoons minced fresh basil

Won Ton Baskets
12 won ton wrappers
peanut oil for deep-frying

Basil Cream
6 garlic cloves, minced
$\frac{1}{4}$ cup ($\frac{1}{2}$ stick) unsalted butter
1 cup heavy cream
$\frac{1}{2}$ cup grated Parmesan cheese
$\frac{1}{4}$ cup minced fresh basil

Garnish
basil leaves

For the filling, sauté the shrimp, shallot and garlic in the butter in a medium skillet over medium-high heat for 2 minutes or until the shrimp begin to turn pink. Add the mushrooms, chicken stock, vinegar and salt. Cook for 1 to 2 minutes longer or until the shrimp are pink and opaque.

Stir in the ricotta cheese, Parmesan cheese, lime juice and basil. Add additional Parmesan cheese if needed to thicken. Cool completely.

For the baskets, arrange 2 won ton wrappers at a time so that all points are visible. Place in a wire mesh strainer or basket and press down in the center to form a basket. Deep-fry in enough 350-degree peanut oil to completely cover for 2 minutes or until golden brown; drain. Repeat with the remaining won ton wrappers.

For the cream, sauté the garlic in the butter in a medium saucepan over medium-low heat for 2 minutes or until tender. Add the cream, cheese and basil. Simmer for 10 minutes or until thickened.

To assemble, fill the baskets with the shrimp filling and place on serving plates. Spoon the basil cream around the basket. Garnish with basil leaves.

Note: The shrimp filling can be prepared several hours in advance, but the filled baskets and cream should be served immediately.

Variation: Chop the shrimp for the filling and spoon a small amount of the filling into the centers of the won ton wrappers. Brush the corners with beaten egg, twist together to enclose the filling and deep-fry in batches.

Serves six

Mesclun with Walnut-Crusted Goat Cheese Rounds

A perfect salad for a sophisticated gathering.

Dijon Vinaigrette
1½ teaspoons minced shallots
1½ teaspoons Dijon mustard
4 teaspoons red wine vinegar
1 tablespoon chopped mixed herbs, such as chives, thyme,
    basil, oregano and/or marjoram
¼ teaspoon sugar
¼ teaspoon salt
⅛ teaspoon freshly ground pepper
2 tablespoons olive oil or 1 tablespoon olive oil and
    1 tablespoon walnut oil

Salad
4 ounces goat cheese
1 egg white, lightly beaten
½ cup finely chopped walnuts, lightly toasted
6 cups packed mixed wild greens or lettuces

For the vinaigrette, combine the shallots, Dijon mustard, vinegar, herbs, sugar, salt and pepper in a small nonreactive bowl and whisk until well mixed. Whisk in the olive oil gradually. Chill until serving time.

For the salad, shape the goat cheese into 4 disks 1½ inches in diameter. Dip the disks in the egg white and then in the walnuts, pressing the walnuts to coat well. Place on a baking sheet. Bake at 425 degrees for 4 to 5 minutes or until just warm.

Combine the greens with the vinaigrette in a large bowl and toss to coat well. Place on 4 salad plates. Top with a disk of goat cheese. Serve immediately.

Serves four

The Art of Saying Thanks

People always remember a thank-you note long after they forget what exactly they did to deserve it. Of course, there are the usual occasions to write thank-you notes, but the unexpected ones are often more interesting and more appreciated. Thank someone for noticing, for being there, and, of course, for having you over for a meal. Even if you are late, send a note; it is a gift in and of itself.

*From Crane's
"The Art of Saying Thanks"*

Creamy Cucumber Soup

This is a perfect first course for six on a warm summer evening. Combine 2 peeled and chopped cucumbers with 2 chopped avocados and 4 chopped scallions in a blender or food processor container. Add 2 cups chicken stock, 2 cups sour cream, 6 tablespoons lime juice and 2 tablespoons chopped chives. Process until smooth. Pour into a bowl and season with Tabasco sauce and salt to taste. Chill for several hours. Ladle into serving bowls and garnish with additional chopped chives.

Pecan-Crusted Chicken with Banana Salsa

A favorite entrée at the world-famous Boca Raton Resort & Club, this recipe is a wonderful marriage of bananas and chicken.

Banana Salsa
3 cups ($1/8$-inch) banana slices
$1/3$ cup chopped red bell pepper
$1/3$ cup chopped yellow
   bell pepper
$1^1/2$ jalapeño chiles, seeded,
   chopped, or to taste
3 tablespoons chopped cilantro
juice of $1^1/2$ limes
$1^1/2$ tablespoons brown sugar
salt and pepper to taste

Chicken
1 egg
$1/2$ cup milk
$1^1/2$ cups bread crumbs
$1^1/2$ cups chopped toasted pecans
6 (6-ounce) boneless skinless
   chicken breasts
salt and pepper to taste
3 tablespoons Dijon mustard
$1/2$ cup flour
3 tablespoons vegetable oil

For the salsa, combine the bananas, bell peppers, jalapeño chiles, cilantro, lime juice, brown sugar, salt and pepper in a bowl and mix well. Let stand for 1 hour or longer.

For the chicken, beat the egg with the milk in a bowl. Mix the bread crumbs and pecans in a bowl. Season the chicken with salt and pepper. Spread with the Dijon mustard and coat lightly with flour. Dip into the egg mixture and then the pecan mixture, pressing to coat well.

Heat the oil in a nonstick sauté pan and add the chicken. Sauté until golden brown on both sides, turning once. Remove to a baking dish. Bake at 350 degrees for 15 to 20 minutes or until cooked through.

Serve with the salsa, smashed potatoes and fresh green beans.

Serves six

J magine that the couple is about to share a final toast after butterflies have been released in their honor. The bride has taken off her gloves to throw the bouquet just as a butterfly lights to wish them luck. The pair will toast their future with champagne flutes from Waterford that feature a design signifying health. What a perfect treasure to pass on to the next generation when the time comes.

Thyme and Treasured Asparagus

Snap off the tough ends of 1 1/2 pounds of asparagus spears and remove the scales with a knife or vegetable peeler. Rub a 9x13-inch baking dish with the cut sides of a garlic clove and place the asparagus in the dish. Drizzle with 2 teaspoons olive oil; sprinkle with 1/2 teaspoon chopped fresh thyme, 1/2 teaspoon salt and 1/4 teaspoon freshly ground pepper. Bake at 400 degrees for 20 minutes, stirring once.

Roasted Herbed Two Potatoes

This is a wonderful marriage of sweet potatoes and red potatoes.

4 or 5 medium red potatoes
3 or 4 medium sweet potatoes
1/4 cup olive oil
2 tablespoons chopped fresh parsley, or
    1 tablespoon dried parsley
1 tablespoon chopped fresh tarragon, or
    1 teaspoon dried tarragon
1/4 teaspoon red pepper flakes
1/2 teaspoon salt
1/2 teaspoon freshly ground black pepper

Cut the peeled or unpeeled potatoes into 1-inch pieces. Spread the red potatoes in a 10x15-inch microwave-safe baking dish coated with 1 tablespoon of the olive oil. Microwave on High for 2 to 3 minutes or bake at 450 degrees for 15 minutes. Add the sweet potatoes to the dish.

Mix the remaining 3 tablespoons olive oil with the parsley, tarragon, red pepper flakes, salt and black pepper in a bowl. Pour over the potatoes, mixing to coat well. Roast at 450 degrees for 45 to 60 minutes or until tender, stirring every 15 to 20 minutes to prevent sticking.

Serves eight

Petite Butter Rolls

These little bread bites are as soft and luscious as a baby.

$^1/_4$ cup sugar
$^1/_3$ cup vegetable shortening
1 teaspoon salt
1 cup boiling water
1 envelope dry yeast
$^1/_4$ cup warm water
1 egg
$3^1/_2$ cups flour
$^1/_2$ cup (1 stick) butter, melted

Combine the sugar, shortening and salt with the boiling water in a large mixing bowl and stir to melt the shortening. Cool to lukewarm.

Sprinkle the yeast over the warm water in a bowl and let stand for 5 minutes. Add to the shortening mixture. Add the egg and mix until smooth.

Add the flour gradually, mixing until smooth and elastic with a dough hook. Sprinkle the surface of the dough with additional flour and cover the bowl with a plate. Let rise in the refrigerator for 24 hours.

Remove the dough to a floured surface and knead 12 times. Roll a small amount at a time to $^1/_4$-inch thickness. Cut with a 1- to $1^1/_2$-inch cutter. Brush with butter and fold each round in half, gently pressing the center. Place in buttered 9-inch round pans with sides touching.

Place the pans on the top rack of an unheated oven and place a large pan of boiling water on the bottom rack. Let the rolls rise for 2 hours or until doubled in bulk.

Brush again with butter. Preheat the oven to 425 degrees and bake the rolls for 7 to 10 minutes or until golden brown.

Makes five dozen

Riesling Sorbet

For a crisp, cool flavor to prepare the palate, combine 1 cup sugar and the strained juice of 1 lemon with 1 cup water in a saucepan and bring to a boil over low heat, stirring to dissolve the sugar. Boil for $1^1/_2$ to 2 minutes. Cool to room temperature and whisk in $^3/_4$ cup water and 2 cups riesling. Freeze, covered, for 4 hours or until firm, whisking several times until smooth. Spoon into 6 chilled serving glasses and garnish with sprigs of mint and lemon twists.

Cake Customs

The wedding cake has been part of the wedding ceremony longer than the wedding ring. While the ring symbolized the couple's unity, the cake looked to fecundity because cakes contain ground wheat or corn flour and symbolize fertility and the earth's bounty.

Using a special knife to cut each birthday cake became such a tradition in one family that the first bride in the clan asked for her birthday knife to cut her wedding cake.

Champagne Truffles

Dazzle your guests with these little jewels!

6 ounces semisweet chocolate, chopped
^{1}/4 cup (^{1}/2 stick) butter, chopped
3 tablespoons heavy cream
1 egg yolk, beaten
3 tablespoons champagne or heavy cream
^{1}/4 cup sifted confectioners' sugar, white
     sprinkles or unsweetened baking cocoa
     mixed with ^{1}/2 teaspoon cinnamon

Combine the chocolate, butter and heavy cream in a medium saucepan. Cook over low heat until the chocolate melts, stirring constantly. Stir a small amount of the hot mixture into the egg yolk; stir the egg yolk mixture into the hot mixture. Cook over medium heat for 2 minutes longer, stirring constantly.

Remove from the heat and stir in the champagne. Spoon into a small mixing bowl. Chill for 1 hour or until completely cool, stirring occasionally.

Beat at medium speed for 1 minute or until the color lightens and the mixture is slightly fluffy. Chill for 30 minutes longer or until the mixture holds its shape.

Shape into 1-inch balls by scraping a small ice cream scoop, melon baller or spoon across the surface of the chilled mixture. Place on a tray lined with waxed paper. Chill until very firm.

Roll the truffles gently in the confectioners' sugar or small white sprinkles or in a mixture of unsweetened baking cocoa and cinnamon. Place in decorative foil cups to serve.

Makes twenty-five to thirty

The tradition of having the bride and groom drink from the same cup at the same time comes from Germany. According to folklore, a German maiden is said to have been planning to wed a goldsmith not to her father's liking. The girl's father told the would-be groom that he could not give his daughter's hand unless the goldsmith could fashion a cup that the pair could drink from at the same time. Fresh roses, lilacs, and hydrangeas add natural elegance to this three-tiered wedding cake. Other beautiful silver touches on the cake table include the Victorian ring box, antique cake basket for the party favors, nosegay cones for the roses, and the English silver-footed champagne cooler from the early 19th century.

Celebration Classics

A Yankee Doodle Dandy Day

Mix the warm summer sun with a soft breeze, add family and friends, and combine with great food for a terrific recipe for a high-flying, flag-raising Fourth of July.

For another key ingredient, this hostess designed brilliant bursts of color to dazzle her guests. After all, the fireworks won't begin until nine o'clock, so she had to set off her own displays of color in the interim.

Lemon yellow is today's twist on the traditional red, white, and blue. And these splashes of sunshine are everywhere: accenting stemware, popping up on serving platters, and garnishing the buffet.

Guests are also delighted by the bold stripes and starbursts. They bring this nostalgic gathering at the country club or favorite park site back to the future.

No matter what the occasion, once you've locked onto a good idea, remember to repeat it. This is a star-studded picnic, and the hostess put stars anywhere she could. Notice the carambola fruit on the Mason jar glasses, the star cutouts on the watermelon, the star-like arrangement of tortilla chips on the Watermelon Salsa (page 44), and the striped star Celestial Sugar Cookies (page 48).

Think about texture too. Comfortable, yet crisp, is the mantra to win the day at a picnic. Here, soft antique quilts and comfortable pillows invite guests to relax on the grass and dream of days gone by. Meanwhile, grosgrain

An all-American family reunion is planned for this Independence Day celebration at the Hillsboro Club in nearby Hillsboro Beach. Soft breezes from the adjacent Intracoastal keep things cool until fireworks begin to burst over the inlet's stately lighthouse.

ribbon, starched cotton cloth, and crepe paper for the bike-decorating contest stand up to the heat of a summer day.

Croquet mallets, tennis racquets, burlap bags for sack races, and a stack of pies for a contest signal arriving guests that there's fun in the air. Don't forget the horseshoes!

Games also break the ice for newcomers, and landscape memories for all ages. The more settled members of this group enjoy chess and backgammon. A station of red, white, and blue beads occupies the little ones as their parents mingle, and they wait eagerly to team up for a turn at bike-decorating for the parade later in the afternoon.

Touches of Yesteryear

Cold drinks are highly prized on a summer's day. This hostess spied this special beer bin in a catalog. It has metal cupholders surrounding it, providing a colorful and convenient option for icing down the drinks. You can get the washtub without the cupholders at the local discount store and spray paint starbursts on it.

Since she started thinking about the party several weeks ahead, this hostess had plenty of time to spray the bamboo trays red. Each is looped with different and colorful fabric, so they're not only festive, but guests won't lose track of theirs because each is a little different.

She also chose simple serving pieces to conjure up that nostalgic feeling again, and to make transporting everything easier. Baskets draped with bright cloth napkins, wooden platters, and canning jars for condiments work in harmony on the buffet. Silver tongs and spoons take the whole look up a notch and are just as easy to pack as stainless or wooden counterparts. She used little red wagons to transport items from the car to the picnic site.

The food for any holiday should be a medley of past and present. Here, an all-American array of grilled corn (page 45), Barbecued Ribs (page 46), and Gold Coast Potato Salad (page 45) evoke memories of Grandma. But Firecracker Chili Cheese Pie (page 42), Watermelon Salsa (page 44), and Bali Wings (page 45) promise that this moveable feast will appeal to the next generation as well. Nudging new traditions in with the tried and true is, after all, the hallmark of a great entertainer. Let the fireworks begin!

Variety Adds Spice

Keep the bursts of color and simplify the food. This is a picnic that can go anywhere from—your own backyard to your favorite place to enjoy the fireworks, parade, or a local band concert. Variations will work well for a gathering of book club members or a fun Girl Scout meeting.

Here's a fun tip for any occasion: Drape the bunting as this hostess has done around the gazebo for a time-honored tradition that can be done in minutes with unseamed fabric and a staple gun. The fabric should be at least two feet wide and at least a foot longer than the space between the posts. And while it's nearly impossible to find tablecloths this vibrant, iron-on seam tape turns any sale fabric into a finished tablecloth in an instant.

You've Just Got to Come

If it's an annual reunion of family and friends, take a color picture or make a color copy of an old favorite of the kids and use for it the cover of the invitation.

Better yet, find a tin mug or something else nostalgic, yet inexpensive, on sale, and buy in quantity. You can print the invitation copy on a label and attach it to the mug. Tie a ribbon on the handle. Complete the package for the mail in a little red or white box with blue ink and a flag stamp. This invitation is the party favor and immediately sets the tone for festive fun upon its receipt.

If you like to invite close friends and neighbors on the spur of the moment, spend most of your time creating the ambiance and go potluck! Keep the bold color scheme with generous use of fabric, and don't forget the ribbons, flags, and flowers. Put anything you can in cloth-covered baskets. Create a couple of eye-catching fruit garnishes and chip displays to go with a grilled entrée and a specialty drink. Ask friends to bring easy salads and desserts or order them from a favorite market. Perhaps each guest could bring a game to share with the group.

What's a picnic without a lawn? Even if you're in a condominium, you can grow your own rye grass or pick some up at a health food store, place it in a basket, and use it as a spot to house the buffet's flatware.

Menu

*Pictured recipes

Fluted Lemon Slices

Use a lemon zester to peel lengthwise strips of lemon rind from a lemon at equal intervals. Cut the lemon into thin slices. For half slices, halve the lemon lengthwise, place it cut side down on a cutting board, and slice crosswise.

Southern Citrus Punch

Southern hospitality never tasted so good!

6 lemons
4 navel oranges
2 (6-ounce) cans frozen
　　lemonade concentrate
1 (6-ounce) can frozen orange
　　juice concentrate

2 liters lemon-lime soda
1 liter sweet bourbon
1 star fruit, thinly sliced

Slice the lemons very thin and layer to fit the size of the punch bowl opening. Place on a baking sheet lined with plastic wrap. Slice the oranges very thin and also layer to fit the punch bowl on a second baking sheet lined with plastic wrap. Freeze for 2 to $2^1/2$ hours or until firm.

Combine the frozen lemonade concentrate and frozen orange juice concentrate in a large punch bowl. Add the lemon-lime soda, bourbon and several handfuls of ice and stir until the concentrates are well mixed. Arrange the frozen fruit over the top of the punch. Add the thinly sliced star fruit. Ladle into punch cups to serve.

Serves ten to twelve

Firecracker Chile Cheese Pie

Light up your taste buds with this festive appetizer.

1 cup crushed tortilla chips
3 tablespoons melted butter
16 ounces cream cheese, softened
2 eggs
1 (4-ounce) can chopped green
　　chiles
2 fresh jalapeños, minced
4 ounces Colby cheese, shredded

4 ounces Monterey Jack cheese,
　　shredded
$1/4$ cup sour cream

Garnish
chopped green onions, chopped
　　tomatoes and sliced
　　black olives

Mix the crushed tortilla chips and melted butter in a bowl. Press over the bottom of a 9-inch springform pan. Bake at 325 degrees for 15 minutes.

Beat the cream cheese and eggs in a mixing bowl. Mix in the green chiles, jalapeños, Colby cheese and Monterey Jack cheese. Pour over the baked layer. Bake at 325 degrees for exactly 30 minutes. Cool for 5 minutes.

Place on a serving plate. Loosen the side of the pan with a knife and remove. Spread the sour cream over the pie. Garnish with green onions, tomatoes and olives. Serve with additional chips.

Serves eight to ten

A good rule of thumb is to let the holiday dictate the color scheme, but choose an accent color such as this lemon yellow to create your own signature and serve as a transition from yesterday to today. Repeat accents over and over for continuity. The stars don't come out only in the night at this party; they're everywhere, even on the watermelon. A sharp metal star-shaped cookie cutter is the fastest way to see these stars.

Bike Decorating Contest

A parade of bicycles is a wonderful idea for a neighborhood celebration! Ask the children to decorate their bicycles at home, days before the picnic. This creates great anticipation for the upcoming event. On the Fourth, all of the children bring their decorated bicycles to be judged–as the most patriotic, most colorful, most creative, most traditional, most contemporary, etc. To keep little ones happy, have lots of categories and a little prize for each. Squirt toys, special balloons, bubbles, pinwheels and red-white-and-blue lollipops or popsicles will all bring smiles. After the judging, all of the children can ride around the block for a showy parade. To make the parade even more festive, invite interested spectators to walk behind the bikers waving crepe paper attached to popsicle sticks.

Watermelon Salsa

Serve as a dip or over grilled fish.

2 cups finely chopped seeded watermelon
1 or 2 jalapeños, minced, or to taste
2 tablespoons minced red onion
2 tablespoons chopped cilantro
1 tablespoon chopped flat-leaf parsley
$1/8$ teaspoon grated gingerroot
$1/2$ teaspoon salt
$1/2$ teaspoon pepper

Combine the watermelon, jalapeños, onion, cilantro, parsley, ginger, salt and pepper in a bowl and mix gently. Let stand for 30 minutes to blend flavors. Serve within a few hours.

Serves eight

Cocobeer Shrimp

These will be gobbled up!

Curry Mustard Sauce
1 cup mayonnaise
2 tablespoons Dijon mustard
2 tablespoons sugar
2 teaspoons minced fresh parsley
2 tablespoons minced onion
2 garlic cloves, minced
2 teaspoons lemon juice
1 teaspoon curry powder
Tabasco sauce to taste

Shrimp
4 eggs
1 cup beer
$1^1/4$ cups flour
2 tablespoons baking powder
$3^1/2$ teaspoons Creole seafood seasoning
48 large shrimp, peeled with tails intact, deveined, patted dry
$1^1/2$ to 2 cups shredded coconut

For the sauce, combine the mayonnaise, Dijon mustard, sugar, parsley, onion, garlic, lemon juice, curry powder and Tabasco sauce in a small bowl and whisk to mix well. Chill until serving time.

For the shrimp, combine the eggs, beer, flour, baking powder and 1 teaspoon of the seafood seasoning in a bowl and mix well. Sprinkle the shrimp with the remaining $2^1/2$ teaspoons of the seafood seasoning. Dip into the beer batter and roll in the coconut, coating well.

Heat $1^1/2$ inches or more oil to 350 degrees in a saucepan. Add the shrimp a few at a time and fry until golden brown. Drain on paper towels. Serve with the sauce.

Serves ten

Bali Wings

Exotic South Sea flavors paint a picture of the tropics.

1 cup soy sauce	1 cup chopped green onions
1 cup pineapple juice	2 tablespoons chopped garlic
1/2 cup white vinegar	2 tablespoons chopped gingerroot
3 tablespoons honey	20 chicken wings
2 tablespoons sesame oil	

Mix the soy sauce, pineapple juice, vinegar, honey, sesame oil, green onions, garlic and ginger in a large bowl. Cut the tip sections from the chicken wings and discard. Add the wings to the marinade. Marinate, covered, in the refrigerator for 2 to 10 hours, stirring occasionally.

Drain the chicken, reserving the marinade. Arrange the chicken on 2 baking sheets. Roast the chicken at 400 degrees for 1 hour, basting with the reserved marinade every 20 minutes.

Pour the remaining marinade into a small saucepan. Bring to a boil and cook for 15 minutes or until thickened and reduced. Serve as a dipping sauce.

Serves ten

Gold Coast Potato Salad

A thoroughly up-to-date picnic potato salad.

Jalapeño Dressing	**Salad**
2 jalapeños, seeded	3 pounds Yukon Gold potatoes
1 garlic clove	2 cups fresh corn kernels
1/2 cup cilantro leaves	1/4 cup olive oil
salt and pepper to taste	1 red bell pepper, chopped
1 cup olive oil	1 large bunch scallions, julienned
	1/4 cup chopped parsley

For the dressing, chop the jalapeños, garlic, cilantro, salt and pepper in the food processor. Add the olive oil gradually, processing until smooth.

For the salad, boil the unpeeled potatoes in water to cover in a saucepan until tender. Drain and cool. Cut into quarters.

Spread the corn kernels on a baking sheet and drizzle with the olive oil. Roast at 400 degrees until the edges of the kernels begin to brown; cool. Combine with the bell pepper and scallions in a bowl. Add the potatoes and chopped parsley. Add the dressing and toss to coat well.

Serves eight to ten

Grilled Corn

Grilled corn is a Fourth of July favorite, and a picnic treat any time. The smoky grilled flavor complements the sweetness of the corn. Many recipes call for the corn to be husked, soaked in cold water, buttered, rewrapped in the husk, and then grilled. This procedure is time-consuming and keeps the smoky flavor away from the corn! It is quicker and easier to simply cook shucked ears directly over the coals.

Removing Corn Kernels from the Cob

Hold the cob vertically over a wide bowl or pan. Slice straight down the kernels with a knife. After the kernels have been removed, turn the knife over and with its dull side scrape the cob on all sides to extract the "milk." For a creamier texture, score the kernels by slicing through the middle of each row before cutting them off. Use milk and sugar to bring out the sweetness of day-old corn.

Barbecued Ribs

The dream entrée that never requires your attention.

1 onion, sliced	½ (12-ounce) bottle horseradish
5 pounds baby back ribs	sauce
salt and pepper to taste	½ cup packed brown sugar
1 (14-ounce) bottle tangy catsup	¼ cup Worcestershire sauce
or chili sauce	

Spread the onion slices in a 9x13-inch baking pan. Sprinkle both sides of the ribs with salt and pepper and arrange over the onion. Cover with foil. Bake at 350 degrees for 2 hours.

Combine the catsup, horseradish sauce, brown sugar and Worcestershire sauce in a bowl and mix well. Spread over the ribs. Bake, uncovered, for 1 hour longer.

Serves eight

Stuffed Bread

Man can live by this bread alone!

1 cup (2 sticks) butter, softened	2 teaspoons lemon juice
1 teaspoon Beau Monde seasoning	1 tablespoon poppy seeds
½ teaspoon dry mustard	1 loaf French or Italian bread
1 small onion, chopped	16 ounces sliced Swiss cheese

Combine the butter, Beau Monde seasoning, dry mustard, onion, lemon juice and poppy seeds in a bowl and mix well.

Slice the bread ½ inch thick, cutting to but not through the bottom. Fold the cheese slices in half and place 1 in each cut. Spread the butter mixture over the top.

Place the loaf on foil and fold up the sides of the foil. Place on a baking sheet. Bake at 350 degrees for 25 to 30 minutes or until the cheese melts.

Serves eight

Raspberry Ribbon Cheesecake

This is sure to win the blue ribbon at the county fair.

Chocolate Crust
2 cups chocolate wafer crumbs
$1/3$ cup melted margarine or
    butter
3 tablespoons sugar

Raspberry Sauce
$2^1/2$ cups fresh red raspberries or
    lightly sweetened frozen red
    raspberries, thawed
$2/3$ cup sugar
2 tablespoons cornstarch
2 teaspoons lemon juice

Cheesecake
24 ounces cream cheese, softened
$1/2$ cup sugar
2 tablespoons flour
1 teaspoon vanilla extract
2 egg whites
1 cup heavy cream
1 cup fresh red raspberries or
    frozen red raspberries,
    thawed
2 tablespoons raspberry liqueur
    or orange juice

For the crust, combine the cookie crumbs, margarine and sugar in a mixing bowl and mix well. Press over the bottom and 1 inch up the side of a greased 8- or 9-inch springform pan. Chill in the refrigerator.

For the sauce, process the raspberries in a blender until smooth. Press through a sieve to remove the seeds. Add enough water to the liquid to measure 1 cup. Combine with the sugar and cornstarch in a small saucepan and mix well.

Cook over medium heat until thickened and bubbly, stirring constantly. Reduce the heat and cook for 2 minutes longer. Stir in the lemon juice. Reserve $1/4$ cup of the sauce for the cheesecake filling and cool slightly without stirring. Cover the remaining sauce and chill until serving time.

For the cheesecake, combine the cream cheese, sugar, flour and vanilla in a large mixing bowl and beat until fluffy. Add the egg whites and beat at low speed just until combined. Stir in the heavy cream.

Pour half the cream cheese mixture into the chilled crust. Drizzle with the reserved $1/4$ cup raspberry sauce and spread the remaining cream cheese mixture carefully over the top. Place the springform pan in a shallow baking pan. Bake at 375 degrees for 35 to 40 minutes or until the center is nearly firm when the pan is shaken.

Cool on a wire rack for 15 minutes. Loosen the side of the pan with a knife and cool for 30 minutes longer. Place on a serving plate and remove the side of the pan. Cool completely. Chill for 4 hours or longer.

Arrange the raspberries over the cheesecake. Combine the liqueur with the reserved $1/4$ cup raspberry sauce. Spoon over the top.

Serves ten to twelve

Picnic Fun

Organize games to entertain kids of all ages at the picnic. For **Find the Flags,** *hide various-sized flags throughout the yard and have plenty of prizes to hand out to all. Offer prizes for the greatest number found, the least number found, the largest flag, and the smallest flag.*

Rainbow Bubbles *is a recipe for quiet fireworks! Just combine 2 cups dish-washing liquid, 6 cups water, and $3/4$ cup white corn syrup in a clean soda bottle. Paper cups and wire wands complete the simple equipment.*

Other festivities could include Sack Races, Beach Ball Blow-up, Frisbees, and Croquet.

Edible Flowers

Edible flowers have become very popular and visually enhance cookies and other baked goods. Any flowers that are used with food should be organically grown and should never be sprayed with chemicals.

To decorate Celestial Sugar Cookies (at right) with edible flowers, gently place a flower on each unbaked cookie and press lightly into the dough. Bake at 350 degrees for 12 to 15 minutes or until the cookies are golden brown.

Celestial Sugar Cookies with Royal Frosting

Sent from heaven, these soft, chewy delights are wonderful to decorate. Use your imagination!

Cookies
^{1}/2 cup (1 stick) butter or margarine, softened
1 cup sugar
1 large egg
1 teaspoon vanilla extract
2^1/2 cups flour
2 teaspoons baking powder
^{1}/4 teaspoon salt

Royal Frosting
3 cups confectioners' sugar
^{1}/3 cup butter, softened
2 tablespoons milk
1^1/2 teaspoons vanilla extract

For the cookies, beat the butter at medium speed in a mixing bowl until light. Add the sugar gradually, beating constantly until fluffy. Beat in the egg and vanilla.

Combine the flour, baking powder and salt. Add to the creamed mixture, mixing just until blended. Shape into a ball and chill, covered, for 1 hour.

Divide the dough into 3 portions and work with 1 portion at a time, leaving the remaining dough in the refrigerator until needed. Roll each portion ^{1}/8 inch thick on a lightly floured surface. Cut with a 3-inch cookie cutter and place on lightly greased cookie sheets.

Bake at 375 degrees for 8 minutes or until the edges are light brown. Cool on the cookie sheets for several minutes and remove to wire racks to cool completely.

For the frosting, combine the confectioners' sugar, butter, milk and vanilla in a large mixing bowl. Beat at medium speed until smooth and of spreading consistency. Spread over the cooled cookies.

Note: You may omit the frosting and sprinkle the cookies with decorator sugar crystals before baking if preferred.

Makes twenty cookies

Spruce up your garden setting with an unexpected display of colorful fresh flowers in a watermelon vase. And if you're going to the park, consider creating a special vignette within a public space. A couple of classic chairs like these pristine white Adirondack chairs, or chairs of teak, wrought iron, or wicker will add flavor. Since they're easy to carry, pile on favorite quilts and plenty of pillows to continue the mood. (See recipe for Celestial Sugar Cookies at left.)

Appetizers & Beverages

Casting off the Day

*F*ive minutes before the guests arrive, take time to feel the gentle breeze against your face. Relax and let your eyes savor the scene. Are the fish jumping? Is the moon rising in the sky? Can you skip a stone across the water?

Now is the time to taste the perfectly chilled martinis. Sneak a bite of the Shrimp with Cajun Rémoulade Sauce (page 80). You've planned a wonderful getaway without leaving town. The waterfront is a world apart, whether dockside or underway. And because you've made a moment for yourself, you'll be radiant when greeting your guests and confident that the memory of this night will linger in each of their daydreams.

All aboard. Turn up the music, drinks all around. A pitcher of Sea Breeze Cocktails (page 75) beckons in one corner. Everyone is going over to spin the silver ferris wheel filled with garnishes. And on deck where space is at a premium, this whimsical serving piece adds a festive focal point while leaving plenty of room for the silver ice bucket and other accessories.

The tropical shades of the drinks, flower petals, and green limes are all the color you need. The beaded coasters add shimmer, and the metals reflect the blending of candlelight and moonlight. Anytime the natural setting can capture the imagination, keep the color palette neutral. Go for the glow.

*T*his chic, elegant setting aboard a yacht in Lake Boca Raton is all done with mirrors and a bit of velcro. For this Art Deco-styled cocktail party, it's all about setting the tone. The Boca Raton skyline in the twilight provides a dramatic ambiance for this escape.

A streamlined Art Deco approach is the design inspiration for the martini bar. A mirrored top, cut to fit over the white shipboard bar, is paired with a mirrored tray to show a simple elegance. This is a bow to Miami's South Beach. But remember, Deco lines began in Paris and were married with the architecture of ships, so they go anywhere. A far cry from insulated acrylic tumblers, it's high style on the high seas or wherever you happen to drift.

Watermelon Margaritas (page 65) might be nearby or on another level. Either way, be sure that guests are offered spirited choices. For entertaining anyone from business associates to best friends, the ambiance at this cocktail party for eight is a refreshing change of pace.

Anchors Aweigh

Aboard ship, you'll need seaworthy accessories and flowers. Think carefully about what moves well, if you'll be hoisting the anchor. The choice is yours to anchor out as the other boats have done or to head south for dinner at a waterfront restaurant. Hurricane lamps keep the candles burning in a strong breeze. Calla lilies are strong enough to stand tall as a little gust goes by. A touch of the nautical, like this round box covered with spokes of a captain's wheel, is just enough when coupled with the nautilus shell for serving stone crabs.

After a toast to the captain, perhaps you'll be underway. This hostess has brought her guests to Lake Boca Raton where the Intracoastal Waterway—which runs the length of the entire east coast—widens as it meets the curves of the ocean inlet. In the background is the pink tower of the Boca Raton Resort & Club, never far from view on the east side of town.

Wherever you are, be sure to plan this party to coincide with the magic hour. It's the time when the sky turns deep blue just before night. Perhaps your party will be on a lake surrounded with dark forests and dotted with houses here and there. Or it could be on a southern river where the moss hangs low on shore. Whatever the backdrop, there is nothing like the wonder of the wind and the water lapping against the side of the boat. All cares stay landside.

On Top of the World

If you're cityside instead of waterside, take this party to a rooftop to capitalize on an urban view. The trickle or babbling of a tabletop fountain would be perfect to soothe the senses. Keep the appetizers simple. You might add something extra to this menu for the land lovers, but keep the Marinated Mussels (page 76) and Smoked Salmon on Potatoes with Dill Sauce (page 74)—they're as easy to balance during conversation as they are to prepare.

The Pleasure of Your Company

What better way to invite your guests to a cocktail affair than with a snapshot showing the evening's view. Design it like a postcard from your little corner of paradise. Whether it's a water scene, cityscape, or garden view, it should be a clever, yet sincere "wish you were here."

You also could focus on one element that symbolizes the party's theme. For example, let the invitation take the shape of a sailboat, city skyline, or garden flower. Or let the music planned for the evening inspire the invitation. Jazz from the Thirties, for instance, moves easily from Paris to Key West, conjuring up anything from Deco lines to palm trees.

Take a look at contemporary serving pieces to make a splash without a fuss. Stainless steel instead of sterling silver won't tarnish your enthusiasm to give this party. The Stone Crab Claws with Mustard Sauce (page 74) seem to float in the naturally elegant mother of pearl shell serving piece. The geometric shapes of the salt and pepper shakers add another special touch to this carefully planned occasion.

Menu

*Pictured recipes

Alligator Eye Dip

Don't be afraid to dip your chip into this zesty vegetarian delight.

1 (15-ounce) can black-eyed peas
1 (15-ounce) can black beans
1 (9-ounce) can chopped
   black olives
2 tomatoes, seeded, chopped
20 green onions, chopped

1 (4-ounce) can chopped
   green chiles
$^{1}/_{2}$ bunch cilantro, chopped
garlic salt to taste
$^{3}/_{4}$ cup salad oil
$^{1}/_{3}$ cup vinegar

Rinse and drain the black-eyed peas and black beans. Combine the peas, beans, olives, tomatoes, green onions, green chiles and cilantro in a bowl and mix well. Add the garlic salt, oil and vinegar and mix well. Chill for 8 hours or longer. Serve with corn chips.
Serves sixteen

Tango Dip

Make your taste buds dance.

2 cups mayonnaise
$^{1}/_{2}$ cup sour cream
1 tablespoon olive oil
1 tablespoon lemon juice
1 tablespoon red wine vinegar
1 tablespoon chopped onion

2 garlic cloves, minced
1 tablespoon chopped fresh chives
1 tablespoon chopped fresh
   parsley
6 ounces bleu cheese, crumbled
salt and pepper to taste

Combine the first 5 ingredients in a bowl and mix well. Add the onion, garlic, chives, parsley, bleu cheese, salt and pepper and mix well. Chill for 8 hours or longer. Serve with fresh vegetables to dip.
Serves twelve

IN 1971, TWENTY-SEVEN FOUNDING MEMBERS WORKED DILIGENTLY TO ESTABLISH THE JUNIOR SERVICE LEAGUE OF BOCA RATON. UNDER THE DIRECTION OF PRESIDENT JOAN MOSELEY, MEMBERS CLOSELY FOLLOWED THE GUIDELINES OF THE ASSOCIATION OF JUNIOR LEAGUES AND PULLED FROM THEIR OWN JUNIOR LEAGUE EXPERIENCE. BY THE FALL OF 1971, THE CHARTER WAS FORMED.

Beef Carpaccio with Green Peppercorn Vinaigrette

Creatively inspired by the Hillsboro Club.

Peppercorn Vinaigrette
1 tablespoon green peppercorns in brine, rinsed
1/4 cup finely minced shallots
1 tablespoon finely chopped red bell pepper
1/2 teaspoon finely minced garlic
1/4 cup champagne vinegar
1 1/2 cups olive oil
salt to taste

Tenderloin
1 (2 1/2- to 3-pound) beef tenderloin, trimmed
1 1/2 tablespoons olive oil
salt to taste
2 tablespoons black peppercorns, cracked

Garnish
grated asiago cheese

For the vinaigrette, crush half the peppercorns. Combine all the peppercorns, shallots, bell pepper, garlic, vinegar, olive oil and salt in a bowl and mix well. Chill until serving time.

For the tenderloin, rub the beef with the oil and sprinkle with the salt and cracked pepper.

Heat a heavy skillet over high heat until very hot. Add the tenderloin and sear on all sides until amost blackened, but do not overcook; the tenderloin should be rare in the center.

Cool on a wire rack. Wrap with plastic wrap or foil and chill in the refrigerator.

To serve, slice the beef very thin and lightly pound with a meat mallet until very thin. Arrange 3 slices on each plate and drizzle with the vinaigrette. Garnish with the cheese and serve with toast points.

Serves sixteen

Sauza Añejo Margaritas

Combine 6 ounces frozen limeade concentrate, 4 ounces Sauza Añejo Tequila and 2 ounces Cointreau in a blender container. Fill the container with ice and process until slushy. Pour into glasses to serve.

Hurricane Punch

Combine one 46-ounce can of Hawaiian Punch, one 12-ounce can frozen orange juice concentrate and one 6-ounce can frozen lemonade concentrate in a pitcher and mix well. Add 3/4 cup sugar if desired.

Fill 16-ounce glasses with crushed ice and add 4 ounces of amber rum to each glass. Fill the glasses with the punch mixture. Garnish with orange slices and maraschino cherries.

Artichoke Cheesecake

A great appetizer for your own party or to take to a friend's party.

1 (3-ounce) jar marinated
    artichoke hearts
24 ounces cream cheese, softened
5 ounces (1¼ cups) feta cheese,
    crumbled
2 garlic cloves, minced
1½ teaspoons chopped fresh
    oregano

3 large eggs
¼ cup chopped green onions
1 teaspoon chopped pimento

Garnish
sliced pimentos
fresh basil leaves

Drain the artichokes, reserving 2 tablespoons of the marinade; chop the artichokes.

Combine the cream cheese, feta cheese, garlic and oregano in a large bowl and beat until smooth. Beat in the eggs just until well mixed. Stir in the artichokes, green onions, pimento and reserved marinade.

Spoon into a greased 9-inch springform pan and cover loosely with foil. Bake at 325 degrees for 35 to 40 minutes or until the edge is firm but the center is still slightly soft when the pan is shaken. Cool on a wire rack. Chill, covered, for 2 to 24 hours.

Place on a serving plate and remove the side of the pan. Garnish with pimentos and basil. Serve slightly chilled or at room temperature.

Serves sixteen

Garlic and Caraway Gouda

You'll feel the need to double dip.

14 ounces Gouda cheese, chopped
1/2 cup beer
1 teaspoon Dijon mustard
1/4 cup (1/2 stick) unsalted butter, softened
2 garlic cloves, chopped

4 ounces cream cheese, softened
1/8 teaspoon grated nutmeg
2 loaves unsliced seedless rye bread
1 tablespoon caraway seeds

Combine the cheese, beer, Dijon mustard, butter, garlic, cream cheese and nutmeg in a food processor container and process for 40 to 50 seconds or until the mixture forms a ball; the cheese may still be lumpy.

Spoon into a bowl, cover and chill for 24 hours. Let stand until room temperature. Hollow out a 3- to 4-inch circle from 1 loaf of bread. Spoon the cheese mixture into the hollow. Sprinkle with the caraway seeds. Cut the remaining loaf of bread into 1-inch cubes. Serve as dippers with the cheese.

Serves twelve to sixteen

Pesto Bleu Cheese Tartlets

A delicious medley of tastes.

1 package frozen puff pastry
8 ounces cream cheese, softened
4 ounces bleu cheese, softened
1/4 cup finely chopped sun-dried tomatoes

1/4 cup prepared pesto
1/4 cup finely chopped walnuts
1/4 cup grated Parmesan cheese

Thaw the puff pastry for 1 hour. Unfold the pastry on a cutting board and cut into 1-inch squares. Place on an ungreased baking sheet. Bake at 350 degrees for 10 minutes or until golden brown. Remove and discard the top halves of the squares.

Combine the cream cheese, bleu cheese and sun-dried tomatoes in a bowl and mix well. Spread about 1/4 teaspoon of the mixture on each pastry square. Top each with pesto; sprinkle with the walnuts and Parmesan cheese.

Broil for 3 to 4 minutes or until the cheeses melt. Serve immediately.

Makes forty squares

Mix Glassware

Don't be afraid to mix and match glassware, especially if you have a large number of guests for cocktails. If you collect Depression glass or colored glass, all the better! Your guests will remember their glasses if they are unique, and the variety of colors will make a beautiful presentation!

Brie in Puff Pastry with Berry Sauce

Festive in both taste and presentation for your next special holiday party.

Berry Sauce
1/4 cup frozen raspberies, thawed
1/4 cup whole cranberry sauce
1 tablespoon spiced rum

Brie
1 package frozen puff pastry, thawed
1 (4-inch) round Brie cheese
1 egg, beaten

Garnish
1 kiwifruit, peeled, cut into wedges

For the sauce, press the raspberries through a sieve to remove the seeds. Combine the purée with the cranberry sauce in a bowl. Add the spiced rum and mix well. Set aside.

For the Brie, place 1 sheet of the pastry on a work surface and place the Brie cheese in the center. Trim 1- to 2-inch triangular pieces off of the corners of the pastry. Roll 1 of the trimmed pieces into a ball and set aside; discard the remaining trimmings. Bring up the pastry to enclose the cheese, overlapping and pleating as needed; there will be an opening over the center of the cheese.

Place the remaining pastry sheet on the work surface and cut 4 lengthwise strips $1/2$ to $3/4$ inch wide. Fold the strips over to form loops and position on the wrapped cheese to form a bow, trimming the ends to resemble trailing ribbons. Place the reserved dough ball in the center of the bow and press to secure.

Place on a baking sheet and brush with the egg. Bake at 375 degrees for 20 minutes or until golden brown. Place on a 12-inch platter. Spoon the sauce carefully around the outer edge. Garnish with kiwifruit and serve with sliced rounds of toasted Cuban Bread (page 138).

Note: For a quick sauce, combine $1/2$ package Ocean Spray cran-raspberry sauce for chicken with 1 tablespoon spiced rum.

Serves ten to twelve

IN 1973, THE JUNIOR SERVICE LEAGUE OF BOCA RATON BEGAN A PUPPET PROGRAM TEACHING THE HISTORY OF BOCA RATON AND OTHER EDUCATIONAL TOPICS IN LOCAL SCHOOLS, AND COMPILED GIFT BASKETS FOR NEIGHBORING MIGRANT WORKERS. JUNIOR SERVICE LEAGUE PRESIDENT JEANNE BAUR SUPPORTED THE CONTINUING EFFORTS TO FURTHER THE ACTIVITIES OF THE BOCA RATON HISTORICAL SOCIETY—BEGUN ONLY A YEAR BEFORE HER TERM.

Goat Cheese and Tomato Tart

Smoky and satisfying served with a salad and crusty bread for a French-style repast.

Bacon Pastry
6 tablespoons (3/4 stick) unsalted butter, softened
2 tablespoons shortening
1 1/4 cups flour
1/4 teaspoon salt
4 ounces bacon, crisp-fried, crumbled
3 to 4 tablespoons ice water

Tart
4 large ripe tomatoes
salt to taste
4 ounces Montrachet cheese, crumbled
4 ounces whole milk mozzarella, shredded
2 eggs, lightly beaten
1/4 cup finely chopped red onion
extra-virgin olive oil

Garnish
basil leaves

For the pastry, beat the butter and shortening in a mixing bowl until light and fluffy. Add the flour and mix until crumbly. Add the salt and bacon gradually, mixing well. Add enough ice water gradually, to form a ball, mixing well after each addition. Wrap in plastic wrap and chill in the refrigerator.

Roll the dough on a lightly floured surface. Fit into a 9-inch tart pan. Bake at 375 degrees for 10 minutes.

For the tart, slice the tomatoes 1/4 inch thick. Place on paper towels and sprinkle with salt. Let stand for several minutes; pat dry. Arrange half the slices in the tart shell.

Combine the Montrachet cheese, mozzarella cheese, eggs and onion in a bowl and mix well. Spread over the tomatoes. Arrange the remaining tomato slices in an overlapping layer over the cheese mixture. Brush with olive oil.

Bake at 350 degrees for 40 minutes. Brush lightly with olive oil. Let stand for 10 minutes before serving. Garnish with basil leaves and slice to serve.

Serves twelve

Orange Bourbon Sours

Combine 2 cups orange juice, 1/2 cup fresh lemon juice, 1/4 cup sugar and 1/2 cup bourbon in a pitcher and mix to dissolve the sugar. Pour over crushed ice in glasses and garnish with thick orange slices.

Bombay Sapphire Martini

Combine 1¹/₂ ounces Bombay
Sapphire Gin with a dash of
Martini & Rossi Extra-Dry
Vermouth with ice in a shaker.
Shake gently and strain into
a chilled martini glass.
Garnish with olives.

Tomato Gorgonzola Torta

*A real eye-catcher. Enjoy each creamy bite of sun-dried tomato
and Gorgonzola teamed with fragrant basil.*

Fresh Pesto
1 cup fresh basil leaves
2 teaspoons fresh parsley
2 garlic cloves
¹/₃ cup grated Parmesan cheese
salt and pepper to taste
¹/₂ cup extra-virgin olive oil

Torta
8 ounces Gorgonzola cheese,
    crumbled
24 ounces cream cheese, softened
1 tablespoon minced garlic
1 (8-ounce) jar marinated sun-
    dried tomatoes, drained,
    chopped
3 tablespoons olive oil
¹/₂ cup pine nuts, toasted

Garnish
fresh basil leaves

For the pesto, combine the basil, parsley, garlic, Parmesan cheese, salt
and pepper in a blender container and process to form a paste. Add the
olive oil gradually, processing until smooth.

For the torta, beat the Gorgonzola cheese and cream cheese in a
mixing bowl until smooth. Spread ¹/₃ of the mixture in an oiled 7-inch
springform pan.

Sauté the garlic and sun-dried tomatoes in the olive oil in a skillet until
tender. Spread over the cheese mixture.

Spread half the remaining cheese mixture over the tomatoes. Layer
the pesto and pine nuts over the layered cheese mixture and top with the
remaining cheese mixture.

Chill, covered, for 3 hours to 3 days. Place on a serving plate and
remove the side of the pan. Garnish with fresh basil leaves. Serve with
French bread which has been brushed with olive oil, sprinkled with basil
and lightly toasted.

Serves twelve

The perfect Bombay Sapphire Martini (page 60) is presented in classic Art Deco style. Mirror on mirror reflects your good design sense and captures the mood in its best light.

Personalizing Caviar Pie

Simply place a cookie cutter
on top of the Caviar Pie and fill the
inside with a different colored
caviar. The many possible designs
and combinations of red, black,
and gold will delight the eye as
well as the palate.

Caviar Pie

*Great served as individual appetizers in crystal
champagne glasses.*

½ cup (1 stick) unsalted butter, softened	2 tablespoons mayonnaise
8 ounces cream cheese, softened	salt to taste
½ cup sour cream	white pepper to taste
4 eggs, hard-cooked, chopped	½ cup red onion, minced
¼ cup drained capers	1 (2-ounce) jar red caviar
	1 (2-ounce) jar yellow caviar

Beat the butter in a mixer bowl until light. Add the cream cheese and mix just until smooth. Stir in the sour cream. Spread half the mixture in a 6-inch springform pan sprayed with nonstick cooking spray. Chill, covered, until firm.

Combine the eggs, capers, mayonnaise, salt and white pepper in a bowl and mix gently. Wrap the onion in a paper towel and twist to remove excess moisture. Spread the egg mixture over the cream cheese layer and top with the minced onion. Press the layers down and top with the remaining cream cheese mixture. Chill, covered, for 8 hours or longer.

Remove the side of the springform pan and place a serving plate on the top. Invert the pan onto the serving plate and remove the bottom. Place a spatula down the center of the pie and spoon the red caviar carefully on one side and the yellow caviar on the other. Chill until serving time. Serve with toast points or plain crackers.

Note: You may layer the ingredients in 8 champagne glasses or ½-cup ramekins if preferred. Dip the ramekins in hot water for 45 seconds and slide a thin knife blade down the side to unmold. Invert onto serving plates. Place champagne glasses directly on serving plates. Top with caviar as above.

Serves eight

Cherry Tomatoes Stuffed with Pesto Orzo

Delicious! The perfect bite to eat while balancing a cocktail.

2 pints cherry tomatoes
4 ounces uncooked orzo
$1/2$ cup fresh basil leaves
1 garlic clove
$1/4$ cup walnuts
$1/4$ cup extra-virgin olive oil
$1/4$ cup grated Parmigiano-Reggiano cheese
$1/4$ cup Romano Locatelli cheese
1 teaspoon sugar
1 teaspoon red wine vinegar
2 teaspoons salt
$1/2$ teaspoon freshly ground pepper

Place the tomatoes stem side down and scoop out the centers with a sharp knife. Invert onto a plate lined with paper towels to drain. Chill in the refrigerator.

Cook the pasta using the package directions; drain.

Combine the basil, garlic and walnuts in a food processor container and process until smooth. Add the olive oil gradually, processing constantly. Combine with the Parmigiano-Reggiano cheese, Romano Locatelli cheese, sugar, vinegar, salt and pepper in a large bowl and mix well. Add the pasta and mix gently. Chill, covered, for 1 hour.

Spoon the mixture into the tomato shells. Arrange on a serving plate.
Serves eighteen

Pearls of the Sea

Beluga is the most highly-valued caviar. Coming from the beluga sturgeon in the Caspian Sea, it has the largest eggs. The beluga sturgeon can be 30 feet long and weigh 3,000 pounds, producing 350 pounds of caviar.

Osetra and sevruga are among the 23 species of sturgeons. They are smaller than the beluga, so the eggs are smaller, but still considered quite desirable.

Alaskan salmon produce a superb red caviar with larger beads.

Whitefish from the Great Lakes produce a golden caviar that is actually more popular for its appearance than its taste.

Spicy Cayenne Toasts with Sun-Dried Tomato Spread

The spiciness is tempered by the amazing tastes of chèvre, sun-dried tomatoes, and basil.

Sun-Dried Tomato Spread
$1^1/2$ ounces dry-pack sun-dried
    tomatoes
$1/4$ cup olive oil
2 garlic cloves, minced
2 tablespoons minced parsley
5 basil leaves, chopped
1 green onion, chopped
sugar to taste
$1/2$ teaspoon salt
1 teaspoon pepper

Toasts
$1/2$ cup olive oil
1 teaspoon sugar
1 teaspoon paprika
$1^1/2$ teaspoons garlic powder
1 teaspoon salt
2 teaspoons cayenne
$1/2$ teaspoon black pepper
1 baguette, sliced $1/4$ inch thick
4 ounces chèvre, crumbled

For the spread, place the sun-dried tomatoes in boiling water to cover and let stand for 5 minutes; drain. Combine with the olive oil, garlic, parsley, basil, green onion, sugar, salt and pepper in a bowl and mix well. Chill, covered, for 4 hours.

For the toasts, combine the olive oil, sugar, paprika, garlic powder, salt, cayenne and black pepper in a food processor container and process until smooth. Arrange the bread slices on a baking sheet. Brush with the olive oil mixture. Bake at 200 degrees for 1 hour or until crisp and golden brown.

Spread the toasts with the spread and top with a sprinkle of chèvre. Arrange on a serving plate.

Serves eight to ten

Wild Mushroom Brie

Mushroom lovers will come back for just one more slice of this flavorful Brie baked in pastry.

16 ounces button mushrooms
8 ounces portobello mushrooms
8 ounces shiitake mushrooms
2 shallots, minced
1/4 cup extra-virgin olive oil
2 tablespoons chopped fresh
    chives

1 (3-ounce) jar pine nuts, toasted
1/4 cup cream sherry
freshly ground pepper to taste
2 pie pastries
1 large round Brie cheese

Wash, trim and chop the mushrooms. Sauté the mushrooms with the shallots in the olive oil in a skillet for several minutes. Add the chives and sauté until the liquid from the mushrooms evaporates. Stir in the pine nuts, sherry and pepper. Cook until the liquid is absorbed.

Place 1 pie pastry in a porcelain quiche pan. Place the Brie cheese on the pastry and spread with the mushroom mixture. Top with the remaining pastry; trim and flute the edge. Shape the leftover pastry into a small mushroom and place in the center of the pastry.

Bake at 400 degrees for 15 minutes or until golden brown. Slice into wedges to serve.

Serves eight

Sauza Hornitos Watermelon Margaritas

Cut enough 1-inch pieces of seeded watermelon to measure 5 cups and place in a sealable plastic bag. Freeze for 3 hours to 1 week. Combine the frozen watermelon with 1 cup of Sauza Hornitos Tequila, 1/2 cup fresh lime juice and 1/4 cup sugar in a 6-cup blender container. Process until thick and smooth. Pour into 5 or 6 glasses to serve.

Walnut and Gorgonzola Crostini

These warm and nutty crostini pack a flavorful bite.

butter, softened
18 (¹/4-inch) diagonally cut
   baguette slices
6 tablespoons chopped toasted
   walnuts
3 tablespoons finely chopped
   fresh arugula

4 ounces Gorgonzola cheese,
   crumbled
freshly ground pepper

Garnish
fresh arugula leaves
18 julienned strips red bell pepper

Spread butter on 1 side of each baguette slice and arrange the slices butter side up on a baking sheet. Bake at 400 degrees until golden brown. Cool completely on the baking sheet. Reduce the oven temperature to 350 degrees.

Combine the walnuts, chopped arugula and cheese in a bowl and mix well. Spread the mixture on the toasted bread, pressing firmly. Sprinkle with pepper. Bake at 350 degrees for 5 to 6 minutes or until the cheese melts. Garnish with the arugula leaves and bell pepper.

Makes eighteen

Spiced Boca Nuts

Love nuts? Coconut? You won't be able to stop munching these.

¹/2 cup sweetened flaked coconut
¹/4 cup sugar
2 teaspoons curry powder
¹/8 teaspoon cayenne, or to taste
1 teaspoon salt

1 large egg white
1 pound mixed nuts such as
   pecans, raw cashews,
   blanched almonds and
   peanuts

Combine the coconut, sugar, curry powder, cayenne and salt in a large bowl, stirring to mix well. Whisk the egg white in a medium bowl until foamy. Add the nuts, tossing to coat well. Add to the coconut mixture and toss to coat well. Spread in a single layer in a buttered shallow baking pan.

Roast at 300 degrees on the middle oven rack for 20 to 30 minutes or until golden brown. Cool in the pan on a wire rack; the nuts will crisp as they cool. Store at room temperature in an airtight container for up to 2 weeks.

Makes four cups

Smoked Salmon Quesadillas

The unexpected combination of boursin cheese and salmon adds a new twist to these delicious quesadillas.

1 cup sour cream
1 tablespoon chopped fresh dill
1 red onion
2 (10-inch) flour tortillas, at room temperature
4 ounces boursin cheese

2 ripe plum tomatoes, seeded, chopped
2 teaspoons chopped fresh dill
1 teaspoon drained capers
4 ounces smoked salmon
1/4 cup olive oil

Combine the sour cream and 1 tablespoon dill in a blender container and process until smooth. Cut the onion into halves and slice into rings.

Place the tortillas on a work surface and spread 2 ounces of cheese over half of each tortilla. Sprinkle each with half the tomato, 1 teaspoon chopped dill, 1/2 teaspoon capers and 2 ounces smoked salmon. Fold the tortillas in half to enclose the filling, pressing lightly to seal.

Heat the olive oil in a skillet over medium heat and add the tortillas. Fry until golden brown, turning once. Cut into wedges and serve with the sour cream mixture and onion.

Serves four

Fontina and Corn Quesadillas

Guests will want another of these south-of-the-border treats.

2 teaspoons olive oil
1 cup frozen corn kernels, thawed
2 jalapeños, seeded, chopped
1 teaspoon dried oregano

olive oil
8 (7-inch) flour tortillas
2 cups grated fontina cheese

Heat 2 teaspoons olive oil in a heavy medium skillet over medium heat. Add the corn, jalapeños and oregano and sauté for 2 minutes.

Heat a medium skillet over medium heat and brush with olive oil. Add 1 tortilla at a time and sprinkle with 1/4 of the cheese and corn mixture. Top with a second tortilla, pressing down lightly.

Cook for 2 minutes on each side or until golden brown and the cheese melts. Repeat the process with the remaining ingredients. Cut into wedges to serve.

Note: The corn mixture can be prepared 1 day in advance and stored, covered, in the refrigerator.

Serves four

Choice Chiles

Choose individual chiles rather than chili powders for a fresher taste. Anchos, with their sweet raisiny flavor are the most common mild chiles for chili con carne. Adding New Mexico Reds and California chiles will add a more complex flavor without turning up the heat. Pasillas are slightly hotter than those already described. For extra fire, you may want to consider guajillo, de Arbol, pequin, japanais, Scotch bonnet, jalapeños, habaneros and cayenne. If you taste as you go, you can build the flavor and avoid a fiery, overly hot chili.

If, however, you want to learn to eat hot foods, try a tiny bit and then take a break for at least two minutes. Try some more, stop again, and repeat. The research shows that a dish with the same amount of chiles will not feel as hot after a brief rest. This phenomenon is called "temporary desensitization." It's generally accepted that the reason that some people can take more heat is because they have fewer taste buds.

Saté with Peanut Sauce

There is something for everyone in this marinated trio. Dip the skewers once in creamy peanut sauce and the party begins.

Saté
1 cup teriyaki sauce
4 garlic cloves, minced
3 tablespoons fresh lime juice
2¹/₂ tablespoons minced
    gingerroot
2 tablespoons brown sugar
1¹/₄ pounds boneless skinless
    chicken breasts
1¹/₄ pounds beef skirt steak or
    filet mignon
24 medium uncooked shrimp,
    peeled, deveined

Peanut Sauce
1 (14-ounce) can chicken broth
1 cup creamy peanut butter
¹/₄ cup fresh lime juice
3 tablespoons brown sugar
2 tablespoons plus 1 teaspoon
    soy sauce
2 tablespoons chopped
    gingerroot
¹/₂ teaspoon crushed dried red
    pepper

Garnish
julienned lime peel
lime slices
hibiscus or gardenia blossoms

For the saté, combine the teriyaki sauce, garlic, lime juice, ginger and brown sugar in a large glass dish and stir until the brown sugar dissolves.

Cut the chicken into ¹/₂-inch strips. Cut the beef skirt into ¹/₂x3-inch strips or filet mignon into ¹/₄x¹/₂x3-inch strips. Add the shrimp, chicken and beef to the marinade, coating well. Marinate, covered, in the refrigerator for 30 to 60 minutes.

Soak 36 bamboo skewers in water for 30 minutes. Drain the shrimp, chicken and beef. Alternate 3 shrimp and 2 pieces of beef and chicken on each skewer. Grill over medium-high heat or broil for 3 minutes on each side or until cooked through.

For the sauce, stir the chicken broth gradually into the peanut butter in a heavy medium saucepan. Add the lime juice, brown sugar, soy sauce, ginger and red pepper. Cook over medium heat for 6 minutes or until thickened, stirring constantly. Thin with water if necessary and reheat to serve. Spoon into a bowl.

To serve, line a large platter with banana leaves or ornamental kale. Place the peanut sauce in the center; garnish with the lime peel. Arrange the skewers around the sauce. Garnish with lime slices and blossoms.

Note: Do not use old-fashioned style or freshly ground peanut butter in this recipe. The sauce can be stored, covered, in the refrigerator for up to 3 days; the prepared skewers can be stored, covered, in the refrigerator for up to 2 hours before grilling.

Serves twelve

Curried Chicken Triangles

It's a good thing.

10 ounces boneless chicken
    breasts
1 tablespoon butter
$1^1/_2$ tablespoons flour
$^1/_2$ teaspoon curry powder
$^1/_2$ cup milk

$^1/_4$ teaspoon kosher salt
$^1/_4$ cup chopped toasted walnuts
$^1/_2$ (16-ounce) package phyllo
1 cup (2 sticks) unsalted butter,
    melted

Wrap the chicken in buttered foil and place in a baking dish. Roast at 375 degrees for 30 to 45 minutes or until cooked through. Open the foil and cool the chicken; cut into small pieces.

Melt 1 tablespoon butter in a small saucepan. Stir in the flour and curry powder. Cook over low heat for 1 to 2 minutes, stirring constantly. Whisk in the milk. Cook until thickened, whisking constantly. Stir in the salt, walnuts and chicken. Cool completely.

Layer the phyllo 3 sheets at a time on a work surface, brushing each with the melted butter. Cut the layers into halves lengthwise, then cut each half crosswise into 6 equal portions.

Spoon 1 teaspoon of the chicken mixture onto the end of each strip and fold over to form a triangle. Continue to fold as for a flag to the end of each strip. Place the triangles on a buttered baking sheet. Brush with butter. Bake at 400 degrees for 10 minutes or until golden brown.

Serves twelve

Sesame Chicken Bites

Serve with heated apricot jam and spicy grainy mustard.

3 tablespoons butter
1 egg
$^1/_3$ cup milk
$^1/_4$ cup flour
$^1/_2$ teaspoon baking powder
$^1/_2$ cup chopped macadamias

$^1/_4$ cup sesame seeds
1 tablespoon paprika
1 teaspoon salt
$^1/_2$ teaspoon pepper
$1^1/_2$ pounds boneless chicken
    breasts, cubed

Melt the butter in a 9x9-inch baking dish. Beat the egg and milk in a small bowl. Mix the next 7 ingredients together.

Dip the chicken in the egg mixture and then in the macadamia mixture, coating well. Arrange in the baking dish, turning to coat with butter and ending with the chicken pieces skin side down. Bake at 400 degrees for 30 minutes, turning after 15 minutes.

Serves six

Curry Sauce

Sauté 1 chopped garlic clove and 1 teaspoon curry powder in $1^1/_2$ tablespoons olive oil. Combine with $^1/_2$ cup mayonnaise, $^1/_2$ cup sour cream, 2 tablespoons orange juice and 1 tablespoon chutney in a blender container and mix until smooth. Store in the refrigerator for up to 2 weeks.

Escargots in Poblanos with Sourdough Croutons

A French favorite with a Southwest flavor from Dakotah 624.
Bon appétit, amigos!

Sourdough Croutons
8 slices sourdough bread
1/4 cup olive oil
1/2 teaspoon Italian seasoning
salt to taste
1/2 teaspoon pepper

Escargots
3 tablespoons olive oil
3 ounces sliced garlic
8 poblanos, split, seeded
72 escargots
5 tablespoons butter
6 tablespoons white wine
salt and pepper to taste

Garnish
2 tablespoons chopped parsley

For the croutons, cut the bread into sixty-four 1/2-inch cubes. Drizzle with the olive oil and sprinkle with the Italian seasoning, salt and pepper in a bowl, tossing to coat well. Spread on a baking sheet. Bake at 350 degrees until golden brown. Turn off the oven and let stand until completely dry.

For the escargots, heat the olive oil in a large skillet until very hot. Add the garlic and sauté just until light brown. Add the peppers, escargots and butter. Add the wine, stirring to deglaze. Cook for 2 to 4 minutes.

Remove the peppers with a slotted spoon. Stir the croutons, salt and pepper into the escargot mixture. Spoon the escargot mixture into the peppers with a slotted spoon. Drizzle with the garlic butter remaining in the skillet. Garnish with the parsley.

Serves eight

IN 1978, THE JUNIOR SERVICE LEAGUE OF BOCA RATON CONTINUED THE EFFORTS OF THE BOCA RATON HISTORICAL SOCIETY TO RESTORE ONE OF BOCA RATON'S TYPICAL "CRACKER" STYLE HOMES INTO A CHILDREN'S MUSEUM. UNDER THE DIRECTION OF PRESIDENT CHRISTINE CRITCHFIELD, JUNIOR SERVICE LEAGUE MEMBERS EXPANDED THE CITY'S FIRST CHILDREN'S MUSEUM AND ESTABLISHED SINGING PINES CHILDREN'S MUSEUM AS AN INDEPENDENT ENTITY.

Macadamia-Stuffed Mushrooms

The essential elegant pass-around appetizer with the unexpected crunch of macadamias.

1 pound medium mushrooms
$^1/_2$ cup chopped sweet onion
2 tablespoons ($^1/_4$ stick) butter
$^1/_2$ cup chopped macadamias
1 tablespoon dry white wine
1 teaspoon salt
$^1/_2$ teaspoon pepper
$^1/_2$ cup (or more) bread crumbs

Remove the stems from the mushrooms, reserving the caps and stems. Chop the stems coarsely. Sauté the stems with the onion in the butter in a skillet until the onion is translucent and the mushrooms are tender.

Add the macadamias, wine, salt and pepper. Add enough bread crumbs to bind the mixture.

Stuff the mixture into the mushroom caps. Arrange on a baking sheet. Bake at 425 degrees for 10 minutes.

Serves twelve

Entertaining Suggestions

To be a good hostess:
Suggest the proper attire based on
the theme, mood, and season.
Have good food, but don't
hide in the kitchen.
Remember that fancy people
like informal parties.
Lighting is everything–there
can't be too many candles.
For place cards, write on
anything from paper to drink
holders to holiday ornaments.
Separate couples at the table.
Invite everyone! People take up
less space than you think.
Use round tables for good
conversation.
Set the table to beckon the guests.
Keep the height of the centerpiece
less than 11 inches.

To be a good guest:
Encourage others to talk about
themselves by asking questions.
They will think you are brilliant.
Be "on," talk, laugh, and have fun.
Bring out the best in others.
R.S.V.P. on time.
Offer the best hostess gift–
a great guest!

Sun-Dried Tomato Mousse

Creamy and cool, elegant to serve with breadsticks or crackers.

1 cup (2 sticks) unsalted butter, softened
16 ounces cream cheese, softened
1/2 cup oil-pack sun-dried tomatoes, drained, chopped
1 garlic clove, crushed
1 (6-ounce) can tomato paste
1 tablespoon dried basil
2 teaspoons salt
1/2 teaspoon pepper

Beat the butter in a mixing bowl until very smooth but not fluffy. Add the cream cheese and mix just until blended. Stir in the sun-dried tomatoes, garlic, tomato paste, basil, salt and pepper; do not overmix.

Spoon the mixture into a 6-inch springform pan. Chill for 8 hours or until very firm.

Place the pan in hot water for 15 seconds. Release the spring and invert the mousse onto a serving plate. Smooth the top with a warm spatula. Garnish by pressing chopped fresh parsley or chopped toasted pine nuts onto the side.

Serves sixteen

In 1979, the Junior Service League of Boca Raton showcased their efforts begun three years earlier with a grand opening celebration at Singing Pines, a children's museum. Under the direction of president Katharine Dickenson and the Boca Raton Historical Society, Junior Service League members also began work on another historic preservation signature project—the restoration of Boca Raton's Old Town Hall.

Baked Grouper Bites with Banana Salsa

Take a trip to the islands with every crunchy bite.

Banana Salsa
$1/2$ cup chopped green bell pepper
$1/2$ cup chopped red bell pepper
3 green onions, chopped
1 tablespoon chopped cilantro
1 small jalapeño, seeded, chopped (optional)
2 tablespoons light brown sugar
3 tablespoons fresh lime juice
1 tablespoon vegetable oil
$1/4$ teaspoon salt
$1/4$ teaspoon pepper
2 medium bananas, chopped

Grouper
$1^1/2$ cups crushed potato chips
$1/4$ cup grated Parmesan cheese
1 teaspoon ground thyme
1 pound grouper fillets, cut into strips
$1/4$ cup milk

For the salsa, combine the bell peppers, green onions, cilantro, jalapeño, brown sugar, lime juice, oil, salt and pepper in a bowl and mix well. Add the bananas and mix gently. Chill, covered, for 3 hours or longer.

For the grouper, mix the potato chips, cheese and thyme in a shallow dish. Dip the fish into the milk and then into the potato chip mixture, coating well.

Arrange in a single layer in a greased baking dish. Bake at 500 degrees for 8 to 10 minutes or until cooked through. Serve with the salsa.

Serves four

Warm and Savory Crab Baguettes

Combine 1 cup mayonnaise, $1/2$ cup grated onion, 1 cup shredded Cheddar cheese, 6 drops Tabasco sauce, $1/4$ teaspoon curry powder and 8 ounces drained crab meat in a bowl and mix well. Cut 2 baguettes into $1/2$-inch slices. Top with the crab mixture. Place on a baking sheet and broil until golden brown. Serve immediately.

Stone Crab Claws with Mustard Sauce

Stone crabs are native to Florida. Fishermen take the smaller claw and return the crab to the ocean to regenerate another claw, a process that takes about 18 months.

Try serving the crab claws with a mustard sauce. Combine $1/2$ cup brown mustard, 1 cup mayonnaise, 1 tablespoon Worcestershire sauce, 2 tablespoons brown sugar, 2 tablespoons dry sherry and 1 teaspoon dry mustard in a bowl and mix well. Chill for 1 hour to 4 days before serving.

Smoked Salmon on Potatoes with Dill Sauce

A dish that will be remembered and requested many times.

Dill Sauce
1 cup sour cream
$1/2$ cup minced fresh dill
2 tablespoons Dijon mustard
2 tablespoons light brown sugar

Salmon and Potatoes
3 pounds small unpeeled new potatoes
6 tablespoons olive oil
2 tablespoons finely grated lemon zest
salt and pepper to taste
1 pound thinly sliced smoked salmon

For the sauce, combine the sour cream, dill, Dijon mustard and brown sugar in a bowl and mix until the brown sugar is dissolved. Chill, covered, in the refrigerator.

For the salmon and potatoes, scoop a depression in the center of each potato, reserving the shells. Combine the shells with the olive oil and lemon zest in a large bowl. Sprinkle with salt and pepper turning to coat well. Arrange in a single layer on large baking sheets.

Bake at 400 degrees for 30 minutes or until golden brown and tender when pierced with the tip of a knife.

Cut the salmon into 1-inch squares. Spoon the dill sauce onto each potato and top with a square of salmon. Arrange on a serving plate. Garnish with dill sprigs.

Serves twenty-four

Baked Crab Cakes with Chunky Peach Salsa

A lighter version of everyone's favorite crab cake with a sassy peach salsa to top it off.

Crab Cakes

1/2 cup finely chopped onion
1/2 cup finely chopped celery
1 garlic clove, minced
1/2 cup chopped scallions
3 tablespoons unsalted butter
1 pound lump crab meat, drained, picked over
2 tablespoons minced fresh parsley
1/3 cup mayonnaise
1/4 teaspoon baking soda
1 teaspoon dry mustard
1 teaspoon salt
cayenne to taste
1/4 teaspoon freshly ground pepper
1 1/2 cups crushed saltines

Chunky Peach Salsa

2 firm medium peaches, peeled, chopped
1 tablespoon fresh lemon juice or lime juice
2 medium tomatoes, peeled, seeded, chopped
4 scallions, chopped
1 tablespoon chopped jalapeño
1 tablespoon coarsely chopped cilantro
1/4 cup extra-virgin olive oil
3 tablespoons sherry vinegar
2 tablespoons honey

For the crab cakes, sauté the onion, celery, garlic and scallions in the butter in a medium skillet over medium heat for 5 minutes. Remove from the heat and stir in the crab meat and parsley.

Combine the mayonnaise, baking soda, dry mustard, salt, cayenne and pepper in a small bowl. Fold into the crab meat mixture with 1/3 cup of the cracker crumbs.

Shape into 6 medium or 12 small cakes and roll in the remaining cracker crumbs. Arrange on a baking sheet lined with baking parchment.

Bake at 450 degrees for 10 minutes or until light brown. Turn and bake for 15 minutes longer.

For the salsa, toss the peaches with the lemon juice in a bowl. Add the tomatoes, scallions, jalapeño and cilantro and toss to mix well. Whisk the olive oil, vinegar and honey in a small bowl. Add to the peach mixture and toss to mix. Serve with the crab cakes.

Serves six

Florida Spritzer

Combine 1 1/2 cups grapefruit juice, 1/4 cup sugar and one 2-inch piece of cinnamon in a saucepan. Bring to a boil, reduce the heat, and simmer for 5 minutes. Discard the cinnamon and cool the syrup. Chill in the refrigerator. Fill four 8-ounce glasses with ice and add about 1/3 cup of the grapefruit syrup to each glass. Fill the glasses with ginger ale and stir gently. Garnish with curls of grapefruit peel.

Sea Breeze Cocktails

Combine 6 ounces vodka, 1/2 cup grapefruit juice and 2 cups cranberry juice in a pitcher. Pour over ice in 4 glasses. Garnish with lime wedges.

Be Known for Something

Some people have an entertaining signature–something for which they are known. Infusing vodka for vodka shooters could be yours! Pour your favorite vodka into a container with a lid. Add raspberries and steep in the refrigerator for 3 or 4 days. Strain it into a bottle, cover, and freeze. It not only tastes great, it's a beautiful treat. And what a signature!

Marinated Mussels

Fresh ginger and soy sauce wake up your taste buds with these orient-inspired mussels topped with crunchy almonds.

2 pounds mussels, cleaned
1/4 cup vegetable oil
1/4 cup soy sauce
juice of 2 limes
1/2 cup chopped onion
1 cup roasted almonds, chopped
2 tablespoons chopped gingerroot
1 tablespoon sugar

Garnish
finely chopped parsley

Combine the mussels with a small amount of water in a large saucepan. Cover and bring to a boil. Cook just until the shells open; discard any shells that do not open.

Cool the mussels and remove from the shells, reserving the same half of each shell.

Combine the oil, soy sauce, lime juice, onion, almonds, ginger and sugar in a bowl and mix well. Add the mussels. Marinate, covered, in the refrigerator for 1 to 8 hours.

Drain the mussels, reserving the marinade. Strain the marinade, reserving the almond mixture. Place each mussel on a shell half. Top with the almond mixture and garnish with the parsley.

Serves eight

*S*pin the ferris wheel for the garnish of your choice. It's a must when space is at a premium and
you want to take every opportunity to entertain your guests.

Orange Vodka Sauce

Combine 1³/4 cups orange
marmalade, 6 ounces vodka,
¹/4 cup packed light brown sugar
and 2 tablespoons marsala
wine in a bowl and whisk
to mix well. Stir in 1 tablespoon
finely chopped cilantro.
Serve with Transcontinental
Shrimp (at right).

Transcontinental Shrimp

*Crisp and tangy! This Damiano's Restaurant specialty will knock
your socks off!*

4 Idaho potatoes	3 eggs
²/3 cup flour	1 to 1¹/2 cups beer
2 teaspoons baking soda	12 medium uncooked shrimp,
¹/8 teaspoon salt	peeled, deveined
cayenne to taste	vegetable oil for deep-frying
¹/8 teaspoon pepper	Orange Vodka Sauce (at left)

Peel and shred the potatoes and place in a bowl of cold water.

Mix the next 5 ingredients in a large mixing bowl. Beat in the eggs and
enough beer to make a batter thick enough to adhere to the shrimp.

Drain the potatoes and press to remove the moisture. Add to the beer
batter and mix well. Dry the shrimp with paper towels.

Heat the oil in a heavy medium saucepan. Dip the shrimp into the
batter and deep-fry in the hot oil until golden brown.

Serve with Orange Vodka Sauce.

Serves four

Scallops with Mango Salsa

*Easy to prepare, beautiful to your guests. Light, healthy,
and delicious!*

¹/2 cup chopped mango	¹/2 teaspoon minced gingerroot
¹/2 cup chopped pineapple	juice of ¹/2 lime
2 tablespoons minced red onion	1 pound sea scallops
¹/4 cup minced red bell pepper	¹/2 tablespoon unsalted butter
1¹/2 teaspoons minced	
jalapeño	**Garnish**
1¹/2 teaspoons chopped cilantro	grated lime zest

Combine the mango, pineapple, onion, bell pepper, jalapeño, cilantro,
gingerroot and lime juice in a bowl and mix well. Chill for up to 24 hours.

Cut the scallops into quarters. Sauté in the butter in a nonstick skillet
over high heat for 1 minute. Spoon into 12 scallop shells or small dishes.
Top with the salsa. Garnish with lime zest.

Serves twelve

Bistro Shrimp Cakes

This alternative to crab cakes is a favorite at Gigi's.

Tomato Corn Relish
$1/2$ cup rice wine vinegar
$1/2$ cup olive oil
1 teaspoon Molido
kernels of 4 ears roasted corn
1 medium tomato, seeded,
    chopped
$1/2$ green bell pepper,
    finely chopped
$1/2$ red bell pepper, finely chopped
$1/2$ red onion, finely chopped
$1/4$ bunch green onions, chopped
$1/4$ teaspoon salt
$1/4$ teaspoon pepper

Shrimp Cakes
2 pounds uncooked shrimp,
    finely chopped
1 ounce chives, minced
juice and grated zest of 1 lemon
1 cup mayonnaise
3 cups bread crumbs
$1/2$ teaspoon salt
$1/2$ teaspoon white pepper
vegetable oil

For the relish, combine the vinegar, olive oil and Molido in a bowl and mix well. Add the corn, tomato, bell peppers, onion and green onions and mix well. Season with salt and pepper.

For the shrimp cakes, combine the shrimp, chives, lemon juice, lemon zest, mayonnaise, bread crumbs, salt and white pepper in a bowl and mix well. Shape into 2-ounce cakes.

Sauté in a small amount of oil in a skillet for 2 minutes on each side or until golden brown. Serve with the relish.

Note: Molido can be found in Spanish markets.

Serves four

Buddha Bowl

This is the Red Bowl's version of Long Island Iced Tea. Combine 2 ounces dark rum, 2 ounces light rum, $1/4$ ounce passion fruit syrup, $3/4$ ounce honey, $3/4$ ounce fresh lime juice, 1 ounce fresh orange juice, 1 ounce fresh grapefruit juice, 1 ounce club soda, and a dash of bitters and grenadine in a pitcher and mix well. Serve over ice in tall frosted glasses.

Shrimp with Cajun Rémoulade Sauce

Piquant marinated and grilled shrimp is a lovely start to any barbecue.

Rémoulade Sauce
1/2 cup mayonnaise
1 tablespoon lemon juice
2 teaspoons minced garlic
2 teaspoons minced shallot
1 tablespoon minced cilantro
1 tablespoon minced parsley
1 tablespoon minced chives
1/2 hard-cooked egg, chopped
1 tablespoon chopped capers
1 to 2 teaspoons Cajun seasoning
cayenne, salt and pepper to taste

Shrimp
3 garlic cloves, chopped
2 shallots, chopped
2 teaspoons lime juice
2 tablespoons minced basil
salt and pepper to taste
vegetable oil
1 to 2 pounds large uncooked
*   shrimp, peeled*

For the sauce, combine the mayonnaise, lemon juice, garlic, shallot, cilantro, parsley, chives, egg, capers, Cajun seasoning, cayenne, salt and pepper in a bowl and mix well.

For the shrimp, combine the garlic, shallots, lime juice, basil, salt and pepper in a shallow dish. Add enough oil to coat the shrimp and mix well.

Add the shrimp, stirring to coat well. Marinate in the refrigerator for 3 hours or longer; drain.

Grill the shrimp until opaque and pink. Serve with the sauce.

Serves four to eight

In 1980, Junior Service League of Boca Raton members continued to work on new projects for alcohol awareness, as well as for runaway and abused teenage girls. Under the direction of president Mary C. Lavalle, the Junior League initiated a Volunteer Career Development Course for its new members—recognizing the opportunity for women to use their Junior League training in career placements.

Spicy Grilled Shrimp

Be sure you have plenty of these bold and flavorful appetizers to take to the game or the beach, wherever the party is!

Shrimp Marinade
$^1/_4$ cup extra-virgin olive oil
2 tablespoons Worcestershire sauce
$^3/_4$ cup catsup
1 garlic clove, crushed
1 tablespoon sugar
2 teaspoons ground cumin
2 teaspoons ground coriander
$^1/_4$ teaspoon cayenne
2 bay leaves
2 pounds (15-count) shrimp

Shrimp
20 pear tomatoes or small plum tomatoes
5 medium red onions, cut into quarters
20 basil leaves

For the marinated shrimp, combine the olive oil, Worcestershire sauce, catsup, garlic, sugar, cumin, coriander, cayenne and bay leaves in a shallow dish and mix well. Peel and devein the shrimp, leaving the tails intact. Add the shrimp to the marinade, turning to coat well. Marinate, covered, in the refrigerator for 2 to 24 hours.

To cook the shrimp, soak 10 bamboo skewers in water for 1 hour. Drain the shrimp and skewers. Thread 3 shrimp, 2 tomatoes, 2 onion quarters and 2 basil leaves onto each skewer. Grill over hot coals for 3 to 5 minutes or until the shrimp are opaque and pink. Serve warm or cold.

Serves ten

Tropical Salsa

Combine 8 to 10 chopped tomatoes, 3 chopped mangoes, 6 chopped garlic cloves and $^3/_4$ cup olive oil in a bowl and mix to get all the garlic in the oil. Microwave on High for 2 minutes and let stand until cool or longer. Add $^1/_2$ cup seasoned rice wine vinegar, $^1/_4$ cup canola oil, 20 to 30 shakes Tabasco sauce, 2 big bunches chopped cilantro and 2 bunches chopped scallions. Serve as an appetizer dip or as a colorful accompaniment to fish, chicken, pork, or steak.

Breads & Breakfasts

French Country Charm

What better way to start the day than with the vibrant allure of a French Country breakfast? Le style Provençal is the haut decor of informal elegance. And it can work just as well for a leisurely brunch.

Designed to warm the hearts of all who greet the day in your home, this savory buffet is a natural beginning, whether entertaining weekend guests, sharing a special welcome home for family, or hosting an early morning meeting of community volunteers.

The irresistible aroma of Ham and Cheese Strata (page 102) in its own whimsical jambon cachepot and baskets of fresh baked Vegetable Bread (page 94), Poppy Seed Bread (page 89) and Strawberry Streusel Muffins (page 90) awaken the senses, while a tempting Honeydew Mimosa (page 101) is an unexpected early morning treat that stirs conversation even while the sun is still rising in the sky.

At this breakfast, the inviting garden view through leaded glass windows and a round portal assures that every guest will look on the sunny side. Even if a vista this fetching is not within sight, you can easily capture the imagination with a vignette of cool stone statues or a stone bench, accents of wrought iron tables and marble boards, and loose bouquets of yellow flowers and fruits.

To recreate the fields of lavender in the French countryside, choose an urn like this hostess procured, or plant the lavender and other herbs to overflow in terra-cotta flowerpots.

In a sunny breakfast room of this historic Boca Raton home, natural colors of sun and sky with earthy and botanical accents dominate at this French Country-style breakfast. The outdoors is brought in with lots of garden flowers and fresh herbs.

Provide scissors so your guests can add a favorite herb to their entrée. Large potted ficus or lemon trees will further bring the outdoors into your "garden" setting, as will lots of ivy, and live topiaries from the garden shop. Small potted herbs tied with ribbon are great party favors. Set them at every place with a guest's name painted on each pot.

The gray and white marble and wrought iron table is a natural for a morning buffet. It works well as a neutral backdrop for the bright colors of the fruit and linens. A marble-topped sofa table or an antique quilt in faded colors over a cherry table would also provide a fitting background.

To add variation in height to this buffet, the French tulips stand loosely in a 15-inch pewter stein, a replica of authentic steins dating back to 1687. An antique cutting board here and a pewter pedestal cake plate there continue the juxtaposition of high and low.

The Promise of a New Day

Set the table with the colors of the French countryside: cerulean blue, sunny yellow, and russet. Add accents of green, ocher, and dusty rose in any combination. For added inspiration, look at the work of van Gogh and Cézanne painted in Arles and around the countryside of Provence. Emphasize the mood of spring with pink zinnias, marigolds, and hydrangeas. For an autumn palette, choose bouquets of yellow solidago and accents in rust.

From chateau to cottage, antique wood block prints on soft cotton fabric can be found on table linens, place mats and pillows in Provence. The ones for this breakfast are bright paisley patterns from Pierre Deux.

Handmade faience plates—pottery with glazing techniques handed down through the generations—characteristically show cheerful village scenes, animals, and botanicals rendered in strong colors. This hostess chose the patterns "La Fleur" and "Provence" for the plates and "Montpellier" flatware, all from Pierre Deux. Hand-blown glassware and a bit of pewter complete the look of an easy, comfortable, yet beautiful, lifestyle with its own seductive sophistication.

Elegance á la Carte

At this dining table, the character of the French countryside is heightened with turn-of-the-century "Quimper" faience figurines from Brittany which stand next to little vases of blue iris and white tulips.

Traditionally, the charm of French Country comes from letting the glow of the polished fruitwood table or the weathered texture of the farm table show. An old rectangular pine farm table and rush seats can provide an instant Country French focal point for any kitchen or dining room. Treasured time spent scouring antique stores to add side tables, a special footstool, and a massive 19th-century hutch will complete the look.

Drawing from the Big Picture

The signature of French Country style is a thoughtful combination of thick, brightly painted and glazed clay pottery, hand blown glass, and paisley cottons in vibrant colors. Tie little bits of fabric around stemware bases to add more character. Use pewter accents or substitute copper if you have a collection. Try colored glass bottles for herb vinegars and oils. Dried lavender bunches are very French.

Clay is everywhere in Provence. Nature inspires the colors. Accents of garden statuary date back to Roman times. As long as you maintain substantial earthy lines and bright clear colors, you can recreate your own version of French Country. This means shying away from cut crystal and fine china, and creating sophisticated elegance with accessories like a lacquered commode and touches of silver.

When French paisley place mats are not available, reinforce the natural look with round grass place mats, or choose an American Calico. Vary and layer the chargers. Try a layer of pewter, then a complementary color like the blue used at this gathering. Not every piece needs to be French.

During the height of the season, send invitations for breakfast rather than lunch because a cheerful, graceful breakfast setting can be created in less time. A dish of strawberries and layers of fresh fruit in a glass trifle dish delight the eye on this beautiful marble and wrought iron table.

Menu

*Pictured recipes

All Buttered Up

Try these flavored butters on your scones, muffins, and waffles for a festive and tasty touch!

For Maple Butter, combine $1/2$ cup softened butter and $3/4$ cup pure maple syrup and mix until fluffy.

For Cinnamon Butter, blend $1/2$ cup softened butter, 1 tablespoon brown sugar and 1 teaspoon cinnamon.

For Orange Butter or Lemon Butter, combine $1/2$ cup softened butter and $1/2$ teaspoon fresh orange zest or lemon zest.

For Strawberry Butter, combine $1/2$ cup softened butter and two large, fresh, ripe, hulled strawberries with confectioners' sugar to taste.

For Honey-Pecan Butter, toast $1/3$ cup of pecans in a shallow pan for about 8 minutes and finely chop. Beat $1/2$ cup softened butter until fluffy, then beat in 2 tablespoons of honey. Mix in the pecans.

Buttermilk Chive Biscuits

Hearty biscuits flavored with fresh parsley and chives.

2 cups flour	1 teaspoon sugar
1 tablespoon chopped fresh chives	$1/2$ teaspoon salt
1 tablespoon chopped fresh parsley	$3/4$ cup buttermilk
	$1/4$ cup vegetable oil
1 tablespoon baking powder	2 tablespoons butter, melted

Mix the flour, chives, parsley, baking powder, sugar and salt in a medium bowl. Add the buttermilk and oil all at once and stir until just blended. Knead about 10 times on a lightly floured surface. Roll $3/4$ inch thick and cut with a floured 2-inch biscuit cutter.

Brush a baking sheet with the melted butter, reserving some for the tops of the biscuits. Place the biscuits 2 inches apart on the baking sheet. Brush the tops with the remaining butter. Bake at 425 degrees for 15 minutes or until golden brown. Cool for 5 minutes before serving.

Serves eight

Lemon Cream Scones

Ideal for brunch or afternoon tea.

2 cups flour	1 teaspoon freshly grated lemon zest
$1/4$ cup sugar	
1 tablespoon baking powder	$1 1/4$ cups heavy cream
$1/2$ teaspoon salt	3 tablespoons unsalted butter, melted
$3/4$ cup dried fruit such as cranberries, cherries, blueberries or chopped apricots	2 tablespoons sugar
	1 tablespoon freshly grated lemon zest

Mix the flour, $1/4$ cup sugar, baking powder and salt in a large bowl. Stir in the dried fruit and 1 teaspoon lemon zest. Add the heavy cream and mix until just moistened. Knead gently on a lightly floured surface. Roll into a 10-inch circle, $1/2$ inch thick. Cut into 12 wedges. Arrange the wedges 2 inches apart on a greased baking sheet. Brush with the melted butter.

Combine 2 tablespoons sugar and 1 tablespoon lemon zest in a small bowl. Sprinkle over the scones. Bake at 425 degrees for 15 minutes or until lightly browned. Remove to a wire rack and cool slightly. Serve warm or at room temperature.

Makes one dozen

Sour Cream Banana Bread

The special topping makes this classic irresistible.

Bread
1^{1}/$_{2}$ cups flour
1 teaspoon baking soda
^{1}/$_{2}$ teaspoon salt
1 cup sugar
2 eggs
^{1}/$_{2}$ cup (1 stick) butter, softened
1 teaspoon vanilla extract
1 cup sour cream
2 ripe bananas, mashed
1^{1}/$_{2}$ cups chopped pecans

Coconut Topping
^{1}/$_{2}$ cup packed brown sugar
5 tablespoons butter
^{3}/$_{4}$ cup chopped pecans, toasted
1 cup sweetened flaked coconut

For the bread, sift the flour, baking soda and salt into a large bowl. Beat the sugar, eggs, butter and vanilla in a medium bowl. Add the sour cream, mashed bananas and pecans and mix well. Add to the dry ingredients and stir until well combined.

Pour the batter into a greased and floured large loaf pan. Bake at 350 degrees for 1 hour or until a wooden pick inserted in the center comes out clean. Cool for 10 minutes before removing from the pan.

For the topping, combine the brown sugar and butter in a saucepan. Cook over medium heat until the butter is melted, stirring to blend well. Remove from the heat and stir in the pecans and coconut. Spoon over the loaf while warm.

Makes one loaf

Seeing Spots

Don't throw those spotted bananas away. Save them for breads and baking by placing them in sealable plastic bags and freezing them. When ready to use, thaw until softened.

Lime Bread with Blueberries

Satisfy your taste whims by substituting raspberries for the blueberries and use lemon juice instead of lime—mmmm...

6 tablespoons (³/4 stick) butter, softened
1 cup sugar
2 eggs
¹/2 cup milk
1¹/2 cups flour
1 teaspoon baking powder
¹/2 teaspoon salt
grated zest of 1 lime
¹/2 cup fresh blueberries
juice of 1 lime
¹/2 cup sugar

Cream the butter and 1 cup sugar in a bowl until light. Beat in the eggs. Add the milk and mix well. Sift the flour, baking powder and salt into a bowl. Add to the butter mixture and beat until smooth. Stir in lime zest and blueberries.

Pour the batter into a greased 4x6-inch loaf pan. Bake at 350 degrees for 1 hour or until a wooden pick inserted in the center comes out clean.

Mix the lime juice and ¹/2 cup sugar in a bowl until the sugar dissolves. Spoon over the hot bread before removing from the pan.

Makes one loaf

A TWO-TERM JUNIOR SERVICE LEAGUE OF BOCA RATON PRESIDENT, CATHERINE C. TOOMEY, SAW THE MEMBERSHIP THROUGH BUSY YEARS IN 1981 AND 1982 AS THE SERVICE LEAGUE READIED TO BECOME AN OFFICIAL JUNIOR LEAGUE. A SERIES OF FUNDRAISERS FOUND THEIR ROOTS DURING THOSE YEARS AND HAVE SINCE BECOME COMMUNITY FAVORITES. THE FIESTA OF ARTS AND CRAFTS, A LEAGUE-SPONSORED EVENT FOR MORE THAN TWENTY YEARS, ATTRACTS AWARD-WINNING ARTISTS AND CRAFTSPEOPLE TO BOCA RATON FOR A WEEKEND OF FAMILY FUN.

Poppy Seed Bread

You can also bake as muffins, if you prefer.

Bread
3 eggs
$1\frac{1}{2}$ cups milk
1 cup plus 2 tablespoons (2 sticks plus 2 tablespoons)
    unsalted butter, softened
$2\frac{1}{3}$ cups sugar
1 tablespoon plus $1\frac{1}{2}$ teaspoons poppy seeds
$1\frac{1}{2}$ teaspoons vanilla extract
$1\frac{1}{2}$ teaspoons almond extract
3 cups flour
1 tablespoon plus $1\frac{1}{2}$ teaspoons baking powder
$1\frac{1}{2}$ teaspoons salt

Almond Orange Glaze
$\frac{3}{4}$ cup sugar
$\frac{1}{4}$ cup orange juice
$\frac{1}{2}$ teaspoon vanilla extract
$\frac{1}{2}$ teaspoon almond extract

For the bread, mix the eggs, milk, butter, sugar, poppy seeds and flavorings in a large bowl. Combine the flour, baking powder and salt in a small bowl. Add the dry ingredients to the egg mixture one cup at a time, mixing well after each addition.

Divide the batter between 5 greased 5-inch loaf pans or 12 greased muffin cups. Bake at 350 degrees for 35 to 45 minutes for bread or for 20 to 30 minutes for muffins or until a wooden pick inserted in the center comes out clean.

For the glaze, mix the sugar, orange juice and flavorings in a bowl. Pour over loaves or muffins while still warm.

Makes five small loaves or one dozen muffins

Best Friends Iced Coffee Frappé

Combine $\frac{1}{4}$ cup instant coffee granules, $\frac{1}{2}$ cup chocolate syrup and $\frac{1}{4}$ cup sugar with $1\frac{1}{2}$ cups boiling water in a pitcher and mix well. Chill for 8 hours or longer. Combine with 2 cups half-and-half and 1 quart vanilla ice cream in a punch bowl and mix gently. Add 2 cups ginger ale.

Which Bean Do You Mean?

Café au Lait: $^1/_3$ *coffee and* $^2/_3$ *steamed milk*

Café Cubano: very sweet espresso

Café con Leche: espresso with steamed milk

Cappuccino: $^1/_3$ *espresso,* $^1/_3$ *steamed milk,* $^1/_3$ *froth, sometimes dusted with ground cinnamon*

Cortadito: a name for a small café con leche in Miami

Espresso: strong, rich coffee from dark-roasted beans

Latte: $^1/_3$ *espresso and* $^2/_3$ *steamed milk*

Macchiato: espresso with a dollop of frothed milk

Mocha: $^1/_3$ *espresso,* $^2/_3$ *steamed milk, a shot of chocolate syrup, and a topping of whipped cream, sometimes dusted with chocolate powder*

Shot: one small espresso cupful

Double or Tall: a double-size drink or a double shot of espresso

Skinny: drink with nonfat milk used in place of whole milk

Strawberry Streusel Muffins

Try using blueberries or raspberries instead of strawberries in the batter and lemon juice in place of Key lime juice in the glaze– FABULOUS!

Muffins
1$^1/_2$ cups flour
$^1/_4$ cup sugar
$^1/_4$ cup packed brown sugar
2 teaspoons baking powder
$^1/_4$ teaspoon salt
1 teaspoon cinnamon
1 egg, lightly beaten
$^1/_2$ cup (1 stick) butter, melted
$^1/_2$ cup half-and-half
1$^1/_4$ cups thinly sliced fresh strawberries
1 teaspoon grated Key lime zest or orange zest

Streusel Topping
$^1/_2$ cup chopped pecans or walnuts
$^1/_2$ cup packed brown sugar
$^1/_4$ cup flour
1 teaspoon cinnamon
1 teaspoon grated Key lime zest or orange zest
2 tablespoons butter, melted

Key Lime Glaze
$^1/_2$ cup confectioners' sugar
1 tablespoon fresh Key lime juice or orange juice

For the muffins, sift the flour, sugar, brown sugar, baking powder, salt and cinnamon into a medium bowl. Make a well in the center. Add the egg, butter and half-and-half to the well and mix just until moistened. Stir in the strawberries and zest; do not overmix. Spoon into 12 greased muffin cups.

For the topping, combine the pecans, brown sugar, flour, cinnamon and zest in a small bowl and mix well. Pour in the butter and mix well. Sprinkle over the muffins.

Bake the muffins at 350 degrees for 20 to 25 minutes or until firm and golden brown. Cool completely.

For the glaze, mix the confectioners' sugar and juice in a bowl. Swirl the glaze over the cooled muffins.

Makes one dozen

Monterey Jack Corn Bread with Basil and Roasted Peppers

Corn bread with a kick!

1 tablespoon unsalted butter
1 cup chopped onion
1³/4 cups yellow cornmeal
1¹/4 cups flour
¹/4 cup sugar
1 tablespoon baking powder
1¹/2 teaspoons salt
¹/2 teaspoon baking soda
7 tablespoons unsalted butter,
    chilled, cut into
    ¹/2-inch pieces

1¹/2 cups buttermilk
3 large eggs
1¹/2 cups (6 ounces) shredded
    Monterey Jack cheese with
    jalapeños
1¹/3 cups frozen corn kernels,
    thawed, drained
¹/2 cup chopped roasted red
    bell peppers
¹/2 cup chopped fresh basil

Melt 1 tablespoon butter in a nonstick skillet over medium-low heat. Add the onion and sauté for 10 minutes or until tender. Cool to room temperature.

Mix the cornmeal, flour, sugar, baking powder, salt and baking soda in a large bowl. Add the chilled butter and rub with fingertips until the mixture resembles coarse meal.

Whisk the buttermilk and eggs in a medium bowl. Add to the dry ingredients and stir until blended. Mix in the cheese, corn, bell peppers, basil and sautéed onion.

Pour into a greased 9x9-inch baking pan. Bake at 400 degrees for 45 minutes or until a wooden pick inserted in the center comes out clean. Cool on a wire rack for 20 minutes before removing from the pan. Cut into squares.

Note: The bread can be prepared up to 8 hours ahead. Cool completely, cover loosely with foil and store at room temperature. If desired, rewarm bread for 10 minutes at 350 degrees before serving.

Serves twelve

Roasted Bell Peppers

Roasting brings out the sweetness of bell peppers, mellows their flavor, and imparts a richness no other method can achieve. After a pepper is roasted, it can be used fresh or frozen.

To broil a pepper, preheat oven on broil. Slice the bell peppers into halves lengthwise and remove seeds and white pith. Cut in half again and press skin side up onto a foil-lined baking sheet. Place baking sheet on the top oven rack and broil for about 8 minutes or until the skins char. Remove from the oven and fold the foil around the peppers to seal in the steam. Let stand for about 10 minutes. Peel the skins off easily with a paring knife.

To cook on a gas range or grill, place the pepper on its side directly on the burner or grill rack, and turn the flame to high. Cook for 6 to 8 minutes or until the skin chars, turning with tongs. Transfer the pepper to a bowl and let stand, covered, until cool enough to handle and peel.

Tomato Focaccia with Basil and Rosemary

An earthy, hearty bread well worth the preparation time. Leftover pieces make delicious croutons for soups and salads.

³/4 cup olive oil
6 garlic cloves, minced
³/4 teaspoon crushed red pepper
1 tablespoon dry yeast
2 cups warm (110-degree) water
5 cups unbleached flour
2 teaspoons salt

8 medium plum tomatoes, seeded,
  cut into 1-inch slices
2 tablespoons coarse salt
2 tablespoons chopped fresh
  rosemary
2 tablespoons thinly sliced
  fresh basil

Combine the oil, garlic and crushed red pepper in a small heavy saucepan. Sauté over medium-low heat for 5 minutes or until garlic is golden brown. Remove from the heat and let stand for 1 hour or longer.

Sprinkle the yeast over the water in a large measuring cup and let stand for 10 minutes or until the yeast dissolves. Whisk in 3 tablespoons of the garlic oil.

Combine 2 cups of the flour and 2 teaspoons salt in the bowl of a heavy-duty mixer. Add the yeast mixture and beat until blended. Mix in the remaining flour 1 cup at a time to form a soft dough. Beat at low speed for 3 minutes or just until the dough is smooth.

Brush a large bowl with 1 tablespoon of the garlic oil. Place the dough in the bowl and turn to coat well. Cover the bowl with plastic wrap and then a damp kitchen towel. Let rise in a warm draft-free area for 1 hour or until doubled in bulk.

Place the tomatoes in a colander set over a large bowl. Toss with 1 tablespoon of the coarse salt. Let stand for 15 minutes. Rinse the tomatoes under cold water. Transfer to paper towels and drain well.

Brush a 10x15-inch baking sheet with 1 tablespoon of the garlic oil. Punch down the dough and knead lightly in the bowl. Place on the prepared baking sheet and stretch with oiled hands to roughly fit in the baking sheet. Press the dough with fingertips to make dimples. Sprinkle the dough with the rosemary and then the tomatoes. Press some of the tomatoes into the dimples. Sprinkle with the basil and remaining 1 tablespoon coarse salt.

Bake at 450 degrees for 30 minutes or until golden brown. Remove to a wire rack to cool. Cut into squares and serve with remaining garlic oil.

Note: The garlic oil can be prepared one day ahead. Store, covered, in the refrigerator. Bring it to room temperature before using.

Serves sixteen

Provolone and Sun-Dried Tomato Basil Bread

A quick bread with savory ingredients. Great as an appetizer or a crusty accompaniment to soups and salads.

$1/3$ cup oil-pack sun-dried tomatoes
$2^1/4$ cups unbleached flour
2 teaspoons baking powder
1 teaspoon salt
1 teaspoon pepper
$1/2$ teaspoon baking soda
1 cup shredded provolone cheese
$1/4$ cup chopped fresh parsley
$1^1/4$ teaspoons chopped fresh basil
2 eggs
3 tablespoons vegetable oil
1 teaspoon sugar
$1^1/4$ cups buttermilk

Drain the sun-dried tomatoes, reserving 2 tablespoons oil; chop the tomatoes. Combine the flour, baking powder, salt, pepper and baking soda in a large bowl. Mix in the cheese, sun-dried tomatoes, parsley and basil with a fork.

Whisk the eggs, vegetable oil, reserved sun-dried tomato oil, sugar and buttermilk in a medium bowl. Add to the dry ingredients and stir until just combined.

Pour into a greased round 8-inch baking pan. Bake at 350 degrees for 50 minutes or until a wooden pick inserted in the center comes out clean. Cool in the pan on a wire rack for 5 minutes. Invert onto the rack and cool completely. Cut into thin slices and serve at room temperature.

Note: The bread can be prepared up to 3 days ahead. Wrap in foil and store in the refrigerator.

Serves eight

Spreads for Bread

For Herbed Cheese Spread, mix 2 tablespoons minced fresh herbs, 2 tablespoons minced sun-dried tomatoes, 1 minced garlic clove and 8 ounces softened cream cheese. Chill for several hours. Serve with crackers or bagel chips.

For Apricot-Almond Spread, mix $1/4$ cup apricot preserves, 8 ounces softened cream cheese, $1/4$ cup chopped toasted almonds and $1/8$ teaspoon ground ginger.

For Garlic Spread, mix 8 ounces softened cream cheese and $1/4$ cup sour cream until smooth. Add 2 crushed garlic cloves, $1/4$ cup sliced green onions with tops and $1/4$ teaspoon salt. Serve at room temperature with warm bread.

Store the spreads in an airtight container in the refrigerator.

Banana Berry Boogie

This smoothie is a great breakfast drink, but you can also pair it with your favorite scones for an afternoon tea treat. For 1 serving, combine 1 small banana, 1 heaping cup of hulled strawberries, $^1/_2$ cup unfiltered apple juice, $^1/_2$ cup low-fat milk or plain low-fat yogurt, 1 teaspoon honey and 2 or 3 ice cubes in a blender container and process at high speed until smooth.

Vegetable Bread

The aroma alone will fill you up!

1 envelope dry yeast
2 cups warm (110-degree) water
2 cups semolina flour
1 red bell pepper
1 green bell pepper
1 small zucchini
4 cups unbleached flour
$^1/_4$ cup olive oil
1 tablespoon salt

Combine the yeast, water and semolina flour in a large bowl. Whisk until creamy. Cover with a towel and let rise in a warm, draft-free area for 1 hour.

Roast the bell peppers and zucchini under the broiler until charred on all sides, turning occasionally. Wrap in paper towels and place in a paper bag until cooled. Remove the charred skins, seed the peppers and chop the vegetables.

Add 1 cup of unbleached flour, olive oil, salt and roasted vegetables to the yeast mixture and mix well. Stir in the remaining unbleached flour $^1/_2$ cup at a time to form a soft dough. Knead the dough on a lightly floured surface until it can hold its shape, adding a few tablespoons of flour, if necessary. Cover the dough with a towel and let rise in a warm draft-free area for 2 hours or until doubled in bulk.

Punch down the dough and shape into two loaves. Place in 2 greased and floured loaf pans. Bake at 375 degrees for 35 to 40 minutes or until golden brown. Remove to a wire rack to cool.

Makes two loaves

*Great collectors are known by their passion for the process. Often described as their owner's obsession,
beautiful collections make the most impact when grouped together. This 19th century English
white pine hutch, purchased at an estate sale, is a natural to house memories of yesterday, such as Majolica,
antique dinner bells, orange juice reamers, and monogrammed silver baby cups.*

"Oh, no, We're Out of" Maple Syrup

Combine 2 cups sugar, 1 cup water and 1 teaspoon maple flavoring in a saucepan. Bring to a boil over medium-high heat; do not boil over. Cool slightly before serving over your favorite breakfast dishes; syrup will thicken as it cools. Store in an airtight container in the refrigerator for several months and reheat to serve. Makes 2 cups.

For Cinnamon Syrup, combine $1^1/3$ cups sugar, $^1/3$ cup water, $^2/3$ cup white corn syrup and 1 teaspoon cinnamon in a saucepan. Boil for 2 minutes. Remove from the heat and stir in one 5-ounce can of evaporated milk and 1 tablespoon butter. Serve warm.

For Honey Pancake Syrup, heat $^1/2$ cup water just to the simmering point in a saucepan over medium heat and stir in 1 cup honey; do not boil. Remove from heat and stir in 1 teaspoon vanilla extract. Store in a covered jar or syrup dispenser in the refrigerator.

Buckwheat Orange Waffles

Forgo the syrup and sprinkle with confectioners' sugar.

4 egg whites
$^1/4$ cup sugar
4 egg yolks
$^3/4$ cup half-and-half
$^1/4$ cup sour cream
$^3/4$ cup sugar
1 cup all-purpose flour

$^3/4$ cup buckwheat flour
1 tablespoon baking powder
$^1/4$ teaspoon salt
$^1/2$ cup (1 stick) unsalted butter, melted
1 tablespoon grated orange zest

Beat the egg whites with $^1/4$ cup sugar at high speed in a mixing bowl until stiff peaks form.

Mix the egg yolks, half-and-half, sour cream and $^3/4$ cup sugar in a large bowl. Sift the all-purpose flour, buckwheat flour, baking powder and salt into a small bowl. Add the dry ingredients to the sour cream mixture and stir until smooth. Stir in the melted butter and zest. Fold in the beaten egg whites.

Coat a waffle iron with nonstick cooking spray and preheat. Spoon enough batter into the center of each waffle grid to spread halfway to the edges, about $^1/3$ cup. Lower the top and bake for 3 to 4 minutes or until golden brown; do not press down on the iron during cooking or the waffles will collapse. Remove waffles with a fork and serve immediately.

Makes about thirteen waffles

German Pancakes

Gather the family for a delicious breakfast.

$^1/2$ cup (1 stick) butter
4 eggs

1 cup milk
1 cup flour

Melt the butter in a 9x13-inch pan in the oven as it preheats. Process the eggs at high speed in the blender for 1 minute. Add the milk gradually, processing constantly. Add the flour gradually, processing constantly. Process for 30 seconds longer.

Remove the baking pan from the oven and tilt to coat the bottom evenly with melted butter. Pour the pancake batter into the hot pan. Bake at 425 degrees for 20 to 25 minutes or until golden brown. Serve hot with lemon slices and confectioners' sugar or maple syrup.

Serves six

French Toast Baked in Honey Pecan Sauce

Easily doubled, this overnight French toast with a praline topping is simple to make and great for brunches. It's very pretty served with a fresh raspberry, strawberry, and blueberry compote.

Honey Butter
$1/2$ cup (1 stick) butter, softened
$2/3$ cup honey
$1/3$ cup packed brown sugar

French Toast
4 eggs, beaten
$3/4$ cup half-and-half
$1^1/2$ teaspoons brown sugar
1 teaspoon vanilla extract
4 thick slices French bread
$1/4$ cup ($1/2$ stick) butter
$1/4$ cup packed brown sugar
$1/4$ cup honey
$1/4$ cup maple syrup
$1/4$ cup chopped pecans

For the honey butter, combine the butter, honey and brown sugar in a mixing bowl and beat until light and fluffy. Spoon into a crock and chill until firm.

For the French toast, mix the eggs, half-and-half, $1^1/2$ teaspoons brown sugar and vanilla in a small bowl. Pour half of the mixture into a shallow dish. Arrange the bread in the dish and top with the remaining egg mixture. Chill, covered, for 8 hours or longer.

Melt $1/4$ cup butter in a 9x13-inch baking pan. Stir in $1/4$ cup brown sugar, honey, maple syrup and pecans. Arrange the bread slices on top. Bake at 350 degrees for 30 to 35 minutes or until puffed and golden brown. Serve immediately with the honey butter.

Serves four

Bee Wise

Before measuring honey, coat the cup or spoon with vegetable cooking spray. The honey will slide off easily. Try the same technique with peanut butter, syrup, and molasses.

Toffee Coffee Cake

Welcome a new neighbor with this easy and delicious coffee cake and make a friend for life.

^{1}/$_2$ cup (1 stick) butter, softened
^{1}/$_2$ cup sugar
1 cup packed brown sugar
2 cups flour
7^1/$_2$ ounces brickle pieces
1 teaspoon baking soda
1 egg
1 teaspoon vanilla extract
1 cup buttermilk
^{1}/$_2$ cup chopped pecans

Cream the butter, sugar and brown sugar in a bowl until light. Stir in the flour and ^{1}/$_2$ cup of the brickle pieces. Remove ^{1}/$_2$ cup of the mixture and set aside. Add the baking soda, egg, vanilla and buttermilk to the remaining mixture and stir well.

Pour into a greased and floured 9x13-inch baking pan. Top with the reserved brown sugar mixture, remaining brickle pieces and pecans. Bake at 350 degrees for 30 minutes or until golden brown.

Note: If buttermilk is not available, add 1 tablespoon of white vinegar or lemon juice to 1 cup of whole milk and let stand for 10 minutes before using.

Serves twenty-four

Viennese Coffee Cake

This recipe was started by a young Indiana housewife more than 30 years ago and has been passed down from neighbor to neighbor. She started a tradition which will also be enjoyed by your family.

Praline Topping
$1/2$ cup chopped pecans
3 tablespoons brown sugar
2 teaspoons instant cocoa mix
2 teaspoons cinnamon

Coffee Cake
$3/4$ cup ($1^1/2$ sticks) butter, softened
$1^1/2$ cups sugar
2 eggs
1 cup sour cream
$1/2$ teaspoon vanilla extract
$1^1/2$ cups sifted flour
1 teaspoon baking powder
$1/4$ teaspoon salt

For the topping, combine the pecans, brown sugar, cocoa mix and cinnamon in a small bowl. Set aside.

For the coffee cake, cream the butter and sugar in a mixing bowl until light and fluffy. Beat in the eggs. Fold in the sour cream and vanilla. Sift the flour, baking powder and salt in a small bowl. Fold into the sour cream mixture; the batter will be very thick.

Spoon half of the batter into a greased and floured 10-inch tube pan. Sprinkle half of the topping over the batter. Add the remaining batter and sprinkle with the remaining topping. Bake at 350 degrees for 50 minutes or until a light golden brown.

Serves twelve

For a great favor for kids of all ages, fill disposable plastic bags with orange jelly beans, shape the bag like a carrot, and tie with a green ribbon. Trim the top of the bag with pinking shears for a finishing touch. For a special treat, bake pound cake in egg-shaped muffin tins, scoop out the centers, and fill with lemon curd; sprinkle the tops with confectioners' sugar.

Maple Sticky Syrup

Combine 1 cup pure maple syrup and 9 tablespoons unsalted butter in a heavy medium saucepan. Cook over medium heat until the butter melts, stirring to blend well. Remove from the heat and stir in 1 cup packed light brown sugar.

Pecan Filling

Combine $3/4$ cup pecans, $1/2$ cup packed light brown sugar, $1/2$ cup raisins and 2 teaspoons ground cinnamon in a food processor container. Pulse until the pecans are finely chopped.

Maple Sticky Buns

A recipe really worth the effort. Better than the bakery.

Maple Sticky Syrup (at left)
$1/2$ cup coarsely chopped pecans
1 tablespoon dry yeast
$1/4$ cup warm (110-degree) water
$1/3$ cup rolled oats
$1/3$ cup sugar
3 tablespoons unsalted butter, cut into pieces
2 teaspoons grated lemon zest

$1^1/2$ teaspoons salt
$1^1/4$ cups whole milk
1 large egg
1 large egg yolk
2 teaspoons vanilla extract
$4^1/2$ cups unbleached flour
3 tablespoons unsalted butter, melted
Pecan Filling (at left)

Pour the Maple Sticky Syrup into 2 buttered 9x13-inch baking dishes. Sprinkle with the pecans.

Sprinkle the yeast over the water in a small bowl. Let stand for 8 minutes or until the yeast dissolves. Combine the oats, sugar, cut-up butter, zest and salt in a large bowl.

Heat the milk in a small saucepan until bubbles form around the edge. Pour over the oats mixture and stir until the butter melts and the sugar dissolves. Cool for 10 minutes. Add the egg, egg yolk, vanilla and dissolved yeast and mix well. Add 3 cups of the flour and beat 100 strokes with a wooden spoon or stiff rubber spatula. Cover with plastic wrap and let rest for 10 minutes.

Stir in the remaining flour $1/4$ cup at a time to make a soft dough. Knead the dough gently on a lightly floured surface for 8 minutes or until smooth and slightly sticky, adding additional flour if needed. Place in an oiled bowl and turn to coat well. Cover with plastic wrap and then a damp kitchen towel. Let the dough rise in a warm, draft-free area for $1^1/2$ hours or until doubled in bulk.

Transfer the risen dough gently to a floured surface; do not punch down. Roll gently to flatten slightly and stretch to a 12x18-inch rectangle. Brush with the melted butter. Sprinkle the Pecan Filling evenly over the dough, leaving a $1/2$-inch edge on one 18-inch side. Roll up the dough from the other long edge; press the seam to seal. Cut into 12 equal pieces with a heavy knife. Arrange 6 pieces cut side up and evenly spaced in each prepared baking dish and press down lightly. Cover tightly with plastic wrap and let rise in a warm draft-free area for 50 minutes or until light.

Remove the plastic wrap and bake at 375 degrees on center oven rack for 25 minutes or until the tops are golden brown and the syrup is bubbly. Invert onto serving plates, cool for 5 minutes and serve hot.

Note: The buns can be prepared ahead. Cool completely and wrap tightly in foil on baking sheets. Freeze for up to 2 weeks. Bake the frozen buns covered at 375 degrees for 15 minutes or until heated through.

Makes one dozen

Strata Oscar

An outstanding combination of crab meat, asparagus, and cheese. Serve with fruit and toasted whole wheat bread for special occasions.

12 to 14 slices firm white bread,
    crusts trimmed
1 pound fresh lump crab meat
1 cup (1-inch diagonally cut)
    asparagus
2 tablespoons finely chopped
    Spanish onion
1/2 cup mayonnaise
1 3/4 cups shredded Gruyère
    cheese and/or Swiss cheese

1/4 cup grated Parmesan cheese
10 eggs
2 cups milk
2 teaspoons Dijon mustard
1/2 teaspoon white Worcestershire
    sauce
1 teaspoon salt
1/2 teaspoon pepper

Arrange half the bread slices in a greased 8x12-inch baking dish. Mix the crab meat, asparagus, onion and mayonnaise in a bowl. Spread over the bread slices. Combine the cheeses and sprinkle 1 1/2 cups over the crabmeat mixture. Top with the remaining bread.

Mix the eggs, milk, mustard, Worcestershire sauce, salt and pepper in a bowl and pour evenly over the bread. Cover with plastic wrap and refrigerate for 2 hours or longer.

Remove the plastic wrap and bake at 350 degrees for 25 to 30 minutes or until puffed and light brown. Sprinkle the remaining cheese over the top; bake for 10 minutes longer or until the cheese is melted and bubbly. Cool for 10 minutes before serving.

Serves eight

Honeydew Mimosas

Cut a honeydew melon into wedges, discarding the seeds and rind; cut into 1-inch pieces. Combine half the melon with 1 cup of ice cubes, 1/2 cup water and 1 tablespoon sugar, or to taste, in a blender container and process until smooth. Repeat with the remaining melon, 1 cup of ice cubes, 1/2 cup water and 1 tablespoon sugar. Measure 3 cups of the liquid and combine with one 750-milliliter bottle of chilled sparkling wine.

Sparkling Kirs

For each serving, pour 1 teaspoon crème de cassis or other black currant liqueur into a large bubble flute and add a couple of ice cubes. Add 8 ounces of champagne. Garnish with rose petals.

Ham and Cheese Strata

Make this dish the night before, and you'll have more time to spend with your guests or family in the morning.

1 loaf French bread, cubed
1 pound ham, cubed
1 pound Cheddar cheese, shredded
1/2 cup grated Parmesan cheese
3 green onions, chopped
15 medium eggs
2 egg yolks
4 cups half-and-half
2 teaspoons Dijon mustard

Combine the bread, ham, Cheddar cheese, Parmesan cheese and green onions in a large bowl. Beat the eggs, egg yolks, half-and-half and mustard in a medium bowl. Pour over the bread mixture and stir until moistened. Cover and refrigerate for 8 hours or longer.

Stir the mixture and pour into an oiled 10-inch springform pan; place on a baking sheet. Bake at 325 to 350 degrees for 1 to 1 1/2 hours, covering with foil if necessary to prevent overbrowning. Cool in the pan for 20 minutes. Place on a serving plate and remove the side of the pan. Cut into wedges to serve.

Serves twelve

*P*ewter is very practical and decorative. Chargers in "Louis XV" pattern at each place setting play on the light and marry well
with silver accents. The Country French look has influences from all over the world. In that tradition, it's perfectly fine
to mix the antique toast holder from across the Channel, and the princess-pattern Depression glass from across the Atlantic.
The block-printed cotton fabric embodies the rich, vibrant colors of Provence. Additions such as the Quimper faience figurines
made in the early 1900s enhance the country charm. Quimper is the only French pottery made continuously since 1690.
(See recipe for Ham and Cheese Strata at left.)

Scrambled Eggs with Shiitake Mushrooms and Herbs

A fabulous recipe for brunch. Your guests will "scramble" for seconds.

1 pound fresh shiitake
    mushrooms
2 tablespoons unsalted butter
½ cup chopped shallots
¾ teaspoon dried thyme
¼ teaspoon dried rosemary,
    crushed
1 tablespoon minced garlic
⅔ cup chicken broth
salt and freshly ground pepper
    to taste

10 large eggs
4 ounces cream cheese or
    reduced-fat cream cheese,
    cubed
2 tablespoons chopped flat-leaf
    parsley
3 tablespoons unsalted butter

Garnish

sprigs of fresh rosemary, thyme
    and parsley

Clean the mushrooms, discarding the stems; coarsely chop the mushroom caps. Melt 2 tablespoons butter in a large heavy skillet over medium-high heat. Add the shallots, mushrooms, dried thyme and dried rosemary. Cook for 5 minutes or until the mushrooms and shallots are tender, stirring constantly. Add the garlic and cook for 1 minute. Add the broth and simmer for 5 minutes or until the liquid evaporates, stirring freqently. Season with salt and pepper.

Beat the eggs lightly in a bowl. Stir in the cream cheese, parsley and mushroom mixture. Season lightly with salt and pepper.

Melt 3 tablespoons butter in the same skillet over medium heat. Add the egg mixture and cook until the eggs are scrambled to a soft texture, stirring constantly. Remove to a serving platter and garnish with sprigs fresh rosemary, thyme and parsley.

Note: The mushroom mixture can be prepared 1 hour ahead. Cover loosely with foil at room temperature.

Serves six

AFTER BECOMING AN OFFICIAL MEMBER OF THE ASSOCIATION OF JUNIOR LEAGUES, THE JUNIOR SERVICE LEAGUE CELEBRATED ITS FIRST FULL YEAR IN 1984 AS THE "JUNIOR LEAGUE OF BOCA RATON." UNDER THE DIRECTION OF PRESIDENT MARSHA L. LOVE, THE JUNIOR LEAGUE INITIATED TWO PROJECTS—CHIPS, A FOSTER GRANDPARENT PROGRAM AND LEAD, A LEADERSHIP COURSE HELD IN LOCAL SCHOOLS.

Farmhouse Benedict

Non-traditional but elegant eggs benedict. Wake up your taste buds with eggs served over Red Pepper Corn Bread and topped with Rosemary Hollandaise.

Red Pepper Corn Bread
2 tablespoons butter
1 cup chopped onion
1 cup chopped shallots
4 cups cornmeal
2 cups flour
2 tablespoons sugar
1 tablespoon salt
2 tablespoons baking powder
1 teaspoon baking soda
1 cup (2 sticks) butter, chopped
3 cups buttermilk
4 eggs
3 cups shredded white
    Cheddar cheese
1 large roasted red bell pepper,
    peeled, chopped (page 91)

Eggs Benedict
2 slices cooked Canadian bacon
2 poached eggs
$1/2$ cup Rosemary Hollandaise
    (at right)
2 slices Red Pepper Corn Bread

Garnish
capers
lemon wedges
fresh rosemary sprigs

For the corn bread, melt 2 tablespoons butter in a heavy skillet. Add the chopped onion and shallots and sauté over medium heat until tender; cool.

Process the cornmeal, flour, sugar, salt, baking powder and baking soda in a food processor until mixed. Add 1 cup butter and pulse until the mixture resembles coarse meal. Transfer to a large bowl.

Beat the buttermilk and eggs in a medium bowl. Add to the cornmeal mixture and mix well. Stir in the Cheddar cheese, bell pepper and onion mixture.

Pour the batter into a greased 9x13-inch baking dish. Bake at 375 degrees for 50 to 60 minutes or until a wooden pick inserted in the center comes out clean. Remove to a wire rack to cool. Slice while warm.

For the eggs benedict, place one slice of warm corn bread on each of two serving plates. Top each with one slice of hot Canadian bacon and one hot poached egg. Pour $1/4$ cup of Rosemary Hollandaise over each. Garnish with capers, lemon wedges and sprigs of fresh rosemary.

Serves two

Rosemary Hollandaise

Combine 2 tablespoons vinegar and $1/4$ teaspoon pepper in a saucepan and cook until reduced by $1/2$. Cool to room temperature and add $1/4$ cup hot water. Add 3 egg yolks and whisk until tripled in volume. Add 6 ounces clarified butter (page 223) gradually, whisking constantly. Stir in $1 1/2$ teaspoons lemon juice and 1 tablespoon ground rosemary. Season with salt and pepper to taste.

Excellent Egg Tips

For the best results, beat egg whites just before ready to use. If beaten whites are not used immediately, the air beaten into them escapes and they become watery.

Uncooked whole eggs, yolks, and whites can be frozen. Beat the whole eggs lightly first to combine yolks and whites.

Simmering, not boiling, prevents hard-cooked eggs from cracking. Place the eggs in cold water in a saucepan. Bring just to the boiling point and reduce the heat to a simmer. Cook for 3 minutes for soft-cooked eggs and 12 minutes for hard-cooked eggs. Cool under cold water until cool enough to handle. The shells will slip off easily.

To get deviled eggs to behave like little angels and not slip around, cut a thin slice from the rounded side of each egg white half—after the yolk has been removed—to make a flat base.

Savory Cheesecake Quiche

Real men—and women—will definitely eat this updated quiche.

1/2 cup sun-dried tomatoes	1 cup shredded Swiss cheese
1 (9-inch) pie pastry	1/2 cup chopped green onions
24 ounces cream cheese, softened	1/4 teaspoon salt
4 eggs	1/4 teaspoon black pepper
1/2 cup milk	1/4 teaspoon cayenne

Soak the sun-dried tomatoes in boiling water in a bowl for 10 minutes. Drain and chop.

Spray a 9-inch springform pan with nonstick cooking spray. Place the pie pastry in the bottom of the pan and trim to fit one inch up the side. Bake at 425 degrees for 5 minutes. Remove from the oven and reduce the oven temperature to 350 degrees.

Beat the cream cheese in a large bowl until light. Beat in the eggs one at a time. Add the remaining ingredients and mix well. Pour into the partially baked piecrust.

Bake at 350 degrees for 60 to 70 minutes or until golden brown. Remove to a wire rack and cool for 20 minutes. Loosen the side of the pan. Cool completely. Place on a serving plate and remove the side of the pan.

Serves six

Sun-Deviled Eggs

The sun-dried tomatoes offer up a new taste.

4 ounces oil-pack sun-dried tomatoes, drained	1/2 teaspoon white wine vinegar salt and pepper to taste
6 hard-cooked eggs	
1/4 cup mayonnaise	**Garnish**
3 tablespoons sour cream	finely chopped fresh parsley

Cut 2 tomatoes into julienne strips and set aside. Finely chop the remaining tomatoes.

Cut the eggs into halves lengthwise and press the yolks through a sieve into a bowl. Mix in the finely chopped tomatoes and remaining ingredients. Spoon into a pastry bag fitted with a 1/2-inch tip. Pipe into the egg white halves. Top with the reserved tomato strips and garnish with parsley.

Serves twelve

Tropical Fruit with Mango Cream

Choose the freshest and ripest tropical fruits you can find at the market. Arranged on your prettiest platter and topped with the luscious mango cream, this simple dish will earn you rave reviews.

Tropical Fruit
2 mangoes
2 nectarines
3 kiwifruit
4 passion fruit
1 pineapple
1 small honeydew melon
juice of 2 oranges, strained

Mango Cream
1 large ripe mango
juice of ½ orange
1 tablespoon kirsch
(optional)
1 tablespoon lemon juice
1 tablespoon superfine sugar
1 cup whipping cream

For the fruit, peel, pit and slice the mangoes. Pit and slice the nectarines. Peel the kiwifruit and slice crosswise. Cut the passion fruit and leave the pulp in the shells. Cut the pineapple into halves, reserving the leaves. Peel, core and slice the pineapple. Cut the melon into halves, discarding the seeds; peel and slice. Arrange the fruit on a serving platter. Sprinkle with the orange juice and cover with plastic wrap. Chill until serving time.

For the mango cream, combine the mango, orange juice, kirsch, and lemon juice in a food processor or blender container and process until puréed. Place the mixture in a bowl and fold in the sugar.

Whip the cream until soft peaks form in a bowl. Fold the whipped cream into the mango purée using a knife to give a marbled effect. Serve with the tropical fruit platter. Decorate with the reserved pineapple leaves.

Serves six

Butter Garnishes

For pretty butter designs, spoon softened butter into a pastry bag fitted with a decorative tip, filling half full. Roll up open end of bag to close. Hold the bag with one hand and squeeze the butter in the desired design onto a waxed paper-lined baking sheet or into candy molds. Chill until serving time.

For butter pats, cut squares from a stick of cold butter with a sharp knife dipped in ice-cold water. Place pats in ice water until serving time.

Make shaped butter cut-outs with miniature cookie cutters. Dip the cutter into cold water, then use it to cut a shape from a square of cold butter.

Soups ⌗ Salads ⌗ Sandwiches

Splendor in the Grass

Tailgating on the polo grounds is a wonderful way to relax and catch up with friends. Maybe an old roommate from college is coming for the weekend. Perhaps you haven't had a get-together with the neighbors in a long time. Or, does the usual gang just need something unusual to do? In any case, everyone likes time to be out in the sunshine or under a tree, and a picnic with panache is the perfect setting to *savor the moment* with those special to you.

Change the accouterments for the other sport of kings, thoroughbred racing. Is there a special spot on the hill, or in the infield? Or, you could invite good friends to an outdoor concert, or even to watch a marathon in a city park. Move waterside, and the party could take on the nautical savoir-faire necessary to enjoy a regatta.

Have you ever thought about transforming the typical tailgate fare before the football game? It could be a fun change. Everyone wants to get away from stadium-sized sausage roasts once in a blue moon. This would be especially appropriate if the big game happened on a special birthday or anniversary.

Of course, a gorgeous golden Rolls Royce is an unprecedented backdrop for a posh tailgate party. But touches of silver and gold, crystal and glass, and classics like Hermès and Ralph Lauren, assure a chic setting, no matter what the transportation.

This smart Hermès cashmere throw with a tone-on-tone horse pattern started it all. Then the hostess found a Dhurrie rug with the polo theme and decided it was time to take tailgating over the top at the Royal Palm Polo fields in Boca Raton.

This hostess mixed sterling silver trays, champagne coolers, and goblets with wicker, leather, and wood to provide a sporty outdoor elegance. The silver and crystal shine in the sunlight. The wood and leather warm things up. Neutral linens here and there assure a subtle, well-bred look. The food and flowers add dimensions of rich texture and color.

Imagine guests sitting on this picnic blanket—a sporty navy blue Dhurrie rug with a mounted polo player—after a sumptuous lunch and enjoying horseshoe-shaped sugar cookies on plates hand-painted with polo scenes.

And what a meal! This menu offers everything from soup to nuts. But you could keep the serving pieces and simplify the menu if you're in a hurry.

The key to making memory points with your guests is to take some planning time to rediscover your most beautiful treasures. Choose the most unexpected, and any that work with your theme. Scouting for a few props from the game at hand makes all of the difference too. This hostess rounded up some mallets, leather riding boots, crops, and helmets. See what you can find to enhance the mood. Borrow the rest, and make sure everything but the signature antique mahogany chairs fits in the trunk of the car.

You'll need to spend some time planning how to pack. An old steamer trunk would be perfect for transporting delicate china and crystal. If you think worrying about breakables will cramp your style, polish the silver goblets from the back of your closet. Find some lovely extra plates at a second-hand shop, or go with glass plates, which you can find on sale after the holidays.

Whoa! It may look too elaborate to fit all of this in your trunk. A secret: the round table comes apart, and the low bamboo table packs easily, holds lots of food, and is within reach for guests on the blanket.

Rules of the Game

If you want to get carried away, rent a limo to pick everyone up, and get a teenager and a couple of friends to drive the van packed with the goodies to the scene. Don't forget the music. "My Old Kentucky Home" works for the horse races, or the team fight song will start things at the football game, and you'll probably be switching to the pregame broadcast on the radio after that.

If you are planning a tailgate for another spectator sport, write a list of the colors and symbols of the game. See how you can bring them in at every turn. Add fine linens, china, silver, and crystal to complement those choices. Don't leave anything to chance, and voila, you're off to the races or the ballgame.

Sporting Ideas

Changing the venue for the sailing enthusiasts, or even a South Florida tradition such as the annual holiday boat parade, is a matter of exchanging the mallets for paddles and boots for anchors, pinning down an old jib to sit on, and baking sailboat cookies. A couple of teak deck chairs, instead of the mahogany ones here, would allow the elegance of wood and mix well with the other accessories chosen by this hostess. If your party will be tailgating at the football game, find a letter sweater, pennants, helmets, and footballs to mix with the team colors.

Sure Bets

Think horseshoes for the invitations and favors. Use them as the emblem on the front cover of typical invitation stock. Or you could send a real horseshoe in a box with an invitation designed like a polo or racing program. Send home horseshoe cookies in pretty boxes tied with a leather bow.

This ornate silver tray is a family antique. The footed crystal punch bowl for the Strawberry Patch Soup (page 113) is another treasured heirloom. Even the wooden salad bowl has a silver base. This is truly tailgating with a silver spoon.

Menu

Black Bottom Soup

*You'll be quick to reach the bottom of the bowl
with this savory soup!*

3 (15-ounce) cans black beans
1 medium onion, chopped
2 garlic cloves, minced
1 medium green bell pepper, chopped
¼ cup olive oil
1 (15-ounce) can Cajun tomatoes
1 (8-ounce) can tomato sauce
1½ cups water
1 tablespoon wine vinegar
Tabasco sauce to taste (optional)
1 teaspoon sugar
2 (5-ounce) packages saffron rice
16 ounces sour cream
1 bunch scallions, sliced
1 tomato, chopped

Rinse and drain the black beans. Sauté the black beans with the onion, garlic and green pepper in the olive oil in a large saucepan until the onion is tender.

Add the tomatoes, tomato sauce, water, vinegar, Tabasco sauce and sugar and mix well. Simmer, covered, for 1 hour. Simmer, uncovered, for 30 minutes longer.

Prepare the rice using the package directions. Spoon the rice into serving bowls. Ladle the soup over the rice. Top with sour cream, scallions and tomato.

Serves eight to ten

In 1987, Junior League of Boca Raton president Judy Hilsmier led the membership's involvement in one of Boca Raton's first community-wide collaborations—the Coalition for Mizner Park. Projects during her term also included Aid to Victims of Domestic Assault and the continuation of a Migrant Health Fair.

Cantaloupe Champagne Soup

A refreshing and elegant summer treat!

2 ripe cantaloupes, peeled,
    seeded, chopped
1 cup (about) fresh orange juice
2 tablespoons honey
sea salt to taste
1 to 2 cups champagne

6 large strawberries, finely
    chopped

Garnish
mint sprigs

Process the cantaloupe in the blender until finely chopped. Add enough orange juice to make a thick purée, processing until smooth. Add the honey and sea salt and process just until mixed.

Pour into a bowl and chill in the refrigerator for 2 hours. Stir in the champagne just before serving. Ladle into chilled bowls; top each serving with the strawberries and garnish with a mint sprig.

Serves eight to ten.

Carrot Soup with Dill

A beautiful soup, rich in color, taste, and appearance.

$3/4$ cup finely chopped onion
2 tablespoons ($1/4$ stick) butter
4 cups (about $1^1/2$ pounds) sliced
    peeled carrots
4 cups chicken stock

2 cups water
salt and pepper to taste
$1/2$ cup ricotta cheese
3 tablespoons port
2 tablespoons chopped fresh dill

Sauté the onion in the butter in a saucepan until wilted. Add the carrots, chicken stock, water, salt and pepper. Bring to a boil and reduce the heat. Simmer for 20 minutes.

Drain, reserving the liquid. Combine the carrot mixture with 1 cup of the reserved cooking liquid and the ricotta cheese in a food processor or blender container; process until smooth.

Combine the purée with the remaining cooking liquid in the saucepan and mix well. Bring to a boil and add the wine and dill. Serve hot or chilled.

Serves six

Strawberry Patch Soup

Combine 16 ounces of fresh strawberries with 1 cup sour cream, 1 cup half-and-half, $1/4$ cup sugar and 2 tablespoons white wine in the blender or food processor container and process until smooth. Chill until serving time. Garnish servings with sliced fresh strawberries and mint.

Bloody Mary Gazpacho

This could be known as a United Nations soup, with the wonderful influences of Mexico and a dash of Russia tossed in!

6 tomatoes
2 cucumbers
2 large red bell peppers
4 large green bell peppers
3 ribs celery
1 large red onion
1/4 cup chopped scallions
1 tablespoon minced garlic
3 cups quality tomato sauce
fresh lemon juice to taste
3 tablespoons Worcestershire
    sauce

Tabasco sauce to taste
horseradish to taste
fresh or dried oregano to taste
1/2 to 1 cup vodka (optional)

Garnish
crab meat, tiny shrimp, or
    skewers of pepperoni
    and sharp white
    Cheddar cheese

Peel, seed and chop the tomatoes and cucumbers. Seed and chop the bell peppers. Chop the celery and onion. Combine the chopped vegetables with the scallions and garlic in a bowl.

Pour 1 cup of the tomato sauce into a food processor container. Add about 1/3 of the vegetables and process to fine chunks or to the desired consistency. Repeat with the remaining vegetables and tomato sauce.

Combine with the lemon juice, Worcestershire sauce, Tabasco sauce, horseradish, oregano and vodka in a large bowl; mix well. Chill, covered, for 4 hours or longer; flavor improves as the mixture stands.

Adjust the seasonings and vodka. Ladle into soup bowls. Garnish with crab meat, tiny shrimp or skewers of pepperoni and cubes of sharp white Cheddar cheese.

Serves ten

IN 1989, THE JUNIOR LEAGUE OF BOCA RATON BEGAN EFFORTS TO OPEN THE DOORS OF BOCA RATON'S MAINSTREAM TEEN CENTER. UNDER THE DIRECTION OF PRESIDENT CAROLE PUTMAN, JUNIOR LEAGUE MEMBERS DEFINED AND FULFILLED A CITY-WIDE NEED TO ESTABLISH THE CITY'S FIRST SAFE AND INVITING PLACE FOR BOCA RATON TEENS TO GATHER AND SOCIALIZE.

Roasted Eggplant and Garlic Soup

Make this in advance so the flavors will marry. Add the red pepper cream at serving time. Mangia!

Red Pepper Cream
2 red bell peppers
1/2 cup heavy cream
salt and pepper to taste

Soup
2 (1 1/2-pound) eggplant
2 garlic bulbs
1 onion, chopped
1/4 cup (1/2 stick) lightly salted butter
salt and pepper to taste
4 cups chicken stock
2 cups heavy cream

For the cream, roast the bell peppers in the oven until the skin is charred; cool in a paper bag. Slip off the skins and chop the peppers. Combine with the cream in the food processor container and process to form a smooth, light red mixture. Season with salt and pepper.

For the soup, roast the eggplant in the oven until the skin is charred. Peel and chop coarsely. Roast the garlic in the oven until very tender. Squeeze the cloves from the skins.

Sauté the eggplant with the garlic and onion in the butter in a large saucepan for 20 minutes. Season with salt and pepper. Add the chicken stock and simmer for 20 minutes.

Process the mixture in a blender until smooth. Combine with the cream in the saucepan and simmer just until heated through. Adjust the seasonings.

Ladle the soup into serving bowls. Drizzle the red pepper cream into the center of the soup and pull a wooden pick through the cream from the center to the outer edge of the bowls to form a spoke design.

Serves eight

Soup Basics

Sauté vegetables in butter or oil before adding them to soup. This seals in their flavor and keeps them firm. Give onions a little extra time, as slow cooking brings out their natural sweetness.

Most soups, with the exception of delicate fresh fruit soups, improve with time and can be made a day or two in advance. Leftovers freeze well.

It is simple to remove fat from a soup if you chill it first; the fat will solidify on top and can easily be removed with a spoon.

Any soup that has a particular herb seasoning should receive a generous dash of that herb just before you are ready to purée. This provides a fresher soup flavor.

The addition of wine frequently enhances the flavor of a soup. A not too dry sherry or madeira blends well with subtle veal or chicken, while a little dry red table wine will complement the flavor of beef.

Mushroom and Tomato Soup with Vermouth

*The earthy flavor of mushrooms brings out the best
in this savory soup.*

3 ribs celery, chopped
white portion of 1 leek, chopped
1 garlic clove, chopped
2 tablespoons vegetable oil
8 ounces mushrooms, chopped
5 cups peeled, seeded, chopped
    tomatoes
3 cups chicken stock
1 cup heavy cream
$^3/_4$ cup vermouth
2 teaspoons tomato paste

$^1/_4$ teaspoon sugar
1 bouquet garni
salt and freshly ground pepper
    to taste
4 ounces mushrooms, sliced
1 tablespoon butter
$^1/_2$ cup chopped watercress

Garnish
chopped fresh chives

Sauté the celery, leek and garlic in the heated oil in a heavy large
saucepan over medium-low heat for 7 minutes or until tender. Increase the
heat to high and add the chopped mushrooms. Sauté for 5 minutes or until
light brown.

Add the tomatoes, chicken stock, cream, vermouth, tomato paste,
sugar and bouquet garni. Season with salt and pepper. Bring to a boil and
reduce the heat. Simmer, covered, for 30 minutes or until the vegetables
are tender. Discard the bouquet garni. Process the soup in a blender
until smooth. Pour into the saucepan.

Sauté the sliced mushrooms in the butter in a small skillet over
medium heat for 5 minutes or until tender. Stir into the soup. Stir in the
watercress and adjust the seasonings. Cook until heated through. Ladle into
soup bowls and garnish with chopped chives.

Note: The bouquet garni for this recipe is made of 2 parsley sprigs,
1 thyme sprig, 1 oregano sprig, 1 basil sprig and 1 bay leaf tied in a
cheesecloth bag.

Serves eight

Spa Soup

Delicious, and it won't attack your waistline.

10 cups bottled water
1$\frac{1}{2}$ cups dried split peas
1 teaspoon chopped fresh thyme
1 bay leaf
2 cups chopped carrots
1 cup chopped onion
1 cup chopped white portion of leeks
2 cups packed fresh spinach
1 cup frozen green peas, thawed
1 teaspoon salt
$\frac{1}{2}$ teaspoon pepper

Bring the water to a boil in a saucepan and add the split peas, thyme and bay leaf. Reduce the heat and simmer, loosely covered, for 30 to 40 minutes or until the peas are tender.

Add the carrots, onion, leeks, spinach, green peas, salt and pepper. Simmer, uncovered, for 30 minutes or until the carrots are tender. Discard the bay leaf.

Reserve 2 cups of the soup and pour the remainder into a blender container. Process until smooth. Combine with the reserved soup in a saucepan and heat just until heated through. Ladle into soup bowls to serve.

Serves twelve

Your Fortune

Your fortune says that you will be doing a lot of eating this year. It says nothing about winning the lottery or meeting a tall, dark, handsome man.

Tortilla Soup with Lime and Tomato

TLT: A dynamite soup!

1 cup chopped onion
4 large garlic cloves, minced or
*   crushed*
3 tablespoons vegetable oil
1 or 2 (1-inch) chiles, chopped,
*   or to taste*
1 teaspoon ground cumin
1/2 teaspoon dried oregano
3 1/2 cups chopped fresh tomatoes

salt to taste
3 cups vegetable stock
1/3 cup fresh lime juice
crushed tortilla chips

Garnish
shredded Monterey Jack cheese
chopped fresh cilantro

Sauté the onion and garlic in the oil in a medium saucepan until the onion is translucent. Add the chiles, cumin and oregano. Sauté for several minutes longer.

Add the tomatoes and sprinkle with salt. Simmer, covered, until the tomatoes begin to release their juices, stirring occasionally. Add the vegetable stock and simmer, covered, for 15 minutes. Stir in the lime juice and season with salt.

Ladle into soup bowls. Top with tortilla chips and garnish with cheese and cilantro.

Serves four

Zucchini Basil Soup

This tasty soup, served with Tuscan Bread Salad (page 129) is a meal in itself.

2 cups chopped onions
3 garlic cloves, minced
2 tablespoons chopped fresh basil
$^1\!/_2$ teaspoon dried thyme
2 tablespoons unsalted butter
8 cups chicken broth
14 small zucchini, chopped (about 8 cups)
3 tablespoons uncooked rice
$^1\!/_3$ cup cream cheese

Garnish
basil leaves
cream cheese

Sauté the onions, garlic, basil and thyme in the butter in a large saucepan over medium-low heat until the onions are tender. Add the chicken broth and zucchini.

Bring to a boil and stir in the rice. Simmer, covered, for 30 minutes or until the rice is tender, stirring occasionally. Stir in the cream cheese until melted.

Process in batches in a food processor for 30 seconds. Combine the batches in a soup tureen and season with salt. Garnish servings with a basil leaf and a dollop of cream cheese.

Serves twelve

Hearts and Flowers on Valentine's Day

Crisp garlic toast can be cut into heart shapes to serve with soup or to top with red and black caviar. Use a cookie cutter to shape the bread. Add a long-stem rose by each plate or have lavender sachets as a favor for your guests.

Popovers

Oil a 6-cup popover pan or spray the pan with nonstick cooking spray and heat on the middle rack in a 400-degree oven for 2 minutes. Blend $1^1/4$ cups flour, 3 large eggs, $1^1/4$ cups milk, 1 tablespoon melted unsalted butter and $1/4$ teaspoon salt in a mixing bowl for 1 to 2 minutes. Place 1 teaspoon butter in each heated popover cup and heat in the oven until the butter is bubbly. Spoon the batter into the cups, filling half full. Bake at 400 degrees for 20 minutes. Reduce the oven temperature to 300 degrees and bake for 20 minutes longer. Serve immediately with butter, jams or other sweet or savory spreads.

White Chicken Chili

Round out the meal with a crisp green salad and hot corn bread.

1 pound dried Great Northern
    beans
$2^1/2$ pounds boneless chicken
    breasts
2 medium onions, chopped
1 tablespoon olive oil
4 garlic cloves, minced
2 (4-ounce) cans chopped green
    chiles, or to taste
2 teaspoons ground cumin
$1^1/2$ teaspoons dried oregano
$1/4$ teaspoon ground cloves
$1/2$ teaspoon cayenne
5 cups chicken broth

1 (12-ounce) can beer
$1/4$ teaspoon lemon pepper
    (optional)
$1/4$ teaspoon white pepper
    (optional)
$1/4$ teaspoon black pepper
    (optional)
3 cups shredded Monterey Jack
    cheese
salt to taste

Garnish
salsa
sour cream

Rinse and pick the beans and combine with water to cover in a large bowl. Let stand for 8 hours or longer.

Combine the chicken with cold water to cover in a large saucepan. Simmer for 15 minutes or until tender. Drain, cool and chop the chicken.

Sauté the onions in the olive oil in a saucepan until transparent. Stir in the garlic, green chiles, cumin, oregano, cloves and cayenne. Sauté for 2 minutes.

Drain the beans and add to the saucepan. Add the chicken broth, beer, lemon pepper, white pepper and black pepper. Bring to a boil and reduce the heat. Simmer for 2 hours or until the beans are tender, stirring occasionally.

Add the chicken and cook until the chicken is heated through. Stir in 1 cup of the cheese. Season with salt.

Ladle into serving bowls. Sprinkle with the remaining cheese. Garnish with salsa and sour cream.

Note: As a time-saver, substitute 2 cans of rinsed white beans for the dried beans.

Serves ten

Asian Salad

An intriguing salad for a special evening.

Lime Vinaigrette
1/4 cup lime juice
3 tablespoons canola oil
1 tablespoon sesame oil
3 tablespoons light soy sauce
2 tablespoons dark brown sugar
1 tablespoon grated orange zest
1 tablespoon minced garlic
1/2 teaspoon cayenne

Salad
8 ounces snow peas,
    trimmed
1 (8-ounce) package dried
    Chinese noodles
2 cups shredded carrots
1/4 cup thinly sliced
    sweet onion

For the vinaigrette, combine the lime juice, canola oil, sesame oil, soy sauce, brown sugar, orange zest, garlic and cayenne in a bowl and mix well.

For the salad, blanch the snow peas until they are tender-crisp and bright green. Rinse until cold water and drain.

Cook the noodles al dente using the package directions. Rinse in cold water and drain.

Combine the snow peas, noodles, carrots and onion in a bowl. Add the vinaigrette and toss gently to mix well. Chill until serving time.

Note: Add 1 1/2 pounds cooked shrimp for a main dish salad.

Serves four to six

Baby Greens with Pears

A refreshing salad with contrasting tastes and textures.

Walnut Oil Vinaigrette
1/3 cup walnut oil or olive oil
3 tablespoons balsamic vinegar
1 teaspoon crushed dried basil
1/4 teaspoon ground cinnamon
1/4 teaspoon salt

Salad
1/4 cup slivered walnuts
8 to 10 cups mixed baby
    greens, torn
1/4 cup crumbled Gorgonzola
2 pears, sliced

For the vinaigrette, combine the walnut oil, vinegar, basil, cinnamon and salt in a small bowl and mix well. Chill until serving time.

For the salad, spread the walnuts on a baking sheet. Toast at 200 degrees for 10 minutes.

Combine the greens in a salad bowl. Sprinkle with the cheese and walnuts. Add the pears and vinaigrette; toss lightly to coat well.

Serves eight

Buying and Storing Greens

The best gauges of freshness when choosing greens are appearance and smell. Greens should be sparkling fresh with a good color, and have no wilted, dry, or yellowing leaves. They should not show excessive ripping or insect damage, and they should smell very, very fresh. Look at the stem base and the center of the head, if possible, because decay sometimes begins there. Weight is another clue: the heavier, the better.

Greens are almost all water—if they feel light, they're drying out. Their high water content makes greens highly perishable. Ideally, you should buy greens close to the time you are planning to use them. Wash them carefully and dry them completely with a salad spinner, cotton tea towels, or paper towels. Divide the dry greens, wrap loosely in paper towels, and place in several plastic bags. Press all the air out of the bags, seal, and store in the crisper. If you store greens unwashed, they may not last as long.

Olive Oil

Olive oil is one of the most delicious and versatile food products. It is the only oil of culinary importance pressed from the flesh of a ripe fruit. Olive oil is made anywhere olive trees grow. Olives, like wine grapes, require a warm climate and particularly sandy soil. The best come from Italy and the south of France. Like most good things, olive trees improve with age. An olive tree must be 35 years old before it bears fruit.

Italian olive oil has a more pronounced olive flavor, giving it a nutty or leafy taste. French oil is fruitier, with a hint of peppery spiciness. Spanish oil has a more intense flavor, while Greek oil has a lighter olive taste but is rich and thick in consistency.

Confetti Salad

A unique asparagus salad–colorful and festive.

Sweet-and-Sour Vinaigrette
4 garlic cloves, crushed
1/2 cup olive oil
1/4 cup balsamic vinegar
1 tablespoon dark brown sugar
salt and freshly ground pepper
   to taste

Salad
1 1/2 pounds asparagus, trimmed
1 head radicchio, thinly sliced
1/2 large yellow bell pepper,
   finely chopped
1/2 large red bell pepper,
   finely chopped

For the vinaigrette, sauté the garlic in the heated olive oil in a heavy small skillet over low heat for 10 minutes or until light brown. Stir in the vinegar and cook for 2 minutes. Stir in the brown sugar until dissolved. Season with salt and pepper; discard the garlic.

For the salad, cook the asparagus in salted boiling water for 3 minutes or until tender-crisp; drain and plunge into ice water until cool; drain. Arrange the radicchio on a large platter. Arrange the asparagus over the top and sprinkle with the bell peppers. Drizzle with the desired amount of vinaigrette; serve with the remaining vinaigrette.

Serves six

Chick-Pea and Cucumber Salad

A delightful combination.

Salad
2 (12-ounce) cucumbers
1 3/4 cups cooked chick-peas
1/2 cup coarsely chopped mint
2 medium carrots, peeled, grated
1/3 cup currants
salt and pepper to taste

Fennel Seed Dressing
1 1/2 teaspoons fennel seeds
3 tablespoons minced shallots
1/4 cup fresh lemon juice
1 1/2 tablespoons olive oil

For the salad, peel waxed cucumbers and cut into halves lengthwise. Scoop out and discard the seeds; cut into 1/4-inch pieces.

Combine the cucumbers with the chick-peas, mint, carrots and currants in a medium bowl. Season with salt and pepper.

For the dressing, combine the fennel seeds, shallots, lemon juice and olive oil in a bowl and whisk until smooth. Add to the salad and toss to coat well. Serve at room temperature.

Serves four

Here is the crème de la crème for champagne and strawberries: a footed silver champagne cooler on a wicker tray with leather handles, crystal flutes, silver and brushed gold mint julep cups, and an antique English pitcher of red tulips. You could appropriately substitute a trophy cup for the pitcher, if you have one. Notice the natural-colored linen table cloth—the color of jodhpurs, the texture of summer. Isn't this more fun than the winner's circle?

Curried Couscous Salad

This salad will elicit rave reviews from your guests.

Curry Dressing
1/2 cup extra-virgin olive oil
2 tablespoons lemon juice
1 1/2 tablespoons red wine vinegar
2 tablespoons water
1 tablespoon sugar
1 tablespoon curry powder
1 tablespoon salt
1/2 teaspoon pepper

Salad
1 (10-ounce) package couscous
1 cup chopped celery
1/4 cup minced sweet onion
1 (15-ounce) can garbanzo
  beans, drained, rinsed
3/4 cup dark raisins
3/4 cup toasted almonds
  with skins

For the dressing, combine the olive oil, lemon juice, vinegar, water, sugar, curry powder, salt and pepper in a bowl and mix well.

For the salad, cook the couscous using the package directions. Combine with the celery, onion, beans, raisins and almonds in a large bowl. Add the dressing and mix gently. Chill until serving time.

Serves eight

Roasted Portobello Salad

Robust flavors beckon!

Basil Vinaigrette
1 cup minus 1 tablespoon olive
  oil
1/2 cup balsamic vinegar
1 teaspoon chopped garlic
1 teaspoon sugar
1 cup chopped fresh basil
juice of 1 lemon

salt and pepper to taste
Salad
4 large portobello mushroom caps
salt and pepper to taste
1 tablespoon olive oil
2 heads radicchio, torn
2 heads Belgian endive, sliced
1 bunch watercress

For the vinaigrette, combine the olive oil, vinegar, garlic, sugar, basil, lemon juice, salt and pepper in a bowl and mix well.

For the salad, scrape the gills gently from the underside of the caps with a teaspoon or a sharp knife. Sprinkle with salt and pepper; brush with the olive oil. Place on a baking sheet. Roast at 450 degrees for 15 to 20 minutes.

Mix the radicchio, endive and watercress in a large bowl. Top servings with the roasted mushrooms. Drizzle with the vinaigrette.

Serves four

Plantation Salad

This recipe is a family favorite that has withstood the test of several generations.

1 cup chopped celery
$^1\!/_2$ cup chopped onion
1 tablespoon butter
$1^1\!/_2$ cups uncooked wild rice
3 cups chicken stock
1 tablespoon parsley flakes
1 tablespoon mixed Italian herbs
$^1\!/_2$ teaspoon poultry seasoning
1 garlic clove, minced
1 tablespoon butter
1 pound fresh mushrooms, sliced
2 tablespoons vermouth

salt and pepper to taste
2 cups chopped cooked chicken breast
2 cups chopped cooked shrimp
1 cup chopped pecans
$^1\!/_2$ cup sliced black olives
$^3\!/_4$ cup mayonnaise
2 tablespoons lemon juice
2 tablespoons red wine vinegar
1 tablespoon sugar
1 tablespoon salt, or to taste
$^1\!/_2$ teaspoon pepper, or to taste

Sauté the celery and onion in 1 tablespoon butter in a large saucepan. Add the wild rice and sauté for 5 minutes. Stir in the chicken stock, parsley flakes, Italian herbs and poultry seasoning. Cook for $1^1\!/_4$ hours or until the rice is tender and the liquid evaporates. Cool to room temperature.

Sauté the garlic in 1 tablespoon butter in a skillet. Add the mushrooms and vermouth. Season with salt and pepper to taste. Cook over high heat until the liquid has evaporated.

Combine the rice mixture, mushrooms, chicken, shrimp, pecans and black olives in a large bowl. Add the mayonnaise, lemon juice, vinegar, sugar, 1 tablespoon salt and $^1\!/_2$ teaspoon pepper and mix well. Chill until serving time.

Serves eight

Types of Olive Oil

There are many types of oil on the market today, but the basic rule remains that you get the quality you pay for.

Extra-extra or extra-virgin olive oil is made from the very first pressing of the olives. It is usually green, sometimes greenish black. Its intense flavor and aroma is that of green olives. Extra-virgin oil is best used in salads or marinades, or tossed with just-cooked vegetables.

Virgin olive oil is also a direct product of the olive fruit, though it may be the result of a second pressing. It should have a sweetish, nutty flavor.

Pure olive oil is made up of oils extracted by treating the previously pressed olive pulp with solvents.

Fine olive oil is oil that has been extracted from the olive pulp, to which water has been added. It is perfect for cooking or frying.

Lettuce Is Not Always Green

A good salad includes a mix of mild and assertive greens.

Boston lettuce has a tightly packed head with green outer leaves and light yellow inner leaves. It offers a subtle, sweet taste and is soft and tender.

Bibb lettuce has a deep, rich green color and is whitish green toward the core. It has a delicate and buttery flavor and is slightly crisper than Boston.

Belgian endive offers a white to whitish-green color with a snappy texture and strong and somewhat bitter taste. The leaves can also serve as a pretty garnish.

Arugula comes in bunches of oak-shaped leaves in a light- to dark-green color, with long stems. It's pungent, peppery, and crisp.

Radicchio adds purple-red color to any salad. A variety of endive, its hearty texture holds up well with chicken salad, imparting a slightly bitter taste.

Shiitake and Warm Corn Salad

A tasty combination to entice friends and family.

Simple Vinaigrette
1¹⁄₂ tablespoons red wine vinegar
1¹⁄₂ tablespoons extra-virgin
    olive oil
sea salt and pepper to taste

Salad
¹⁄₄ cup extra-virgin
    olive oil

1¹⁄₂ cups shiitake mushrooms,
    sliced
3 cups blanched fresh corn kernels
6 ounces smoked slab bacon,
    julienned, crisp-fried
³⁄₄ cup chopped walnuts
sea salt and pepper to taste
4 bunches arugula, torn
³⁄₄ cup grated aged goat cheese

For the vinaigrette, whisk the vinegar and olive oil in a nonreactive bowl until smooth. Season with salt and pepper.

For the salad, heat the olive oil in a 12-inch sauté pan over high heat. Add the mushrooms and cook for 1 minute. Add the corn and bacon and cook for 1 minute. Stir in the walnuts and season with salt and pepper. Spoon onto 6 plates.

Toss the arugula with the vinaigrette in a bowl. Pile in the center of the corn mixture; sprinkle with the cheese.

Serves six

Southern Salad

This salad was a hit among our testers.

Raspberry Dijon Vinaigrette
2 tablespoons raspberry
    vinegar
¹⁄₂ teaspoon Dijon mustard
¹⁄₂ teaspoon sugar
¹⁄₂ teaspoon salt
freshly ground pepper to taste
6 tablespoons (or less) olive oil

Salad
6 cups mixed baby greens
¹⁄₂ to 1 cup dried cranberries
1 cup pecan halves or chopped
    pecans
¹⁄₂ medium red onion, thinly
    sliced
crumbled feta cheese to taste

For the vinaigrette, combine the raspberry vinegar, Dijon mustard, sugar, salt and pepper in a bowl and mix until the sugar and salt dissolve. Whisk in the olive oil.

For the salad, combine the greens, cranberries, pecans, onion and cheese in a salad bowl. Add the vinaigrette and toss gently to coat well.

Serves six

Sun-Dried Tomato Potato Salad

Try to eat this slowly to relish the flavors.

10 new potatoes, cut into quarters
4 garlic cloves
4 shallots, cut into halves
1/4 cup virgin olive oil
salt and pepper to taste
1 cup green beans
1/2 cup julienned red onion
1/4 cup chopped sun-dried tomatoes
3 tablespoons chopped fresh basil
3 tablespoons chopped fresh parsley

Combine the potatoes with the garlic, shallots, olive oil, salt and pepper in a bowl and mix well. Place in a baking pan and cover with foil. Bake at 475 degrees for 40 to 45 minutes or until the potatoes are tender; cool to room temperature.

Cook the beans in salted boiling water in a medium saucepan for 5 to 6 minutes or until tender-crisp. Rinse under cold water and drain.

Combine the potatoes, beans, onion, sun-dried tomatoes, basil and parsley in a serving bowl and mix gently.

Serves eight to ten

Balsamic Vinaigrette

Combine 1 tablespoon Dijon mustard, 1/4 cup balsamic vinegar, 2 tablespoons red wine vinegar and 1/4 cup water in a mixing bowl or blender container and mix well. Mix in 2 teaspoons sugar. Add 1/2 cup extra-virgin olive oil and 1/4 cup canola oil gradually, blending or whisking constantly until well mixed. Season with 2 teaspoons salt and 1 teaspoon coarsely ground pepper.

Tropical Tomato Salad

Delicious, light, easy to prepare, and impressive.

3 large ripe mangoes
3 large ripe tomatoes
5 tablespoons extra-virgin olive oil
4 teaspoons white vinegar
1/4 teaspoon curry powder

8 to 10 large fresh basil leaves
salt and pepper to taste

Garnish
basil leaves

Peel the mangoes and slice into 18 long strips. Cut the tomatoes into 18 thin slices. Arrange alternately on a serving platter.

Combine the olive oil, vinegar, curry powder and basil leaves in a blender container. Add the salt and pepper and process until smooth. Pour over the tomatoes and mangos. Garnish with additional basil leaves.

Serves six

Zeus' Pasta Salad

A salad offering from the gods.

Basil Dressing
2/3 cup olive oil
3 tablespoons red wine vinegar
2 tablespoons chopped
    fresh basil
2 tablespoons chopped
    green onions
2 tablespoons grated Parmesan
    cheese
1 1/4 teaspoons salt
1/4 teaspoon freshly ground
    pepper

Salad
1 each small red, yellow and green
    bell pepper
12 ounces rotelle, cooked, drained
1 medium tomato, cut into thin
    wedges
1/4 cup pine nuts
1/4 cup Greek olives
8 ounces feta cheese, crumbled
2 tablespoons chopped fresh basil
1/4 teaspoon crumbled dried
    oregano leaves

For the dressing, combine the olive oil, vinegar, basil, green onions, Parmesan cheese, salt and pepper in a blender or food processor container and process until smooth.

For the salad, cut the bell pepper into halves and then into thin strips. Combine with the pasta, tomato, pine nuts and olives in a large bowl. Add the dressing and toss to coat well. Roll the feta cheese in the basil. Add to the salad and sprinkle with the oregano. Serve at room temperature.

Serves four

Mushroom and Gnocchi Salad

A fabulous combination from Nick and Max's.

Truffle-Thyme Vinaigrette
1/2 cup chicken stock
1/4 cup minced shallots
1/4 cup sherry vinegar
2 tablespoons chopped
    fresh thyme
3/4 cup olive oil
1/4 cup truffle oil
salt and pepper to taste

Salad
2 (16-ounce) packages dried
    gnocchi
2 tablespoons butter
12 ounces wild mushrooms
    such as morels, porcini or
    hedgehog
1/4 cup sliced shallots
4 cups torn frisée

For the vinaigrette, cook the chicken stock in a saucepan until reduced by half. Combine with the shallots, vinegar and thyme in a bowl. Whisk in the olive oil gradually. Add the truffle oil, salt and pepper and mix well.

For the salad, prepare the gnocchi using the package directions; drain. Heat a sauté pan and add the butter. Cook until the butter begins to brown and add the gnocchi. Cook until golden brown. Add the mushrooms and cook until tender. Add the shallots and cook until tender.

Combine the frisée with enough vinaigrette to coat lightly. Add the gnocchi mixture and toss to coat well.

Serves eight

Tuscan Bread Salad

An aria of flavors destined to become an Italian classic.

2 large tomatoes, chopped
1 large yellow or red bell pepper,
    cut into 3/4-inch pieces
6 ounces mozzarella cheese, cut
    into 1/2-inch pieces
1/3 cup coarsely chopped basil

6 tablespoons extra-virgin olive oil
3 tablespoons balsamic vinegar or
    red wine vinegar
3 garlic cloves, minced
salt and pepper to taste
4 ounces Italian or French bread

Combine the tomatoes, bell pepper, cheese and basil in a bowl. Whisk the olive oil, vinegar and garlic in a small bowl. Season with salt and pepper. Add to the tomato mixture and mix well.

Cut the bread into 1-inch cubes. Spread on a baking sheet. Broil for 1 minute or just until the cubes begin to brown, stirring once. Add to the salad and mix gently. Spoon onto serving plates.

Serves two

Storing Olive Oil

As important as your choice of oil is the care you take of it. Even good oil can go stale or turn rancid if not stored carefully. After two weeks, opened oil should be stored in a refrigerator, especially in the summer. It may become cloudy, but it will clear rapidly upon returning to room temperature.

Stilton Dressing

*Mash $^1/_3$ cup Stilton cheese
in a small bowl. Add $^1/_3$ cup
mayonnaise, $^1/_4$ cup sour cream,
1 tablespoon rice wine vinegar and
1 tablespoon Worcestershire sauce
gradually and mix well. Season
with Tabasco sauce and freshly
ground pepper to taste. Chill until
serving time. Serve on Beef and
Stilton Salad (at right).*

Roast Beef and Stilton Salad

You'll love the heartiness of this main dish salad.

1 tablespoon sesame oil
1 tablespoon vegetable oil
2 cups thinly sliced cooked roast
    beef, trimmed
2 medium carrots, julienned
1 cup sliced mushrooms
1 red bell pepper, thinly sliced

Stilton Dressing (at left)
mixed salad greens

Garnish
grated carrots
red bell pepper slices
chopped parsley

Heat the sesame oil and vegetable oil in a wok or large skillet over
medium-high heat. Add the beef, carrots, mushrooms and bell pepper.
Cook until heated through, tossing to coat evenly with the oil.

Combine the beef mixture with the dressing in a bowl and mix lightly.
Spoon onto mixed greens on serving plates. Garnish by arranging grated
carrot and red bell pepper slices around the salad and top with parsley.

Serves six to eight

Chutney Chicken Salad

*As an alternative, serve on French bread and enjoy with a glass
of chardonnay.*

2 pounds bone-in chicken breasts
salt to taste
$^1/_2$ cup plus 2 tablespoons
    mayonnaise
1 teaspoon curry powder
3 tablespoons mango chutney

1 tablespoon fresh lime juice
$^1/_4$ cup raisins
$^1/_4$ cup sliced almonds
$^1/_4$ cup finely chopped celery
$^1/_4$ cup finely chopped scallions

Cook the chicken in salted water in a large saucepan for 30 minutes or
until tender. Cool and cut into pieces, discarding the skin.

Combine the mayonnaise, curry powder, chutney, lime juice, raisins
and almonds in a large bowl. Add the chicken, celery and scallions and mix
well. Serve on a bed of lettuce.

Serves four

Fiesta Shrimp Salad

This will make you dance with its delightful flavors.

Marinated Shrimp
1 tablespoon soy sauce
1 teaspoon grated gingerroot
1 garlic clove, minced
sugar and dried red pepper flakes
    to taste
24 uncooked large shrimp, peeled
    with tails intact, deveined

Sesame-Ginger Dressing
2 tablespoons fresh lemon juice
2 tablespoons rice vinegar
1 tablespoon beaten egg
1 teaspoon grated gingerroot
1 garlic clove, minced
$1/2$ cup olive oil
1 teaspoon sesame oil
salt to taste
1 tablespoon chopped fresh chives
    or green onion tops

Salad
8 cups loosely packed torn salad
    greens such as curly endive,
    radicchio, arugula and/or
    red leaf lettuce
1 large ripe avocado, sliced
    lengthwise into 16 strips
1 papaya, sliced lengthwise into
    16 strips
sections of 1 large grapefruit

To marinate the shrimp, combine the soy sauce, gingerroot, garlic, sugar and pepper flakes in a shallow dish and mix well. Add the shrimp and toss to coat well. Marinate, covered, in the refrigerator for 1 hour.

For the dressing, combine the lemon juice, vinegar, egg, gingerroot and garlic in the blender or food processor container and process until smooth. Add the olive oil gradually, process until well mixed. Mix in the sesame oil and season with salt. Combine with the chives in a small bowl. Adjust the seasonings.

For the salad, drain the shrimp. Heat a heavy large nonstick skillet over medium heat and add the shrimp. Cook for 2 minutes or until light brown. Turn and cook for 1 minute longer; keep warm.

To serve, toss the greens with enough dressing to coat lightly. Mound in the centers of 4 large plates. Arrange the avocado and papaya alternately in a pinwheel design over the greens. Arrange 6 shrimp in an overlapping cluster in the center; drizzle with additional dressing. Arrange the grapefruit sections around the edges of the plates. Serve with the remaining dressing.

Serves four

Marinated Tomatoes

Cut 2 or 3 large tomatoes into thick slices and arrange overlapping on a platter. Combine $1/2$ cup olive oil, 2 tablespoons red wine vinegar, 2 tablespoons chopped fresh basil, 2 tablespoons chopped fresh parsley, 1 tablespoon minced red onion, 1 tablespoon drained capers, 1 crushed large garlic clove and 1 teaspoon salt in a bowl and mix well. Drizzle over the tomatoes and garnish with additional parsley. Marinate in the refrigerator for 1 hour or longer.

Chile Oil

Prepare fresh poblanos, jalapeños, and serranos or dried pasillas by the warm-infusion method. Roast one of the fresh or dried chiles to add flavor. Add black pepper to the mix. It makes a truly amazing oil.

Select 4 fresh hot chiles with seeds or 8 dried chiles of a single type or mix for a more complex flavor. Chop the chiles in a food processor. Heat with 1 cup olive oil in a saucepan until mixture begins to bubble. Cook for 10 to 15 seconds and remove from heat. Swirl until just warm. Strain into a bowl through 4 layers of cheesecloth, pressing to extract as much oil as possible. Pour into a sterilized jar or bottle, seal tightly, refrigerate, and use within 1 week for the best flavor.

Sesame-Seared Tuna Salad

A light dinner option from Max's Grill.

Oriental Vinaigrette
1/3 cup rice wine vinegar
1 tablespoon minced garlic
2 tablespoons minced gingerroot
1 teaspoon prepared wasabi
1 tablespoon catsup
1/4 cup soy sauce
1 tablespoon lemon juice
1/2 cup vegetable oil
3 tablespoons sesame oil
salt and pepper to taste

Salad
8 (2-ounce) pieces tuna
1/2 cup black and white
  sesame seeds
1 tablespoon vegetable oil
4 cups mesclun or mixed greens
1/2 cup julienned carrot
1 cucumber, thinly sliced
4 teaspoons wasabi
4 teaspoons pickled gingerroot

For the vinaigrette, combine the vinegar, garlic, gingerroot, wasabi, catsup, soy sauce and lemon juice in the food processor container and process for 30 seconds. Add the vegetable oil and sesame oil gradually, processing constantly. Add salt and pepper to taste.

For the salad, coat the tuna with the sesame seeds. Heat the oil in a sauté pan just until it begins to smoke and add the tuna. Sear for 10 seconds on each side.

Combine the mesclun with the carrot in a bowl. Add half of the vinaigrette and toss to coat well, reserving remaining vinaigrette for another use. Spoon into the centers of 4 serving plates. Arrange the cucumbers around the greens. Slice the tuna pieces into halves and arrange around the greens. Serve with the wasabi and gingerroot.

Serves four

The memory of being pampered like this on a beautiful day out with good friends will last a lifetime. The horsey set will love this hand-hammered silver tray with its leather-strap handles. Savory Brie in Puff Pastry with Berry Sauce (page 58), bunches of grapes, baskets of bread, and bowls of fruit add nature's bounty to last the afternoon.

Bleu Cheese Vinaigrette

This tangy vinaigrette allows the bleu cheese flavor to come alive.

1 tablespoon olive oil
2 teaspoons minced garlic
1 cup crumbled bleu cheese
$1/4$ cup white wine vinegar
1 tablespoon water
1 tablespoon sugar

$1/2$ teaspoon Tabasco sauce
$1/2$ teaspoon salt
$1/4$ teaspoon pepper
6 tablespoons olive oil
1 tablespoon chopped fresh basil

Heat 1 tablespoon olive oil in a skillet over medium heat. Add the garlic and sauté until golden brown. Combine with the cheese, vinegar, water, sugar, Tabasco sauce, salt and pepper in a blender container. Process until smooth. Add 6 tablespoons olive oil gradually, processing constantly.

Combine with the basil in a bowl and mix well. Store, covered, in the refrigerator for up to 2 days.

Makes two cups

Phoenician Dressing

The Phoenicians should be remembered in history for this flavorful dressing.

1 egg yolk
$1^1/2$ teaspoons minced shallots
$1^1/2$ teaspoons minced garlic
$1^1/2$ teaspoons Worcestershire
    sauce
$1^1/2$ teaspoons Dijon mustard

3 tablespoons red wine vinegar
1 tablespoon tarragon
$1^1/2$ teaspoons thyme
salt and pepper to taste
$1^1/2$ cups vegetable oil

Beat the egg yolk in a mixing bowl. Add the shallots, garlic, Worcestershire sauce, Dijon mustard, vinegar, tarragon, thyme, salt and pepper and mix well. Add the oil gradually beating constantly until the dressing is of the consistency of thin mayonnaise.

Makes one and three-fourth cups

Japanese Ginger Dressing

This Pacific Rim inspired dressing transforms any salad into a trip to the Orient.

1/4 cup minced onion	2 tablespoons rice wine vinegar
1 tablespoon minced celery	1/4 cup peanut oil
1 tablespoon minced gingerroot	1 teaspoon lemon juice
1 1/2 teaspoons tomato paste	1 1/2 teaspoons sugar
1 tablespoon soy sauce	1/4 teaspoon salt
2 tablespoons water	1/4 teaspoon pepper

Combine the onion, celery, gingerroot, tomato paste, soy sauce, water, vinegar, peanut oil, lemon juice, sugar, salt and pepper in a blender or food processor container. Process until smooth and thick.

Makes one cup

Poppycock Dressing

Great served over salad greens and strawberries.

1 1/2 teaspoons chopped onion	1 teaspoon salt
3/4 cup sugar	1 cup olive oil
1/3 cup balsamic vinegar	1 1/2 tablespoons poppy seeds
1 teaspoon dry mustard	

Combine the onion, sugar, balsamic vinegar, dry mustard and salt in a blender container and process to mix well. Add the olive oil gradually, processing constantly until smooth. Add the poppy seeds and process until mixed.

Makes two cups

Lemon Vinaigrette

Combine 1 cup best-quality olive oil, 2/3 cup lemon juice, 1/2 cup chopped fresh chives, 2 tablespoons finely minced shallots and 2 tablespoons Dijon mustard in a covered container. Add salt and freshly ground pepper to taste and shake to mix well. Serve immediately.

Pan Bagna

A hearty treat from Provence.

3 tablespoons olive oil	6 kalamata olives, sliced
1 tablespoon balsamic vinegar	1 cup arugula leaves
1 garlic clove	3 large radishes, sliced
salt to taste	pepper to taste
1 (16-inch) sourdough or whole wheat baguette	1 (6-ounce) tuna steak, cooked, sliced
1 tablespoon olive oil	3 small tomatoes, thinly sliced
3 ounces mild goat cheese	8 large fresh basil leaves, shredded

Combine 3 tablespoons olive oil, vinegar, garlic and salt in a blender container and process until smooth.

Cut the bread into halves horizontally. Hollow the bread from both halves, leaving 1¹/₂-inch shells. Brush the bottom shell with 1 tablespoon olive oil.

Spread the cheese in the bottom shell. Layer the olives, arugula and radishes over the cheese. Sprinkle with salt and pepper and drizzle with ¹/₃ of the dressing.

Arrange the tuna over the layers. Sprinkle with salt and pepper and drizzle with half of the remaining dressing. Layer the tomatoes and basil over the tuna. Sprinkle with salt and pepper and drizzle with the remaining dressing.

Fit the top shell over the layers and wrap tightly with plastic wrap. Place in a shallow dish and place a baking sheet on the top. Weight the baking sheet with several 1-pound weights.

Chill for 1 to 6 hours. Cut into 2-inch slices to serve.

Serves four

IN 1990, THE JUNIOR LEAGUE OF BOCA RATON CONCENTRATED ITS COMMUNITY OUTREACH IN ONE OF ITS MAJOR FOCUS AREAS—CHILD HEALTH AND WELFARE. UNDER THE DIRECTION OF JUNIOR LEAGUE PRESIDENT MARY CSAR, MEMBERS ESTABLISHED A TASK FORCE TO RESEARCH AN ALARMING RATE OF CHILD INJURIES AND DEATHS IN THE NEIGHBORING FARMWORKER COMMUNITY. THIS RESEARCH ULTIMATELY CULMINATED IN THE OPENING OF THE FARMWORKER CHILD DEVELOPMENT CENTER.

Garden Sandwich

Try this on a sunny day when the outdoors beckons.

2 (10-ounce) packages frozen chopped
    spinach, thawed
1/2 cup minced green onions
1 tablespoon minced green bell pepper
1/4 cup plus 2 tablespoons mayonnaise
1 tablespoon lemon juice
1/4 teaspoon salt
8 ounces fresh mushrooms, sliced
1/4 cup plus 1 tablespoon butter, softened
12 slices pumpernickel bread
3/4 cup alfalfa sprouts
2 tablespoons salted sunflower kernels
6 slices provolone cheese
6 slices Cheddar cheese
6 slices Swiss cheese

Squeeze the spinach to remove excess liquid. Combine with the green onions, green pepper, mayonnaise, lemon juice and salt in a bowl and mix well.

Sauté the mushrooms in 1 of the tablespoons butter in a skillet until tender.

Spread 1 teaspoon of the remaining butter on one side of each bread slice. Place 6 bread slices butter side down on a hot griddle and grill until light brown. Spread the spinach mixture evenly on the unbuttered side of the grilled bread; sprinkle with the alfalfa sprouts, sautéed mushrooms and sunflower kernels.

Layer 1 slice of provolone, Cheddar and Swiss cheese on the unbuttered side of the remaining bread. Place butter side down on the hot griddle and grill over medium heat just until the cheeses begin to melt and the bread is light brown.

Place the cheese-topped bread and spinach-topped bread together to form sandwiches. Serve immediately.

Serves six

Flower Ice Ring

Layer edible flowers in the bottom of a metal mold or bundt pan. Add 1 1/2 inches of distilled water. Freeze until firm. Continue to add layers of flowers and water to the mold, freezing each layer before adding another. Place briefly in a bowl of hot water and invert to remove from the mold. Ice cubes can be prepared in the same manner. Freezing in layers keeps the flowers from floating to the top, which becomes the bottom when inverted. The distilled water insures that the ice will freeze clear.

Roasted Garlic

Simmer garlic in milk before roasting to sweeten the flavor. Place 4 garlic bulbs on their bases in a saucepan and add 4 cups milk. Bring to a boil and reduce the heat. Simmer, uncovered, for 10 minutes; drain. Place the garlic in a deep baking dish. Pour $^1/_4$ cup olive oil over the garlic and sprinkle lightly with salt and pepper. Cover with foil and bake at 350 degrees for $1^1/_2$ hours. Cool the garlic and squeeze the cloves from the skins. Serve with crusty bread.

Cuban Bread

Bring Havana home with this wonderful base for sandwiches; try it with your favorite spread or flavored butters (page 86).

2 tablespoons dry yeast
2 tablespoons sugar
1 tablespoon salt
5 to 6 cups bread flour or all-purpose flour
2 cups (120- to 130-degree) water
sesame seeds or poppy seeds (optional)

Combine the yeast, sugar and salt with 4 cups of the flour in a large mixing bowl and stir to mix well. Add the water and beat for 3 minutes with a mixer flat beater or 100 strong strokes by hand. Add enough of the remaining flour $^1/_2$ cup at a time to form a dough that is no longer sticky, mixing after each addition.

Knead on a floured surface for 8 minutes with floured hands or knead with a dough hook until smooth and elastic. Place in a greased bowl, turning to coat the surface. Let rise, covered, in a warm place for 15 minutes or until doubled in bulk.

Punch dough down on a floured surface and divide into 2 portions. Shape into 2 round loaves. Place on baking sheets which have been greased or sprinkled with cornmeal. Slash an X on the tops with a sharp knife. Brush with water and sprinkle with sesame seeds.

Place on the middle shelf of a cold oven. Place a large pan of hot water on the lower shelf and set the oven to 400 degrees. Bake for 50 minutes or until the loaves are deep golden brown and sound hollow when thumped on the bottom. Remove to wire racks to cool.

Note: Because this bread has no shortening, it will only keep fresh for a couple of days. After that, it makes excellent toast and freezes well.

Serves eight

Game Day Muffuletta

This sandwich always scores a touchdown!

1 (16-ounce) jar marinated
    mixed vegetables, drained,
    chopped
1/2 cup chopped pimento-stuffed
    green olives
1 garlic clove, finely chopped
1/4 teaspoon dried oregano leaves,
    crumbled

1 tablespoon olive oil
1 unsliced round loaf of bread
3 ounces sliced lean baked ham
3 ounces sliced lean turkey
    breast
3 ounces sliced salami
3 ounces sliced provolone cheese

Combine the mixed vegetables and olives in a small bowl. Sauté the garlic and oregano in the heated olive oil in a skillet for 2 minutes or until the garlic is tender but not brown.

Cut the bread into halves horizontally; create a pocket by removing some of the bread. Brush the bottom half with the garlic oil.

Spread half of the vegetable mixture on the bottom half. Layer the ham, turkey, salami and cheese over the vegetables and spread with the remaining vegetable mixture. Top with the remaining bread half. Serve at room temperature or toast under the broiler. Cut into pieces to serve.

Serves six to eight

Mermaid Tea Sandwiches

Salmon is a refreshing alternative to tuna.

1 bunch watercress, chopped
2/3 cup mayonnaise
juice and grated zest of
    1 lemon
1 tablespoon chopped fresh
    tarragon

14 ounces fresh salmon, poached,
    or 2 (7-ounce) cans pink
    salmon
grated nutmeg, salt and pepper
    to taste
1 loaf white bread

Combine half the watercress with the mayonnaise, lemon juice, lemon zest and tarragon in a bowl and mix well. Flake the salmon and stir into the mayonnaise mixture. Add the nutmeg, salt and pepper and mix gently. Chill until serving time.

Trim the crusts from the bread and cut into fish or starfish shapes with cookie cutters. Spread with the salmon mixture and top with the remaining watercress.

Serves sixteen

The Great Outdoors

Try some of these pointers for successful outdoor entertaining:

Grill! It's the preferred way to cook in South Florida and people love it everywhere. Make sure the coals are ready before everyone gets too hungry.

Create a special "room" with your outdoor setting. Bring fun collections outdoors. Browse thrift shops for vintage tablecloths, stemware, and flatware. Use pitchers for flowers, to hold utensils, or for wine, water, or lemonade. Consider double-sided tape to attach linens to your tables in case of high winds. Use live flowers and herbs for accents and plant them in your plant beds after the party.

Provide lots of seating. Slipcovers for chairs add festive personality and charm. If you entertain outdoors often, consider making sets in varying prints to match the mood of the party.

Piazza Portobello Sandwich

An open-face sandwich with an elegant presentation.

Red Pepper Vinaigrette
1 red bell pepper, roasted
    (page 91)
1 tablespoon white wine vinegar
1 tablespoon water
2 tablespoons extra-virgin olive oil
salt and pepper to taste

Sandwich
1½ pounds fresh portobello
    mushroom caps
5 tablespoons balsamic vinegar

6 large garlic cloves, minced
2 tablespoons chopped fresh
    thyme, or 2 teaspoons
    dried thyme
½ cup olive oil
2 ounces (about ¼ cup)
    Gorgonzola cheese, at room
    temperature
1 tablespoon unsalted butter,
    softened
4 large diagonal slices crusty
    bread, ½ inch thick

For the vinaigrette, combine the bell pepper, vinegar, water, olive oil, salt and pepper in a blender container and process until smooth.

For the sandwich, place the mushrooms in a single layer in 2 sealable plastic bags. Whisk the vinegar, garlic, thyme and olive oil in a small bowl. Add half to each plastic bag; seal the bags, pressing out the air. Marinate at room temperature for 1 to 2 hours, turning several times.

Combine the cheese and butter in a bowl and mix until smooth. Place the bread on a rack 5 to 6 inches above coals and grill for 1 minute or until golden brown. Place on 4 serving plates and spread with the cheese mixture.

Drain the mushrooms and grill for 2 to 3 minutes on each side or until tender. Cut into thin slices and arrange on the toasts. Drizzle with the vinaigrette.

Serves four

IN 1991, JUNIOR LEAGUE OF BOCA RATON MEMBERS WORKED TIRELESSLY TO SECURE GRANTS AND RAISE FUNDS FOR A PRESCHOOL—THE FARMWORKER CHILD DEVELOPMENT CENTER—TO BE HOUSED ON THE GROUNDS OF IN THE PINES FARMWORKER CAMP. UNDER THE DIRECTION OF PRESIDENT SUSAN SAXTON, JUNIOR LEAGUE MEMBERS PROUDLY OPENED THE DOORS OF THE CENTER AND HELPED GIVE FARMWORKER CHILDREN AN EQUAL START IN LIFE.

Persian Chicken Sandwich

A burst of delight with the flavor of the Middle East.

Marinated Chicken
$1/2$ small onion
2 tablespoons fresh lemon juice
1 teaspoon paprika
2 teaspoons dried oregano
1 teaspoon minced garlic
$1/4$ cup olive oil
salt and freshly ground pepper
    to taste
4 (8-ounce) skinless boneless
    chicken breast halves

Lemon-Dill Mayonnaise
$2/3$ cup plain yogurt
1 teaspoon grated lemon zest
1 tablespoon fresh lemon juice
2 tablespoons chopped fresh dill
$1/2$ cup mayonnaise
salt and pepper to taste

Sandwich and Filling
$1/3$ cup chopped toasted walnuts
4 pita bread rounds
8 ($1/8$x3x3-inch) slices feta cheese
16 each large mint leaves, basil
    leaves and watercress sprigs

For the marinated chicken, combine the onion, lemon juice, paprika, oregano and garlic in a food processor or blender container; process until chopped. Spoon into a nonreactive bowl and stir in the olive oil, salt and pepper. Add the chicken and mix well. Marinate in the refrigerator for 8 hours or longer.

For the mayonnaise, place the yogurt in a cheesecloth-lined sieve and let drain for 1 hour; measure $1/2$ cup thick yogurt. Combine with the lemon zest, lemon juice, dill, mayonnaise, salt and pepper in a bowl and mix well. Chill until serving time.

For the filling, drain the chicken and place on a rack in a broiler pan and broil for 3 minutes on each side. Cool slightly and cut into $1/2$-inch pieces. Combine with the lemon-dill mayonnaise and walnuts in a bowl and mix well. Adjust the seasonings.

To assemble the sandwich, cut the pita rounds into halves and open the pockets. Place the feta cheese, mint leaves, basil leaves and watercress sprigs into the pockets. Add the chicken mixture.

Note: Serve the chicken salad filling in 8 miniature pita rounds for appetizers.

Serves four

Homemade Mayonnaise

Combine 1 egg, $1/2$ teaspoon dry mustard, 2 tablespoons lemon juice and $1/2$ teaspoon sea salt in a blender container and process until smooth. Add 1 cup extra-virgin olive oil gradually, processing constantly at high speed until thickened. Store in an airtight container in the refrigerator for up to 7 days.

Entrées

A Night to Remember

There's something magical about gathering around a beautiful dinner table in your own home. When you take the time to offer your finest and arrange everything just so, it puts a sparkle in everyone's eyes. Guests love to be entertained in style. It lets them know they are important to you—so special, in fact, that you want to give them the most precious gifts of your time and your creative spirit. And if you schedule far enough in advance, it can be a lot of fun to play around with special touches here and there.

Celebrating special birthdays or anniversaries with close friends are wonderful reasons to throw formal dinner parties. You don't have to wait for the holidays, a rehearsal dinner, or the arrival of an honored guest for inspiration. If you love to entertain, offer to throw a formal dinner party as your donation to a favorite charity auction, and let them sell tickets for each seat at the table. Or schedule a black tie dinner with the gourmet group.

At this elegant dinner party for ten, the evening began with Cosmopolitans and passed hors d'oeuvres on the terrace. In the background, the CD player was preprogrammed with classics from Old Blue Eyes and Tony Bennett. The guests then moved into the dining room for the first course of Caviar Pie (page 62) served in crystal champagne glasses.

To set the mood in the dining room, this hostess chose white candles and roses and an ecru tablecloth, so the beauty of the gilded china and sterling silver would sparkle. These neutral tones also would be a beautiful backdrop for china accented in any jewel tone.

An opulent Old-World backdrop, like this one at the Boca Raton Resort & Club's Cathedral Dining Room, will enchant all who enter. Yet an elegant table also can be set in an intimate dining room at home. In a simpler setting, the table itself will command most of the attention.

To enhance even the prettiest chinas, set the dinner plates on gold chargers or service plates. Chargers are purely decorative, employed to make a dazzling impression, and are removed after the soup course. They work equally well for the traditional Lenox or antique Limoges china and the many beautiful contemporary chinas.

Crystal is also an elegant accent for any formal dinner table. There's something wondrous about the way the light dances off the facets. The effect is as delightful as champagne bubbles. You can mix different patterns for the water, white wine, and red wine, but repeat the same combination at each place setting to provide continuity of design.

While it doesn't have to take more than a couple of hours to set an elegant table, it's much more enjoyable to start a few days ahead, so you can try different accessories. As the hostess, you deserve to *savor the moment* too. You may not often set out all your treasured things, but there is nothing like this process to create new combinations and traditions.

Setting a formal table is not synonymous with being austere. Adding treasures like this pair of silver pheasants between the centerpiece and the candles is a light-hearted touch for a formal scene. Little antique ivory Japanese figurines and a beautiful porcelain vase give guests a bit of art to admire as they dine. They also promote conversation with dining partners, and give the hostess a chance to tell a story. See if you have a collection that works for the season of your party.

Remember Plan B

When choosing the menu, this hostess wrote down simpler selections next to her first choices in case she started to run out of time. Shrimp cocktail or smoked salmon with lemon and capers, for example, could easily be substituted for the Caviar Pie (page 62).

Rosemary Roasted Rack of Lamb with Cabernet Sauce (page 154) and Potatoes Anna (page 223), on tonight's menu, are wonderful choices for an intimate gathering. The combination is delectable, but fairly easy to prepare, saving the hostess for her guests.

If you think you might be running out of time, visit a good pastry shop for dessert. A simple cake with berries or a sorbet with sauce can be beautifully presented on individual plates. Your guests will wonder how you can do it all so well.

Not Just Conversation

After dinner take your guests into the living room for dessert and coffee. Create a coffee bar. Serve the latest coffees accompanied by a silver bowl of whipped cream, chocolate shavings, and several liqueurs.

This is the time when you can let your personal style shine. If you like classical music, bid on an evening with a couple of musicians who are donating their services to a school fund-raiser. Students from the local conservatory also might be tapped to perform. See if they'll tell a brief story about each piece. Or perhaps you'll hire a piano player for dancing or singing around the piano.

Is there something interesting to do in your neighborhood? You could rent a couple of antique cars and visit the local chocolate shop for a tour and tasting.

An expert on rare liqueurs also could conduct a tasting. Or this might be a chance to play games. Pictionary, your favorite board game, bridge, Bunko or charades are great, especially if the evening is taking a more informal tone. Or buy a book of discussion questions and go around the room filling in the blanks on what everyone's sport would be if they were competing in the Olympics.

You Are Cordially Invited

Telephone a few close friends to make sure they will be available for the date you're considering. Follow up with hand-written invitations on personal note cards. Consider printed or engraved invitations for a special occasion like a formal engagement party or rehearsal dinner.

Not everything has to match. Here, each of the sterling and gold water goblets is different, although they are all the same shape, height, and made by Galmer. Czech crystal and gold wine glasses blend perfectly.

Menu

Caviar Pie
(page 62)

Baby Greens with Pears
(page 121)

Rosemary Roasted
Rack of Lamb with
Cabernet Sauce*
(page 154)

Potatoes Anna*
(page 223)

Red Beet Rose*
(page 165)

Five-Vegetable Napoleons
(page 224)

Clos du Bois Alexander Valley
Cabernet Sauvignon

Fallen Chocolate
Soufflé Cakes
(page 254)

Coffee with Kahlúa

*Pictured recipes

Paradise in Pink

The Boca Raton Resort & Club started with noted architect Addison Mizner's dream to create a pink paradise south of Palm Beach in the mid 1920s. Replete with pink stucco, terra-cotta tile, and pecky cypress beams, this Mediterranean Revival structure is also a showcase of archways, colonnades, and tiled and fountain gardens. (See photographs in the Appetizers and Beverages, Entrées, and Pasta chapters.)

Since it opened in 1926, the 100-room Cloister Inn, as the Resort & Club was originally known, has undergone numerous renovations and additions– including the application of 5,000 square feet of gold leaf to the ceiling of the Cathedral Dining Room (see pages 142–143), which was modeled after a 15-century Catalonian hospital. The original furniture, wrought iron chandeliers and candleholders, and precast architectural elements were fashioned at the Mizner Industries in West Palm Beach.

Mizner Meat Loaf

This is not your mother's meat loaf.

1 pound lean ground beef
1 pound lean ground veal
2 eggs
$1/2$ cup bread crumbs
$1/2$ onion, chopped
2 tablespoons chopped fresh herbs, such as basil, chives and/or parsley
2 teaspoons salt
1 teaspoon pepper
4 slices smoked bacon
$1/2$ cup molasses
$1/2$ cup catsup
$1/3$ cup packed brown sugar

Combine the ground beef, ground veal, eggs, bread crumbs, onion, herbs, salt and pepper in a bowl and mix well. Shape into a loaf and place in a loaf pan. Bake at 350 degrees for 45 minutes.

Arrange the bacon over the top. Combine the molasses, catsup and brown sugar in a bowl and mix well. Spread over the meat loaf and bacon. Bake for 45 minutes longer. Remove from the loaf pan and slice to serve.

Serves eight

Beef Tenderloin with Bleu Cheese Stuffing

Rest assured of the success of this classic tenderloin with robust flavor.

1 (2-pound) beef tenderloin
^{1}/2 cup crumbled bleu cheese
2 tablespoons chopped walnuts
2 tablespoons chopped parsley
2 teaspoons dried oregano

salt and pepper to taste
^{2}/3 to ^{3}/4 cup beef broth

Garnish

parsley sprigs

Cut a long pocket in the top of the tenderloin, starting and ending ^{1}/2 inch from the ends and cutting to within 1 inch of the bottom.

Combine the bleu cheese, walnuts, parsley and half the oregano in a bowl and mix well. Spoon into the pocket in the tenderloin. Press the sides of the pocket together and secure with string. Rub with the remaining oregano, salt and pepper.

Place in a 9x13-inch roasting pan and insert a meat thermometer in the thickest portion of the beef, not the filling. Roast at 425 degrees to 135 degrees on the meat thermometer for medium-rare. Let stand for 5 minutes. Remove to a platter. Place the roasting pan over medium-high heat and add the beef broth. Cook until heated through, stirring to deglaze the pan. Pour into a sauce boat.

Slice the tenderloin and garnish with parsley sprigs. Serve with the heated pan juices.

Serves six

Sesame Beef Tenderloin

Marinate the beef for as long as possible for the best flavor.

^{3}/4 cup soy sauce
^{1}/4 cup vegetable oil
^{1}/4 cup flour
^{1}/2 cup sugar
^{1}/2 cup toasted sesame seeds

2 scallions, sliced
2 garlic cloves, crushed
^{1}/4 teaspoon pepper
1 (4-pound) beef tenderloin

Combine the soy sauce, oil, flour, sugar, sesame seeds, scallions, garlic and pepper in a bowl and mix well. Cut the tenderloin into fillets and add to the marinade. Marinate, covered, in the refrigerator for 1 hour or longer.

Drain the beef, reserving the marinade. Grill the fillets until done to taste, basting with the reserved marinade.

Serves six to eight

Menu Pointers

Keep a file with past parties, recording the menu, guest list, and theme.

Plan the menu so much of the work can be done in advance, such as a sauce that can be made two or three days ahead, or have a frozen soufflé for dessert.

Plan a balanced meal, avoiding several heavy courses.

Choose recipes you have made before.

Plan hors d'oeuvres; will they be passed or stationary?

As guests RSVP, note any allergies or dislikes.

Have a simpler alternative in mind in case something unexpected grabs your time.

Practice presentation touches for vegetables and garnishes with your family: stuffing potatoes and fanning vegetables are fun, but they take a little practice.

Herbed Beef Tenderloin with Shallot Wine Sauce

Preparation the day before serving makes this an excellent choice for a party.

Herb Marinade and Tenderloin

2 tablespoons chopped fresh
    rosemary
2 tablespoons chopped fresh
    thyme
4 large garlic cloves
1 large shallot, cut into quarters
1 tablespoon grated orange zest
2 bay leaves
$1/2$ teaspoon ground nutmeg
$1/4$ teaspoon ground cloves
1 tablespoon coarse salt
1 teaspoon freshly ground pepper
2 tablespoons olive oil
2 (2-pound) thick beef
    tenderloins, trimmed

Shallot Wine Sauce

reserved pan drippings
3 tablespoons unsalted butter
$1/2$ cup chopped shallots
2 tablespoons chopped fresh
    chives
1 tablespoon red wine vinegar
$3/4$ cup dry red wine
1 tablespoon unsalted butter
salt and pepper to taste

Garnish

chopped fresh parsley, rosemary
    and/or chives

For the marinated tenderloin, combine the rosemary, thyme, garlic, shallot, orange zest, bay leaves, nutmeg, cloves, salt and pepper in a food processor container and process until chopped. Add the olive oil gradually, processing constantly until smooth. Spread the mixture evenly over the tenderloins and place in a shallow dish. Marinate, covered with foil, in the refrigerator for 8 hours or longer.

Place the tenderloins on a rack in a large roasting pan. Insert a meat thermometer in the thickest portion of one tenderloin. Roast at 400 degrees to 130 degrees on the meat thermometer for rare or to 140 degrees for medium.

Remove the tenderloins to a platter and cover with foil, reserving the pan drippings. Let the tenderloins stand for 10 minutes. Cut into $1/2$-inch slices.

For the sauce, pour the reserved pan drippings into a medium saucepan. Add 3 tablespoons butter, shallots and chives. Cook for 1 minute or until the shallots are tender, stirring constantly. Stir in the vinegar and wine. Simmer for 1 minute. Stir in 1 tablespoon butter and season with salt and pepper. Remove from the heat. Spoon over the beef. Garnish with fresh herbs.

Serves eight

Filet Mignon with Shallot Sauce

A different grilled steak. Try this with crispy onions for a crunchy seasoning.

^{1}/2 *cup thinly sliced shallots*
2 tablespoons olive oil
^{1}/4 *cup sugar*
^{1}/2 *cup balsamic vinegar*
1 cup chicken stock or canned broth
1 cup beef stock
2 tablespoons chopped fresh thyme, or 2 teaspoons dried thyme
salt and pepper to taste
4 (8- to 10-ounce) 1-inch beef filets

Sauté the shallots in the heated olive oil in a skillet over medium heat for 15 minutes. Add the sugar and cook for 5 minutes, stirring constantly. Add the vinegar and cook for 1 minute or until reduced to a syrupy consistency. Stir in the chicken stock and beef stock. Boil for 10 minutes. Season with the thyme, salt and pepper.

Season the steaks with salt and pepper. Grill until done to taste. Serve with the shallot sauce and Crispy Onions (at right).

Note: The shallot sauce can be prepared up to 1 day in advance and reheated to serve.

Serves four

Crispy Onions

Cut 3 onions into ^{1}/4-inch slices and divide into rings. Soak in ice water for 2 hours, adding additional ice as it melts. Combine 1 egg, 1 cup buttermilk, 1 cup flour, ^{1}/2 teaspoon baking powder and ^{1}/2 teaspoon salt in a bowl and mix well. Drain the onion rings and pat dry. Dip into the batter and deep-fry a few at a time in 375-degree vegetable oil until brown. Drain on paper towels and keep warm until all the onions are cooked. Serve immediately.

Look What Happens When You Play with Fire

Fire gives food another life, another layer of flavor. So by all means, fire up that grill!

Before you start, clean your grill; spray or rub it with oil; and always preheat.

For better browning, pat your meat dry before placing it on the grill.

Know when to baste. Oil and vinegar, or citrus-based marinades can be brushed on meat throughout the cooking time. When using sugar-based barbecue sauces, apply it toward the end of your cooking time.

Turn, don't stab! The juices will run. Invest in a set of spring-hinged tongs for best results.

Keep it covered, and don't desert your post! When cooking larger cuts of meat and poultry, find a low heat zone and keep the grill covered. Resist the temptation to peek! Every time you lift the lid, you add five to ten minutes to the total cooking time.

Beef Tenderloin with Spicy Rub and Barbecue Mop

Even your mother-in-law will love this!

Barbecue Mop
1 cup beef stock or canned beef broth
$^1/_4$ cup dry red wine
3 tablespoons prepared barbecue sauce
2 tablespoons Worcestershire sauce
2 tablespoons vegetable oil
2 large garlic cloves, minced
1 tablespoon minced serrano chile

Tenderloin and Spicy Rub
$^1/_4$ cup chopped fresh parsley
2 tablespoons minced garlic
1 tablespoon paprika
2 tablespoons crumbled bay leaves
$1^1/_2$ teaspoons dry mustard
3 tablespoons coarse salt
$1^1/_2$ teaspoons cayenne
3 tablespoons coarsely ground black pepper
1 (4-pound) beef tenderloin
vegetable oil

For the mop, combine the beef stock, wine, barbecue sauce, Worcestershire sauce, oil, garlic and chile in a bowl and mix well. Store, covered, in the refrigerator for up to 24 hours

For the tenderloin and rub, combine the parsley, garlic, paprika, bay leaves, dry mustard, salt, cayenne and black pepper in a small bowl. Brush the tenderloin with oil and press the rub over all sides. Let stand for 40 minutes.

Insert a meat thermometer in the thickest portion of the tenderloin. Grill for 20 minutes or to 125 degrees on the thermometer for rare, turning and basting with the barbecue mop every 5 minutes. Move the tenderloin to the coolest part of the grill and cover with foil. Cook for 10 minutes longer. Remove to a platter and let stand for 10 minutes. Slice and serve hot.

Note: You may also cut the tenderloin into 10 fillets. Wrap each fillet with 2 slices of partially cooked bacon and secure with wooden picks. Prepare as above, adjusting the grilling time as needed.

Serves six

Grilled Sirloin with Sunshine Citrus Salsa

A true Florida dish with fresh ingredients; serve it al fresco to complete the mood.

Citrus Salsa

sections of 2 oranges, chopped
2 tablespoons fresh orange juice
1/2 teaspoon chopped lemon zest
1/2 small lemon, peeled, seeded,
    finely chopped
1/2 teaspoon chopped lime zest
1/2 small lime, peeled, seeded,
    finely chopped
1/4 cup chopped green onions
1 tablespoon chopped fresh
    cilantro
2 tablespoons rice vinegar
1 tablespoon sugar
1/8 teaspoon salt

Steak

1/2 cup reduced-sodium soy sauce
1/4 cup chopped green onions
3 tablespoons fresh lime juice
1 garlic clove, minced
1/8 teaspoon hot sauce
1 (1 1/2-pound) boneless lean top
    sirloin steak

Garnish

lemon and lime slices
fresh cilantro

For the salsa, combine the oranges, orange juice, lemon zest, lemon, lime zest, lime, green onions, cilantro, vinegar, sugar and salt in a bowl and mix gently. Chill, covered, for 2 hours.

For the steak, combine the soy sauce, green onions, lime juice, garlic and hot sauce in a shallow dish. Add the steak, turning to coat well. Marinate, covered, in the refrigerator for 2 hours or longer, turning occasionally.

Drain the steak, discarding the marinade. Grill over medium-hot, 350- to 400-degree, coals in a covered grill for 5 to 6 minutes on each side or until done to taste. Remove to a platter and let stand for 5 minutes.

Cut the steak diagonally into thin slices. Top with the salsa. Garnish with lemon and lime slices and cilantro.

Serves six

How to Section Citrus

Cut a slice from the top and bottom of each piece of fruit with a freshly sharpened knife to expose the pulp. Cutting from top to bottom in a curving motion around the fruit, remove all the peel and pith. Working over a bowl to catch the juices, free each section of fruit by cutting it away from the membrane on both sides. Lift out the section and discard the seeds.

Zesting Tips

When zesting citrus fruits, it's always a good idea to use fruit that is fresh, cold, dry, and firm enough to peel or grate easily. The zest can be removed in strips or grated off the whole fruit. To take off zest in strips, use a vegetable peeler and remove the colored part of the rind only, without any of the bitter white pith. The pieces of zest may be used as is, cut into julienne strips, or chopped.

Drying Herbs

Dried herbs have a shelf life of about six months if stored in a cool dark place. Stored near a hot oven, they have a life of six days. Herbs that are more than a year old have lost their flavor.

To air-dry herbs, tie small bunches of each herb together and put them in a brown paper bag. Leave for a few weeks until completely dry. Do not dry herbs in the sun or the oils and fragrance will be lost.

To dry herbs in the microwave, arrange a single layer of the herbs between three or four thicknesses of paper towels and microwave on high for two minutes or until dry.

Cajun Rub

Mix 6 tablespoons paprika,
$1/4$ cup garlic powder,
3 tablespoons onion powder,
$1/4$ cup salt, 2 tablespoons cayenne
and 2 tablespoons black pepper.
Use to rub on chicken or beef before
grilling or add to mayonnaise or
sour cream for a taste lift.

Roast Prime Rib with Horseradish Crust

Simple and delicious, the horseradish is the perfect complement to this tender roast.

1 (8-pound) 4-rib standing rib roast, trimmed
3 tablespoons drained horseradish
1 tablespoon Dijon mustard
1 teaspoon crumbled dried thyme
1 teaspoon crumbled dried rosemary
1 teaspoon salt
1 teaspoon coarsely ground pepper
$2/3$ cup dry red wine
2 cups reduced-sodium beef broth
salt and pepper to taste

Garnish
fresh rosemary sprigs

Let the roast stand at room temperature for 1 hour. Combine the horseradish, Dijon mustard, thyme, rosemary, salt and pepper in a small bowl and mix well. Place the roast rib side down in a roasting pan. Rub the fat side with the horseradish mixture. Insert a meat thermometer in the thickest portion, not touching a bone.

Roast at 450 degrees on the middle oven rack for 25 minutes. Reduce the oven temperature to 300 degrees. Roast for $2^3/4$ hours longer or to 135 degrees on the meat thermometer for medium-rare. Remove to a cutting board and cover loosely. Let stand for 20 to 30 minutes.

Skim the fat from the drippings in the roasting pan. Add the wine, stirring to deglaze the pan. Bring to a boil and boil on the stove top until reduced by $1/2$; pour into a saucepan. Add the beef broth. Bring to a boil and boil for 5 minutes. Season with salt and pepper.

Carve the roast and garnish with rosemary. Serve with the sauce.
Serves eight

Hacienda Skirt Steak

Feed the whole corral with this spicy recipe from Café Maxx.

Steaks and Adobo Marinade
1 cup fresh cilantro
$1/3$ cup chopped yellow onion
$1/4$ cup chopped garlic
$1/2$ cup white vinegar
1 bay leaf
1 teaspoon ground cumin, toasted
1 teaspoon ground oregano
1 teaspoon ground thyme
$1^1/2$ teaspoons salt
1 teaspoon pepper
$1/4$ cup olive oil
6 (8-ounce) skirt steaks

Chimichurri
$1^1/2$ garlic cloves
1 bay leaf
2 jalapeños
$1/2$ teaspoon salt
2 tablespoons white vinegar
$1/4$ cup minced fresh parsley
$1/4$ cup minced fresh flat-leaf
 parsley
$1/4$ cup minced fresh oregano
3 tablespoons virgin olive oil

To marinate the steaks, combine the cilantro, onion, garlic, vinegar, bay leaf, cumin, oregano, thyme, salt and pepper in a food processor container and process until smooth. Combine with the olive oil in a bowl and whisk until well mixed. Pour over the steaks in a nonreactive dish. Marinate, covered, in the refrigerator for 12 hours.

For the chimichurri, combine the garlic, bay leaf, jalapeños and salt with a small amount of the vinegar in a blender container and process until chopped. Combine the mixture with the parsleys and oregano in a bowl and mix well. Whisk in the olive oil and remaining vinegar.

Grill the steaks over hot coals for 3 minutes on each side for medium-rare to medium. Remove to a warm plate and top with the chimichurri. Serve with rice and beans.

Serves six

Flank Steak Marinade

Process $1/4$ cup vegetable oil, $1/4$ cup soy sauce, $1^1/2$ tablespoons chopped gingerroot, 3 chopped garlic cloves, 2 tablespoons red wine vinegar, 3 onion slices and 6 tablespoons honey in a blender until smooth. Use as a marinade for flank steak or skirt steak, marinating for 2 hours or longer before grilling.

Rosemary Roasted Rack of Lamb with Cabernet Sauce

Elegant; the perfect dish for company or a romantic evening.

Lamb
2 (7-rib) racks of lamb, trimmed
salt and pepper to taste
1 cup fresh white bread crumbs
2 teaspoons finely chopped fresh rosemary
4 garlic cloves, minced
1/4 cup (1/2 stick) unsalted butter, softened

Cabernet Sauce
2 shallots, finely chopped
2 tablespoons (1/4 stick) unsalted butter
1 cup cabernet
1 1/2 cups unsalted fresh or canned beef broth
1/2 teaspoon Dijon mustard
1 tablespoon unsalted butter
reserved pan drippings

For the lamb, ask the butcher to remove the cap and backbone from the racks and to french the ribs. Season both sides of the racks with salt and pepper. Mix the bread crumbs, rosemary, garlic and butter in a small bowl. Spread over the top and sides of the lamb. Insert a meat thermometer in the thickest portion of 1 rack, not touching the bone. Place in a roasting pan.

Roast at 400 degrees on the middle oven rack for 25 to 30 minutes or to 125 to 130 degrees on the meat thermometer ; lamb should be pink and juicy. Let stand in the roasting pan for 10 to 15 minutes, reserving the juices that drip from the lamb.

For the sauce, sauté the shallots in 2 tablespoons heated butter in a sauté pan for 2 to 3 minutes or until tender. Add the wine and cook over high heat for 2 minutes to reduce. Stir in the beef broth, mustard, 1 tablespoon butter and the reserved pan drippings. Cook until heated through.

Carve the lamb into 3- and 4-chop portions. Spoon the sauce onto the serving plates and place the lamb in the sauce.

Serves four

In 1992, based upon extensive community research, the Junior League of Boca Raton formed a partnership with the Children's Place and Connor's Nursery to establish a child-abuse crisis shelter in South Palm Beach County. Under the direction of president Pattie Damron, plans for what would become Children's Place South were developed to offer shelter to abused, abandoned, and neglected children—inspired and funded through the efforts of the Junior League of Boca Raton.

Bridgehampton Lamb

A grilled boneless leg of lamb with wonderful flavor.

1 (5-pound) leg of lamb	2 garlic cloves, minced
1/4 cup lemon juice	2 tablespoons brown sugar
3 tablespoons olive oil	Tabasco sauce to taste
3 tablespoons soy sauce	1/2 teaspoon salt
3 tablespoons Dijon mustard	1/2 teaspoon pepper

Ask the butcher to bone and butterfly the leg of lamb. Pat dry with paper towels.

Combine the lemon juice, olive oil, soy sauce, Dijon mustard, garlic, brown sugar, Tabasco sauce, salt and pepper in a bowl and mix well. Brush some of the mixture over the lamb.

Grill the lamb over hot coals for 40 minutes, basting several times with the lemon juice mixture. Remove to a platter and let stand for 5 to 10 minutes. Carve diagonally and serve immediately.

Serves eight

Herbed Leg of Lamb

A dish with an incredibly flavorful combination of herbs and a simple preparation.

1 garlic clove, crushed	1 teaspoon dried marjoram
1 teaspoon salt	1 teaspoon dried rosemary
2 tablespoons olive oil	2 tablespoons flour
1 (5- to 6-pound) leg of lamb	1 cup white wine
1 teaspoon dried thyme	1 cup water

Mix the garlic, salt and olive oil in a small bowl. Spread over the lamb. Sprinkle with the thyme, marjoram, rosemary and flour. Place on a rack in a shallow roasting pan and add the wine and water to the pan. Roast at 325 degrees for 2 1/2 hours, basting frequently with the pan juices.

Serves eight

Marinating Meats and Vegetables

For best results, use your marinade immediately after the ingredients have been combined. Place meats or vegetables with the marinade in a resealable bag, and remove as much air as possible before sealing and refrigerating.

You may want to prick the meat with a fork to allow the marinade to permeate deeply into the cut of steak, pork, or chicken.

Discard meat marinade once it has been used. If it is to be served with the grilled food, it should be boiled to remove any danger of contamination from the uncooked meat.

What Wine When?

The old rule of white with fish, red with meat doesn't always apply. In a good match, delicate foods show best with lighter wines; heavier foods need richer wines. Try mixing and matching from the following lists. In each case, pair foods from the first list with wines from the second.

Delicate Foods

*Clams or oysters
Fish, such as sole or snapper
Grilled vegetables
Pasta with oil-based or
vegetable sauces*

Wines

*Pinot Blanc
Riesling
Chardonnay*

Dijon Lamb Chops with Shallot Sauce

A gourmet dish for lamb lovers.

*1¹/₃ cups dry white wine
2 cups canned beef broth
¹/₂ cup minced shallots
1 teaspoon crumbled dried rosemary
8 small (1¹/₂-inch) double-rib lamb chops
salt and pepper to taste
6 tablespoons Dijon mustard
1¹/₂ cups dry bread crumbs
¹/₄ cup (¹/₂ stick) unsalted butter, sliced*

Combine the wine, beef broth, shallots and rosemary in a saucepan. Bring to a boil and reduce the heat. Cook until the sauce is reduced to ¹/₃ cup. Keep warm.

Sprinkle the lamb chops with salt and pepper; spread with the Dijon mustard and coat with the bread crumbs. Place on a rack in a broiler pan.

Broil the lamb chops 4 inches from the heat source for 5 minutes on each side for medium-rare. Remove to a platter and let stand for 5 minutes.

Add the butter to the shallot sauce and swirl the pan to melt the butter. Serve with the lamb chops.

Serves four

Spicy Grilled Lamb Chops with Marinated Tomatoes

A satisfying and colorful main dish for a springtime barbecue.

2 tablespoons cider vinegar
1 or 2 garlic cloves, crushed
$^{1}/_{4}$ teaspoon curry powder
$^{1}/_{2}$ teaspoon dry mustard
$^{1}/_{8}$ teaspoon cayenne
3 tablespoons olive oil
6 (1$^{1}/_{2}$-inch) lamb chops
Marinated Tomatoes (page 131)

Garnish
6 parsley sprigs

Combine the vinegar, garlic, curry powder, dry mustard and cayenne in a small bowl and whisk to mix well. Add the olive oil gradually, whisking constantly. Brush over both sides of the lamb chops and let stand at room temperature for 30 minutes or longer.

Grill the lamb chops 6 inches from hot coals for 6 to 7 minutes on each side or until done to taste but still pink in the center. Remove to a warmed platter. Serve with Marinated Tomatoes. Garnish the chops with the parsley.

Serves four to six

What Wine When?

Medium Foods

Crabs or lobster
Fish, such as salmon or tuna
Roasted chicken
Roasted pork
Pasta with cream or seafood sauce

Wines

Pouilly-Fumé
Sauvignon Blanc

Heavy Foods

Beef
Stews
Roast Veal or Pork

Wines

Red Bordeaux
Zinfandel
Cabernet Sauvignon

Baked Bananas

Cut 4 ripe bananas into halves crosswise, then into halves lengthwise; arrange in a single layer in a 9x11-inch baking dish. Melt $1/4$ cup unsalted butter in a small saucepan over medium heat. Stir in 2 tablespoons dry sherry and 1 tablespoon fresh lime juice. Pour over the bananas; sprinkle with $1/3$ cup loosely packed brown sugar and 1 teaspoon ground cinnamon. Bake at 375 degrees for 12 to 15 minutes or until golden brown and bubbly.

Cuban Pork Roast

A south Florida favorite. Serve with Havana Black Beans, Baked Bananas, and Mojito Cocktails for an authentic Cuban meal.

6 garlic cloves
4 scallions with tops, minced
$1/2$ cup pine nuts
1 jalapeño, seeded, minced
2 cups minced fresh cilantro leaves
$2/3$ cup fruity olive oil
3 tablespoons fresh lime juice
$1/3$ cup Niçoise or Greek olives, minced
salt and freshly ground pepper to taste
1 (4-pound) boneless pork loin roast
$1/2$ cup fresh grapefruit juice
$1/2$ cup fresh orange juice
$1/2$ cup fresh lime juice
$1/2$ cup hot pepper jelly

Combine the garlic, scallions, pine nuts, jalapeño and cilantro in a food processor and process to a thick paste. Add the olive oil gradually, processing constantly. Combine with the lime juice, olives, salt and pepper in a small bowl.

Unroll the roast if it has been tied and spread with $2/3$ of the cilantro paste. Reroll the roast and tie with string. Make shallow incisions over the surface of the roast with the tip of a sharp knife. Place in a shallow dish.

Stir the grapefruit juice, orange juice and lime juice into the remaining cilantro paste. Pour over the roast. Marinate, covered, in the refrigerator for 24 hours, turning occasionally.

Drain the roast, reserving the marinade. Place the roast in a roasting pan. Roast at 375 degrees for $1^3/4$ hours, basting occasionally with the reserved marinade. Brush the roast with the pepper jelly and roast for 15 minutes longer or until done to taste.

Remove the roast to a platter and let stand for 10 minutes. Cut into $1/2$-inch slices and serve.

Serves eight

Havana Black Beans

The perfect accompaniment to the Cuban Pork Roast.

1 pound dried black beans
1½ tablespoons annatto seeds
    (optional)
⅓ cup olive oil
1 medium onion, chopped
2 scallions with tops, minced
4 garlic cloves, minced
½ green bell pepper, seeded,
    chopped
½ red bell pepper, seeded,
    chopped

1 jalapeño, seeded, minced
2 tablespoons tomato paste
3 tablespoons red wine vinegar
1 tablespoon dried oregano leaves
1 tablespoon ground cumin
3 tablespoons minced fresh
    cilantro
1 tablespoon salt
2 teaspoons freshly ground
    pepper

Rinse and sort the beans. Combine with cold water to cover in a large bowl. Soak for 8 hours or longer. Drain the beans and combine with fresh water to cover in a large saucepan. Bring to a boil over medium-high heat and reduce the heat. Simmer for 1½ hours, adding additional water if necessary to cover the beans.

Heat the annatto seeds in the olive oil in a small saucepan over medium heat for 5 to 7 minutes or just until the seeds color the oil. Strain the oil, discarding the seeds.

Heat the strained oil in a medium skillet over medium-high heat. Add the onion, scallions, garlic, bell peppers and jalapeño and sauté for 7 minutes. Stir in the tomato paste and vinegar. Add the oregano, cumin, cilantro, salt and pepper. Reduce the heat to medium and cook for 5 minutes longer. Add to the beans and simmer for 30 minutes or until quite thick.

Note: The beans may be made in advance and stored in the refrigerator to improve the flavor. Reheat in a covered saucepan over low heat to serve.

Serves eight

Mojito Cocktail

Combine 5 chopped fresh mint leaves, the juice of ½ lime, 2 teaspoons sugar and 2 teaspoons water in a tall glass and mix well. Fill the glass with ice and add 2 ounces light rum; mix gently and top off the glass with soda water.

Centerpiece Anxiety

*Follow your next party's theme
from the invitation to the
centerpiece. A unique centerpiece
beckons your guests to the table.
Think past the traditional and
choose items from your own
collections. Even if you don't think
you have a collection, you probably
do. If you or someone you live with
is a hunter, try ducks. If you are a
reader, it could be books. Open the
books at different angles and place
a fun flowering plant next to your
arrangement. Add a magnifying
glass and maybe a dictionary or a
thesaurus. Grab whatever you have
adorning your house and put it on
the table in a new combination.
Presto! Like magic, you have a
striking and unusual centerpiece!*

Pork Roast with Drunken Apricot and Prune Stuffing

Try this little piggy stuffed with fruit and bourbon!

Apricot and Prune Stuffing
1/2 cup dried apricots
1/2 cup pitted prunes
1/2 cup bourbon
1 1/2 cups fresh bread crumbs
3/4 cup finely chopped walnuts
2 shallots, minced
1 teaspoon dried sage
2 tablespoons chopped fresh
    rosemary, or 1 tablespoon
    dried rosemary
salt and freshly ground pepper
    to taste
1 large egg, lightly beaten

Pork
1 (4- to 5-pound) pork loin roast,
    boned, tied
1/4 cup Dijon mustard
1/2 cup packed light brown sugar
1 cup dry white wine
2 to 3 cups beef broth
1/2 cup bourbon
2 bay leaves

For the stuffing, combine the apricots, prunes and bourbon in a small saucepan. Bring to a simmer over medium heat and simmer for 10 minutes. Combine with the bread crumbs, walnuts, shallots, sage, rosemary, salt and pepper in a large bowl and mix well. Add enough of the beaten egg to bind the mixture; it should just stick together but not be soggy.

For the pork, untie the roast and spread the stuffing evenly over the center. Retie the roast and place in a roasting pan. Spread with the Dijon mustard and press the brown sugar over the mustard. Season with salt and pepper. Pour the wine, 2 cups of the broth and bourbon into the roasting pan and add the bay leaves. Insert a meat thermometer into the thickest portion of the meat.

Roast, covered, at 425 degrees for 45 minutes. Remove the cover and roast for 45 to 60 minutes longer or to 160 degrees on the meat thermometer, basting occasionally with the pan juices and adding additional broth if necessary.

Remove the roast to a platter and cut into thick slices. Degrease the pan drippings, discarding the bay leaves; spoon over the roast.

Serves eight

Pork Roast with Mustard Glaze and Savory Apples

A crowd pleaser; great tasting and easy to prepare.

Pork

1/4 teaspoon dried marjoram
1 tablespoon crumbled
   dried sage
2 garlic cloves, chopped
2 tablespoons soy sauce
1/2 cup Dijon mustard
1 (5-pound) rolled boneless pork
   loin roast
salt and pepper to taste

Savory Apples

1 medium sweet onion, cut into
   halves, sliced
2 tablespoons (1/4 stick) butter
2 tablespoons cider vinegar
1/2 cup white wine
4 Granny Smith apples, peeled,
   sliced 1/4 inch thick
3/4 cup packed dark brown sugar
2 tablespoons (1/4 stick) butter

For the pork, combine the marjoram, sage, garlic, soy sauce, and Dijon mustard in a bowl and whisk to mix well. Place the pork loin fat side up in a shallow roasting pan and season with salt and pepper. Spread with the mustard mixture.

Insert a meat thermometer in the thickest portion of the roast. Roast at 325 degrees for 2 hours or to 160 degrees on the meat thermometer. Remove to a cutting board and let stand for 5 minutes.

For the apples, sauté the onion in 2 tablespoons butter in a large sauté pan over medium to medium-high heat for 3 minutes or until translucent. Stir in the vinegar and then the wine. Cook for 1 minute or until slightly reduced.

Add the apples and brown sugar, stirring to mix well. Bring to a boil and reduce the heat to medium. Cook for 5 to 7 minutes, stirring occasionally. Swirl in 2 tablespoons butter. Spoon with a slotted spoon into the center of a large platter, reserving the juices.

Cut the roast into 1/2-inch slices. Arrange around the apples. Pour the reserved juices from the apples over the top. Serve immediately.

Serves ten

Choosing Chargers

Chargers, also known as service plates or place plates, are strictly decorative and add another layer of elegance to your table. Since food is never served on them directly, they can be fashioned of many different materials, including silver, china, pewter, brass, straw, pâpier mâché, and even leaves from the garden. It is customary to first clear the charger with the soup or salad plate on top of it. Then, present the next course.

Grilled Rosemary Pork Tenderloin with Pineapple Salsa

Traditional pork with an updated southwestern salsa. The salsa will also add a fresh taste to any grilled steak, fish, or chicken.

Pineapple Salsa
$^1/_2$ cup chopped pineapple with juice
1 garlic clove, minced
1 tomato, chopped
$^1/_3$ cup chopped onion
$^1/_3$ cup chopped red bell pepper
10 to 15 sprigs of fresh cilantro, chopped
1 jalapeño, chopped (optional)
$^1/_4$ cup chopped green chiles

Pork
2 tablespoons olive oil
1 teaspoon soy sauce
1 teaspoon fresh lime juice
2 garlic cloves, minced
2 tablespoons chopped fresh rosemary
pepper to taste
1 (1-pound) pork tenderloin

For the salsa, combine the pineapple and juice, garlic, tomato, onion, bell pepper, cilantro, jalapeño and green chiles in a bowl and mix well. Chill for 1 to 2 hours.

For the pork, combine the olive oil, soy sauce, lime juice, garlic, rosemary and pepper in a small bowl. Pour over the pork tenderloin in a shallow dish. Marinate, covered, in the refrigerator for 1 hour or longer.

Drain the pork. Grill over hot coals for 30 minutes or until done to taste. Serve with the salsa.

Serves four

Bourbon-Marinated Pork Tenderloin with Sour Cream Sauce

The savory sauce complements the pork beautifully. Plan enough for seconds; everyone is sure to want more.

Bourbon Marinade and Pork
1/2 cup bourbon
6 tablespoons reduced-sodium
*   soy sauce*
3 tablespoons peanut oil
3 tablespoons honey
1 1/2 tablespoons red wine vinegar
2 garlic cloves, chopped
1 1/2 teaspoons ground ginger
3 (1-pound) pork tenderloins

Sour Cream Sauce
1/3 cup sour cream
1/3 cup mayonnaise
1 tablespoon finely chopped
*   scallions*
1 1/2 tablespoons vinegar
1 tablespoon dry mustard
salt to taste

To marinate the pork, combine the bourbon, soy sauce, peanut oil, honey, vinegar, garlic and ginger in a bowl and mix well. Pierce the tenderloins with a fork and combine with the bourbon marinade in a sealable 1-gallon plastic bag. Marinate, covered, in the refrigerator for 12 to 24 hours.

For the sauce, combine the sour cream, mayonnaise, scallions, vinegar, dry mustard and salt in a bowl and mix well. Chill, covered, until serving time.

To cook the pork, drain, reserving the marinade. Place the pork on a rack in a shallow roasting pan. Roast at 325 degrees for 30 to 60 minutes or until done to taste, basting several times with the reserved marinade. Carve into thin diagonal slices. Serve with the sauce.

Note: You may also grill the pork, covered, for 20 to 30 minutes if preferred.

Serves eight

Marinades

Acidic marinades are best for tenderizing and flavoring meats and need several hours to do so.

Oil marinades add moisture to lean meats and give them a crisp skin.

Paste marinades create a savory crust and, if left on overnight, will leave a penetrating flavor.

Rubs or bastes will give foods a burst of flavor on the outside.

Ironing a Large Tablecloth

To iron a large tablecloth, position the ironing board next to the dining room table. As you finish ironing, spread the cloth from the board directly onto the table to eliminate any creases or wrinkles.

Roasted Pork Tenderloin with Tangy Sauce

The soy sauce and ginger give this a wonderful Eastern flair. The sauce is also good with baked ham, roasted chicken, or roasted duck.

Tangy Sauce
1/4 cup finely chopped onion
1/4 cup finely chopped peeled
   carrot
1/4 cup applesauce
1/2 cup tomato sauce
2 tablespoons tarragon vinegar
1/2 cup packed brown sugar
1/4 teaspoon minced
   gingerroot
3 drops of Tabasco sauce
cayenne to taste

Pork
2 teaspoons soy sauce
1 teaspoon Dijon mustard
2 teaspoons honey
1 garlic clove, minced
1 (2-pound) pork tenderloin
freshly ground pepper to taste

Garnish
1/4 cup chopped scallions

For the sauce, combine the onion and carrot with the applesauce, tomato sauce, vinegar, brown sugar and gingerroot in a saucepan. Simmer for 10 minutes. Stir in the Tabasco sauce and cayenne. Store, covered, in the refrigerator for up to 3 weeks.

For the pork, combine the soy sauce, Dijon mustard, honey and garlic in a shallow dish and mix well. Add the pork and brush with the marinade to coat well; sprinkle with pepper. Marinate, covered, in the refrigerator for 2 hours or longer.

Drain the pork and place in a roasting pan, folding the narrow end of the tenderloin under; insert a meat thermometer in the thickest portion. Roast at 350 degrees for 55 minutes or to 160 degrees on the meat thermometer. Slice the pork and serve with the sauce. Garnish with the scallions.

Serves four

Mustard Pork Chops with Brie

Simple but elegant, this will delight even the most discriminating of palates.

¹/₃ cup flour
¹/₄ teaspoon ground coriander
¹/₂ teaspoon salt
¹/₄ teaspoon pepper
4 (1-inch) boneless pork chops
2 tablespoons Dijon mustard
2 teaspoons olive oil
1 (4-ounce) round Brie cheese

¹/₂ cup seasoned Italian bread crumbs
2 tablespoons chopped parsley
2 tablespoons (¹/₄ stick) melted butter
2 garlic cloves, minced
¹/₄ teaspoon crushed dried thyme

Combine the flour, coriander, salt and pepper in a shallow bowl. Spread both sides of the pork chops with mustard and coat with the flour mixture. Brown on both sides in the heated olive oil in a large skillet. Remove to a baking dish.

Trim the rind from the Brie cheese and cut into halves crosswise. Split the halves horizontally. Place a half-circle of Brie on each pork chop. Mix the bread crumbs, parsley, butter, garlic and thyme in a small bowl. Spoon over the pork chops.

Bake at 400 degrees for 20 to 24 minutes or until the crumb mixture is golden brown and the pork chops are cooked through.

Serves four

Raspberry and Thyme-Glazed Pork Medallions

A light and fruity flavor for the other white meat.

4 (3-ounce) pork medallions
1 teaspoon canola oil
¹/₂ cup chopped red onion
2 tablespoons balsamic vinegar
3 tablespoons orange juice

¹/₃ cup raspberry preserves
1¹/₂ teaspoons chopped fresh thyme
salt and coarsely ground pepper to taste

Sauté the pork medallions in the heated canola oil in a sauté pan for 3 minutes on each side. Add the onion, vinegar, orange juice and raspberry preserves. Cook for 2 minutes longer. Stir in the thyme, salt and pepper. Cook until the pork is glazed.

Serves two

Red Beet Rose

Cook a large red beet in water to cover until tender. Peel in a spiral strip about ³/₄ inch wide with a sharp knife. Begin by rolling up the strip tightly for the center of the rose, then loosening at the outer edge. Soak in cold water to freshen and set the color, and use as a garnish.

Dinner Party Checklist

*Plan the party as far in advance
as possible.
Make lists for everything.
Consider the chemistry of the
people on your guest list.
Plan a theme for the party. Carry
it out from start to finish.
Choose an invitation that reflects
the elegance of the occasion.
Arrange for extra help
for the evening.
Arrange for music–either
preprogrammed CDs or a live
pianist or harpist, etc.
Plan with your florist to match the
floral arrangements with your
china and linens.
Set the table at least a day
in advance.
Plan for traffic flow if using
buffet tables.
Make sure everything shines
and is positioned properly. Align
all of the flatware.
Purchase or make mementos or
favors for your guests.
Take a snapshot of the table
after it's set. Keep your menu
and guest lists with the photo
in a binder with plastic sleeves.*

Pork with Cherry Sauce

The cooking process will ensure moist and tender pork.

4 (8-ounce, 1-inch) bone-in pork loin chops,
    trimmed
1 tablespoon olive oil
2 cups canned reduced-sodium chicken broth
$1/3$ cup dried cherries, about 2 ounces
$1/3$ cup balsamic vinegar
salt and pepper to taste
1 tablespoon olive oil
$1/2$ cup canned reduced-sodium chicken broth

Cut the bones from the pork chops with a sharp knife. Cover the pork and chill until needed. Sauté the bones in 1 tablespoon heated olive oil in a heavy medium skillet for 15 minutes or until brown; drain.

Add 2 cups broth to the skillet. Simmer over low heat for 25 minutes or until the broth is reduced to 1 cup, stirring to deglaze the skillet. Remove the bones with a slotted spoon. Add the dried cherries and vinegar to the skillet. Simmer for 8 minutes or until reduced to $2/3$ cup.

Sprinkle the pork with salt and pepper. Sauté in 1 tablespoon heated olive oil in a heavy large skillet over medium-high heat for 2 minutes on each side or until brown. Add $1/2$ cup chicken broth and reduce the heat to low. Simmer, covered, for 6 minutes or until the pork is cooked through. Remove to a plate and tent with foil to keep warm.

Pour the cherry mixture into the skillet in which the pork was cooked and bring to a boil. Reduce the heat and simmer for 5 minutes or until the sauce is reduced to $3/4$ cup and coats the back of the spoon, stirring frequently. Season with salt and pepper. Spoon over the pork.

Serves four

Grilled Stuffed Veal Chops

Simple, yet sophisticated.

12 thin green beans, trimmed
1 tablespoon salt
4 (1-inch) veal rib chops
1 cup Tomato Concassé (at right)
4 ounces fontina cheese or mozzarella cheese,
    sliced 1/4 inch thick
4 large basil leaves
salt and pepper to taste
1 tablespoon extra-virgin olive oil

Cook the green beans with 1 tablespoon salt in water to cover in a small saucepan for 3 minutes or until tender-crisp. Drain and pat very dry.

Scrape any protruding veal bones clean. Split each veal chop horizontally with a sharp thin knife, cutting from the outer edge to the bone and leaving on the bone. Pound each side at a time as thin as possible with a meat mallet, starting at the bone. Open the halves of the veal chops and place 1/4 of the Tomato Concassé, 1/4 of the sliced cheese, 3 green beans and 1 basil leaf in each. Season with salt and pepper to taste and replace the halves to enclose the filling, which should not hang over the edges. Secure the edges with 3 wooden picks as if with straight pins in a hem.

Brush with the olive oil. Grill over hot coals for 2 minutes. Season with salt and turn. Season the remaining sides and grill for 2 minutes longer or just until cooked through.

Note: The veal chops may be stuffed earlier in the day and grilled just before serving.

Serves four

Tomato Concassé

Cut off the stem ends of the tomatoes and score the bottoms with an X. Drop into a saucepan of boiling water and leave for 10 to 30 seconds, depending on the ripeness of the tomato. Remove with a slotted spoon and plunge into ice water. Slip off the skins. Cut round tomatoes into halves crosswise and plum tomatoes into halves lengthwise. Gently squeeze out the seeds. Chop or julienne the pulp.

Tomato concassé can be made in advance, but prepare only enough for the recipe in preparation, as tomatoes begin to lose some of their flavor and texture when they have been peeled and chopped.

Sausage and Pepper Paella

Chock full of delicious, nutritious vegetables, this is a great one-dish meal to serve the family or company.

3 or 4 garlic cloves, minced
1 small onion, chopped
$1/2$ tablespoon olive oil
1 red bell pepper, chopped
1 green bell pepper, chopped
6 ounces hot and/or sweet Italian
    sausage, casing removed
$3/4$ cup uncooked arborio rice
$1/2$ cup dry white wine
1 cup drained canned tomatoes,
    coarsely chopped

$1/2$ (10-ounce) package frozen
    peas, cooked
1 zucchini, chopped (optional)
1 yellow squash, chopped
    (optional)
$1^1/2$ cups canned chicken broth or
    vegetable broth
salt and pepper to taste

Sauté the garlic and onion in the olive oil in a heavy 10-inch ovenproof skillet or Dutch oven over medium-high heat until tender. Add the bell peppers and sauté for several minutes.

Add the sausage. Cook for 5 minutes, stirring until the sausage is crumbly and the vegetables start to brown. Add the rice and sauté for 1 minute. Stir in the wine, tomatoes, peas, zucchini, yellow squash and chicken broth. Bring to a boil, stirring to deglaze the skillet.

Bake at 400 degrees for 25 minutes or until most of the liquid is absorbed. Season with salt and pepper.

Serves three or four

Sausage and Chicken Jambalaya

Spicy, but not overpowering. A Creole cookery hallmark.

2 bay leaves
1 teaspoon garlic powder
1 teaspoon salt
1/2 teaspoon cayenne
1 teaspoon white pepper
1/4 teaspoon black pepper
1 1/2 cups chopped onions
1 1/2 cups chopped celery
1 1/2 cups chopped green
    bell peppers

1/4 cup (1/2 stick) butter
Tabasco sauce to taste
1 1/2 pounds andouille sausage,
    thinly sliced
1 1/2 pounds boneless skinless
    chicken breasts, cut up
2 cups uncooked rice
3 cups chicken stock
3/4 cup tomato sauce

Mix the bay leaves, garlic powder, salt, cayenne, white pepper and black pepper in a small bowl. Sauté half the onions, half the celery and half the green peppers in the butter in a large saucepan. Add the seasoning mixture, Tabasco sauce and sausage. Cook over high heat for 20 minutes or until the onions are brown, stirring constantly.

Add the chicken. Cook for 15 minutes. Stir in the rice and reduce the heat. Simmer for 12 minutes. Stir in the chicken stock, tomato sauce and the remaining onions, celery and green peppers. Bring to a boil and reduce the heat to low. Simmer, covered, for 15 to 20 minutes or until the rice is tender. Let stand for 10 minutes. Ladle into serving bowls, discarding the bay leaves.

Serves six to eight

Mise En Place

This French kitchen term means "put in place" and refers to readying all of your ingredients at hand for the preparation of a dish. Chinese cooking is the perfect example of "mise en place." It requires having all ingredients, previously prepared by chopping, etc., in small bowls, ready before you start cooking. Chefs often refer to having your "mise en place" prepared, meaning that all sauces, garnishes, and ingredients are ready to cook. Not only is this more convenient, but it avoids missing an ingredient in more complex recipes.

Cutting Up a Whole Chicken

With a sharp chef's knife, cut through the skin around the leg where it attaches to the breast.

Using both hands, pop each leg out of its socket.

Use the chef's knife to cut through the flesh and skin to detach each leg from the body.

Cut through the joint at the point where a line of fat separates the thigh and drumstick.

Using poultry sheers, cut down the ribs between the back and the breast to separate the back and wings from the breast.

Place a chef's knife directly on the breast bone, then apply pressure to cut through the bone and separate the breasts.

Herb and Lemon-Roasted Chicken

The secret to this is the herbs under the skin.

2 tablespoons finely chopped fresh thyme	salt and pepper to taste
1 tablespoon finely chopped fresh rosemary	1 lemon, cut into halves
1 teaspoon salt	6 unpeeled garlic cloves, lightly crushed
1/2 teaspoon pepper	1 small sprig of fresh rosemary
2 tablespoons olive oil	6 small sprigs of fresh thyme
1 (3 1/2- to 4-pound) chicken	2 tablespoons olive oil
	1 cup water

Mix the chopped thyme, chopped rosemary, 1 teaspoon salt, 1/2 teaspoon pepper and 2 tablespoons olive oil in a small bowl. Remove and discard the wing tips of the chicken. Loosen the skin carefully from the breast and legs, taking care not to tear the skin. Spread the herb mixture carefully under the skin and over the breast and legs.

Season the chicken cavity with salt and pepper to taste. Squeeze and reserve the juice from the lemon. Stuff the lemon rinds, garlic and sprigs of thyme and rosemary into the cavity. Place in a medium roasting pan; rub with 2 tablespoons olive oil and drizzle with half the reserved lemon juice. Season generously with salt and pepper to taste.

Roast at 450 degrees for 20 minutes. Drizzle with the remaining lemon juice and reduce the oven temperature to 350 degrees. Roast for 40 minutes longer or until the juices run clear when a thigh is pierced, basting once or twice; cover loosely with foil if necessary to prevent overbrowning. Remove to a cutting board or platter and let stand for 15 minutes.

Skim the fat from the pan drippings and place the pan over 2 burners set at medium-high heat. Add the water and bring to a boil, stirring to deglaze the pan. Cook until the drippings are reduced to 3/4 cup. Strain and serve with the chicken.

Serves four

Citrus Chicken Caribbean

Citrus juice makes a flavorful fresh accent for this chicken.

½ cup lemon juice	1 teaspoon ground ginger
½ cup orange juice	1 teaspoon dried tarragon leaves
2 tablespoons vegetable oil or olive oil	salt and pepper to taste
6 garlic cloves, minced	6 boneless skinless chicken breast halves

Combine the lemon juice, orange juice, oil, garlic, ginger, tarragon, salt and pepper in a bowl. Add the chicken, coating well. Marinate, covered, in the refrigerator for 2 hours or longer; drain. Grill, bake or broil the chicken until cooked through.

Serves four to six

Gingersnap Chicken

It's as quick and easy as it is light and aromatic.

¼ cup soy sauce	4 tablespoons vegetable oil
2 tablespoons vegetable oil	4 teaspoons minced gingerroot
pepper to taste	2 cups thinly sliced scallions
2 whole skinless boneless chicken breasts	2 garlic cloves, minced
	2 tablespoons fresh lemon juice

Combine the soy sauce, 2 tablespoons oil and pepper in a shallow dish and whisk until smooth. Cut the chicken breasts into halves and pound ⅓ inch thick between plastic wrap. Add to the soy sauce mixture and marinate, covered, in the refrigerator for 15 minutes. Drain and pat dry.

Heat 1 of the 4 tablespoons oil in a heavy large skillet over medium-high heat and add the chicken. Sauté for 1 minute on each side or until brown and cooked through. Remove to a platter and keep warm.

Add the remaining 3 tablespoons oil, the gingerroot, scallions and garlic to the skillet. Sauté for 1 minute. Stir in the lemon juice. Serve over the chicken.

Serves four

Chicken Stock

Combine 4 pounds of chicken carcasses, backs, wings or necks with 2 quarts of cold water in a large saucepan. Add 2 quartered onions, 2 quartered carrots, 2 quartered celery ribs, 8 parsley stems, 5 peppercorns, 1 bay leaf and 1 sprig of fresh thyme or ½ teaspoon dried thyme. Bring to a boil, skimming the foam that rises. Reduce the heat and simmer for 2 hours. Strain, reserving only the liquid. Chill for up to 1 week or freeze for longer periods. Skim the fat from the surface before using.

Trussing a Chicken

Place four feet of kitchen string on a work surface and place the chicken breast down in the center. Draw the ends around the shoulders, meeting at the backbone; tie securely, pinning the wings against the sides. Turn the chicken breast up. Wrap the ends of the string around the ends of the drumsticks to hold them close together and tie securely.

Chicken Veronique with Fresh Peaches

The natural sweetness of the fruit enlivens this classic dish. Try serving fruit with each course, adding oranges or strawberries to a green salad and finishing with a fresh fruit tart.

1 cup seedless grapes
2 fresh peaches, peeled, cut into halves
1/4 cup white wine
1 teaspoon sugar
2 tablespoons flour
1/2 teaspoon paprika
1/4 teaspoon ground ginger
1 teaspoon salt
1/4 teaspoon pepper
1 (2 1/2-pound) chicken, cut up
1 garlic clove, minced
3 tablespoons butter

Combine the grapes and peaches with the wine and sugar in a bowl and marinate at room temperature for 1 hour.

Mix the flour, paprika, ginger, salt and pepper in a paper bag. Add the chicken and shake to coat well. Brown the chicken on both sides with the garlic in the butter in an ovenproof skillet. Drain the fruit and add the marinade to the skillet.

Bake, covered, at 375 degrees for 25 minutes or until the chicken is tender and cooked through. Add the grapes and peaches. Bake, uncovered, just until the fruit is heated through.

Serves four

Barbecued Chicken with Mango Salsa

An unusual blend of flavors makes this a noteworthy dish.

Mango Salsa

1 cup chopped peeled mango
1 cup chopped seeded tomato
1/2 cup finely chopped onion
1/4 cup finely chopped green
    onions
2 tablespoons chopped cilantro
1 jalapeño, seeded, minced
2 tablespoons fresh lime juice
2 tablespoons olive oil
salt and pepper to taste

Chicken

1 cup crushed canned tomatoes
1/2 cup chopped peeled mango
2 tablespoons white vinegar
1 tablespoon sugar
2 teaspoons chopped canned
    chipotle chile in adobo
    sauce
salt to taste
6 boneless skinless chicken breast
    halves

For the salsa, combine the mango, tomato, onion, green onions, cilantro, jalapeño, lime juice and olive oil in a bowl and mix well. Season with salt and pepper. Chill, covered, for up to 2 hours.

For the barbecued chicken, combine the tomatoes, mango, vinegar, sugar and chipotle in a food processor container. Process until smooth. Season with salt. Brush some of the mixture over the chicken. Grill the chicken for 4 minutes on each side or until cooked through, brushing frequently with the remaining barbecue mixture. Serve with the salsa.

Note: The barbecue mixture can be prepared 1 day in advance and stored, covered, in the refrigerator. The chipotle chile in adobo sauce is available in big supermarkets, specialty food stores and Latin-American markets.

Serves six

Mango Peach Chutney

Combine 1 coarsely chopped peeled large mango and 2 cups peeled and coarsely chopped fresh or frozen peaches in a nonreactive saucepan. Add 1/2 cup unsweetened apple juice, 1/2 cup cider vinegar, 1/2 cup packed brown sugar, 1 chopped medium red onion, 2 teaspoons grated fresh gingerroot, 1/2 teaspoon dried red pepper flakes, 1/4 teaspoon ground cardamom, 1/2 teaspoon ground cinnamon and 1/4 teaspoon salt. Bring to a boil. Reduce the heat and simmer for 45 minutes or until thick and translucent, stirring occasionally. Cool or chill before serving. Store in a tightly covered jar in the refrigerator for up to several weeks.

Salt Sense

Coarse salt, or kosher salt, has many advantages over table salt. The grains are rough and do not melt on contact with other foods, making it perfect to sprinkle on greens or on pretzel or bagel dough before baking, and for coating the rim of a margarita glass. Table salt is treated with anti-clumping agents that allow it to seep into foods. Ironically, the larger crystals of kosher salt impart a less salty flavor because they cannot permeate the food.

Salt is an effective retainer of heat and moisture, and coarse salt can be used much like clay for baking foods because it forms a crusty casing that seals in flavor and juices. It also absorbs melting fat and thereby provides a method of fat-free cooking.

Chicken with Goat Cheese and Roasted Bell Peppers

A new classic, this fabulous, flavorful, and colorful combination will be everyone's favorite.

$1/2$ red bell pepper
$1/2$ yellow bell pepper
3 ounces goat cheese
toasted slivered almonds or pine nuts
4 boneless skinless chicken breast halves
2 tablespoons olive oil
1 teaspoon chopped shallot
1 teaspoon chopped garlic
$1/4$ cup olive oil
$1/2$ cup dry white wine
2 teaspoons chopped rosemary, or $1/2$ teaspoon dried rosemary
$1/2$ cup (1 stick) unsalted butter, sliced
salt and pepper to taste

Place the bell peppers cut side down on a baking sheet. Broil until the skins are charred. Transfer to a bowl, cover with foil and let stand for 10 minutes. Remove the skins and cut the peppers into strips.

Cut the cheese into 8 rounds. Roll in the almonds, coating well.

Brush the chicken with 2 tablespoons olive oil. Grill for 10 minutes on each side or until cooked through. Remove to a baking sheet and top with the peppers and cheese.

Sauté the shallot and garlic in $1/4$ cup olive oil in a large skillet for 30 seconds. Add the wine and rosemary. Cook for 3 minutes or until reduced by $1/2$. Whisk in the butter gradually. Season with salt and pepper and keep warm.

Bake the chicken at 350 degrees for 5 minutes or just until the cheese melts. Place on serving plates and top with the wine sauce.

Serves four

Papaya Chicken

A burst of tropical flavors.

Papaya Salsa
1/2 papaya, chopped
1 garlic clove, minced
1/2 cup finely chopped
    red onion
1/2 red bell pepper, finely
    chopped
1 tablespoon chopped fresh
    cilantro
2 tablespoons rice vinegar
salt and pepper to taste

Chicken
1 cup fresh orange juice
1 small onion, chopped
1/2 to 3/4 teaspoon crushed
    red pepper
1/2 teaspoon ground allspice
1/2 teaspoon curry powder
1/4 teaspoon salt
1/4 teaspoon black pepper
6 (4-ounce) boneless skinless
    chicken breast halves

For the salsa, combine the papaya, garlic, onion, bell pepper, cilantro, vinegar, salt and pepper in a bowl and mix well. Chill until serving time.

To marinate the chicken, process the orange juice, onion, red pepper, allspice, curry powder, salt and black pepper in a food processor until almost smooth. Place the chicken in a sealable plastic bag in a shallow dish. Add the marinade to the bag, turning to coat the chicken well. Marinate in the refrigerator for 2 to 24 hours.

Drain the chicken, reserving the marinade. Place the chicken on a rack in a broiler pan. Broil 4 inches from the heat source for 5 minutes. Turn and brush with the reserved marinade. Broil for 7 to 10 minutes or until cooked through. Serve with the salsa.

Serves six

Cooking with Peppercorns

One-fourth teaspoon or one tablespoon? How much cracked pepper is enough? It depends. When pan-frying steak, for example, most of the peppery oils are burned off during the high heat searing process. For the best results, just add the pepper according to your own taste. Reduce the amount (especially for children) or change from black peppercorns to white peppercorns, which are not as hot as black, but which are very aromatic.

To crack pepper, enclose peppercorns in a clean kitchen towel or in a heavy-duty sealable plastic bag, then pound with a mallet until the peppercorns are lightly crushed. You could also pound the peppercorns with the bottom of a heavy skillet, crush them in a mortar with a pestle, or use an electric spice grinder. Of course, after a lazy day at the beach, you can always resort to your tried-and-true pepper mill.

Roasted Cornish Hens with Port

A delightfully different study in flavors and textures.

Port Marinade and Cornish Hens

1 cup semidry port
1 cup dry red wine
$^{1}/_{2}$ cup olive oil
$^{1}/_{4}$ cup balsamic vinegar
$^{1}/_{4}$ cup dark molasses
2 bay leaves, crumbled
several sprigs of fresh thyme, or 2 teaspoons dried thyme
Juniper berries to taste
2 garlic cloves, crushed
2 teaspoons cracked pepper
4 Cornish game hens

Port Sauce

2 carrots, coarsely chopped
1 onion, coarsely chopped
3 ribs celery, coarsely chopped
1 garlic clove, chopped
4 cups chicken stock
1 bay leaf
fresh thyme to taste
1 cup plus 2 tablespoons port
2 tablespoons ($^{1}/_{4}$ stick) unsalted butter
salt and pepper to taste

To marinate the hens, whisk the port, dry red wine, olive oil, vinegar and molasses in a medium bowl. Add the bay leaves, thyme, juniper berries, garlic and pepper and mix well. Pour into 2 large sealable plastic bags and place in shallow dishes. Add the hens and seal the bags; turn the bags to coat well. Marinate in the refrigerator for 3 hours or longer.

To roast the hens, drain and discard the marinade. Arrange the hens breast side up in a shallow roasting pan. Insert a meat thermometer in the thickest portion of the thigh of 1 hen. Roast at 375 degrees for 30 to 40 minutes. Place foil over the hens to prevent overbrowning. Roast for 30 to 45 minutes longer or until the juices run clear and the meat thermometer registers 180 degrees.

For the sauce, combine the carrots, onion, celery, garlic, chicken stock, bay leaf and thyme in a large saucepan. Bring to a boil and reduce the heat. Simmer for 30 minutes or until reduced by $^{1}/_{2}$. Strain into a saucepan, discarding the vegetables. Add 1 cup of the port. Bring to a boil and boil gently for 15 minutes. Reduce the heat to very low and add the remaining 2 tablespoons port. Whisk in the butter and season to taste with salt and pepper. Serve with the hens.

Serves four

Tomato Basil Seafood Stew

Serve with bread to soak up every bit of this delicious broth.

¼ cup olive oil
1¼ cups chopped onions
2 tablespoons chopped garlic
4 teaspoons dried oregano
1½ teaspoons fennel seeds
2 (6½-ounce) cans clams
2½ cups bottled clam juice
2½ cups crushed tomatoes with added purée
1 cup dry white wine
16 ounces uncooked large shrimp, peeled, deveined
1 (6-ounce) can crab meat, drained
½ cup chopped fresh basil
salt, cayenne and black pepper to taste

Heat the olive oil in a heavy large saucepan over medium heat. Add the onions, garlic, oregano and fennel seeds and sauté for 8 minutes or until the onions are tender. Drain the clams, reserving the liquid. Add the reserved clam liquid, bottled clam juice, tomatoes and wine to the saucepan. Increase the heat and cook for 15 minutes or until slightly thickened.

Chop the clams and add to the saucepan with the shrimp and crab meat. Simmer for 2 minutes. Stir in the basil. Simmer for 2 minutes longer or just until the shrimp are opaque in the centers. Season with salt, cayenne and black pepper. Serve immediately.

Serves four

Port Possibilities

Port is brandy-fortified wine made from the grapes of the Douro Valley in the north of Portugal. Brandy is added to the wine to stop fermentation before the yeasts eat all the grape sugar, thus yielding a sweeter wine, which also has a higher alcohol content of at least 33 proof. It is typically served after dinner.

Ruby or red port is named for its dark, rich red color. Ruby port is the simplest form of port–aged three years in a wooden cask and bottled for immediate sale and consumption.

Tawny port is also named for its color. It is a blended variety of wine aged in wooden casks– generally for five years–until the color fades and the wine takes on a nutty character. The three types are basic, aged, and colheita.

Imperial Sauce

Combine 2^1/$_2$ tablespoons minced
fresh parsley, 2^1/$_2$ tablespoons
minced cilantro, 2 tablespoons
minced green onions, ^{1}/$_2$ minced
garlic clove, ^{1}/$_8$ teaspoon dried
oregano, ^{1}/$_8$ teaspoon black pepper
and cayenne to taste in a bowl.
Add 1 tablespoon red wine vinegar
and 1 cup mayonnaise and mix
well. Spread over your favorite
fish fillets and broil for 5 to
7 minutes or until the mayonnaise
browns and bubbles.

Roasted Sea Bass in Prosciutto

*A creative combination of flavors and textures that will have your
guests marveling at your culinary talents.*

^{1}/$_4$ cup (^{1}/$_2$ stick) unsalted butter, softened
2 teaspoons dried rosemary leaves, crushed
^{1}/$_2$ teaspoon dried thyme leaves
1 tablespoon grated lemon zest
^{1}/$_2$ teaspoon salt
freshly ground pepper to taste
4 (6-ounce, ^{1}/$_2$-inch-thick) pieces Chilean sea bass fillet,
    cod or other firm white fish
4 teaspoons fresh lemon juice
5 or 6 (or more) very thin slices prosciutto

Garnish
shaved fresh Parmesan cheese
4 rosemary sprigs

Combine the butter, rosemary, thyme, lemon zest, salt and pepper in a
small nonreactive bowl and mix well. Arrange the fish on a foil-lined baking
sheet. Sprinkle with the lemon juice and spread with the butter mixture.
Arrange the prosciutto over the fish, covering the tops and sides.

Roast at 450 degrees on the middle oven rack for 15 minutes or until
the fish is opaque and flakes easily with a fork. Remove to a serving platter
and garnish with the Parmesan cheese and rosemary sprigs.

Note: The herb butter can be prepared in advance and chilled until
needed; let stand at room temperature for 30 minutes before using. The
fish can be prepared in advance and stored, wrapped in plastic wrap, in
the refrigerator for 1 hour. Let stand at room temperature for 15 minutes
before roasting.

Serves four

*Y*ou never know what kind of history you can make at a party . . . . *This formal setting mixes glasses from the Czech Republic with antique salt cellars that might have been used in Julia Tuttle's time. Tuttle, an Ohio widow turned Miami landowner, is fondly known as the "Mother of Miami." She is credited with enticing oil baron Henry Flagler to build his railroad all the way down to the Florida Keys. She caught Flagler's interest with a fragrant bouquet of live orange blossoms, which she sent him from Miami while he was assessing the orange crop damage during the 1894–1895 freeze in northern Florida.*

Compound Butters

All of the following combinations require 1 stick ($^1/_2$ cup) of softened unsalted butter.

For Chive Butter, *add 2 heaping tablespoons minced fresh chives, salt and freshly ground black pepper.*

For Herb Butter, *add 2 tablespoons minced fresh herb leaves, 1 teaspoon fresh lemon juice, salt and freshly ground black pepper.*

For Lemon Butter, *add the juice of $^1/_2$ lemon, 1 tablespoon minced fresh lemon zest, salt and freshly ground white pepper.*

For Pecan Butter, *add $^1/_3$ cup toasted and minced pecans, salt and freshly ground black pepper.*

After adding the seasonings of your choice, blend in the flavorings with a wooden spoon. Place the butter on a sheet of waxed paper or aluminum foil, fold the top half over it, and form the butter into a 6-inch log by rolling in the paper. Twist the ends and chill until firm or freeze for several months.

Mahi Mahi with Bananas and Almonds

Easy and light with a Caribbean flair.

4 (6-ounce) mahi mahi fillets
lime juice, salt and pepper to taste
$^1/_2$ cup flour

$^1/_4$ cup ($^1/_2$ stick) butter
2 ripe bananas, chopped
$^1/_2$ cup toasted sliced almonds

Season the mahi mahi lightly with lime juice, salt and pepper. Dust with the flour, shaking off the excess. Melt the butter in a heated skillet over medium heat. Add the fish and sauté over low heat until cooked through and golden brown on both sides.

Remove the fish to warmed plates with a spatula. Add the bananas and almonds to the skillet. Sauté for 1 minute or just until the bananas are softened. Spoon over the fish. Serve with rice and vegetables.

Serves four

Lemon Soy Swordfish

A luscious, lemony broiled fish.

8 small swordfish steaks, or
    4 large swordfish steaks,
    cut into halves
$^1/_3$ cup soy sauce
$^1/_4$ cup lemon juice
1 teaspoon grated
    lemon zest

1 garlic clove, crushed
2 teaspoons Dijon mustard
$^1/_2$ cup vegetable oil

Garnish
lemon wedges
parsley sprigs

Pierce the fish with a fork and place in a shallow 9x13-inch dish. Combine the soy sauce, lemon juice, lemon zest, garlic, Dijon mustard and oil in a small bowl and mix well. Pour over the fish. Marinate in the refrigerator for 1 to 3 hours, turning occasionally and piercing again with a fork.

Drain the fish and place in a preheated broiler pan. Broil for 5 to 6 minutes on each side or until the fish flakes easily. Garnish with lemon wedges and parsley.

Note: To grill the fish, reserve the marinade. Grill over medium coals for 5 to 6 minutes on each side, brushing occasionally with the reserved marinade.

Serves eight

Vanilla Rum Butter Salmon

Graciously provided by Café Maxx. If salmon is not available, substitute other firm fish such as sea bass, snapper, grouper, or mahi mahi.

Citrus Marinade

2 tablespoons olive oil
juice of $^{1}/_{2}$ lemon
juice of $^{1}/_{2}$ lime
juice of 1 orange
2 tablespoons white wine
1 teaspoon chopped shallot
salt and pepper to taste

Salmon

6 (7- to 8-ounce) salmon
   fillets
1 cup fish broth
$^{1}/_{2}$ cup white wine
1 or 2 bay leaves
1 star anise clove
2 or 3 slices fresh gingerroot
1 teaspoon chopped lemon grass

Vanilla Rum Butter Sauce

$^{1}/_{4}$ cup white wine
$^{3}/_{4}$ cup dark rum
1 star anise clove
1 vanilla bean, split
juice of $^{1}/_{2}$ lemon
juice of $^{1}/_{2}$ lime
1 teaspoon chopped shallot
2 tablespoons cream
reserved cooking liquid
4 to 6 tablespoons
   ($^{1}/_{2}$ to $^{3}/_{4}$ stick) butter
salt and pepper to taste
2 tablespoons chopped chives

For the marinade, combine the olive oil, lemon juice, lime juice, orange juice, wine, shallot, salt and pepper in a small to medium bowl and mix well. Add the fish to the marinade. Marinate, covered, in the refrigerator for 30 to 60 minutes.

To cook the fish, combine the fish broth, wine, bay leaves, star anise, gingerroot and lemon grass in a small saucepan. Bring to a boil over medium heat and remove from the heat. Let stand for several minutes to blend flavors. Place the fish in a medium baking dish and pour the remaining marinade over the top. Add the broth mixture to the dish. Bake at 350 degrees until the fish flakes easily. Remove to a serving platter, reserving the cooking liquid.

For the sauce, combine the wine, rum, star anise, vanilla bean, lemon juice, lime juice, shallot and cream in a small nonreactive saucepan. Cook over medium-low heat for 12 to 15 minutes or until reduced to the desired consistency. Stir in the reserved cooking liquid. Bring to a boil over medium-high heat and cook for 2 to 3 minutes. Stir in the butter and remove from the heat. Strain through a fine strainer and season with salt and pepper. Stir in the chives. Spoon over the fish. Serve with Purple Mashed Potatoes (at right).

Serves six

Purple Mashed Potatoes

Combine 6 cups of chopped, unpeeled purple potatoes with salted water to cover in a medium saucepan and bring to a boil. Reduce the heat and simmer for 30 to 40 minutes or until tender; drain and place the potatoes in a bowl. Combine $^{3}/_{4}$ cup coconut milk and 1 tablespoon butter in the saucepan and bring to a boil. Remove from the heat and add the potatoes; mash with a potato masher. Season with salt to taste.

Grilled Swordfish with Tomato and Arugula Salsa

This versatile Mediterranean-style salsa will add flavor to any meat dish as well.

Tomato and Arugula Salsa

1 pound plum tomatoes, seeded, cut into $^1/_4$-inch pieces
$^3/_4$ cup chopped arugula
1 shallot, finely chopped
$^1/_4$ cup olive oil
2 tablespoons lemon juice
$4^1/_2$ teaspoons capers
salt and pepper to taste

Swordfish

4 or 5 (6-ounce) swordfish steaks
2 tablespoons olive oil
salt and pepper to taste

For the salsa, combine the tomatoes, arugula, shallot, olive oil, lemon juice, capers, salt and pepper in a bowl and mix well. Chill in the refrigerator for 2 hours.

For the swordfish, brush both sides of the steaks with the olive oil; sprinkle with salt and pepper. Grill over medium-high heat for 4 minutes on each side or until the fish flakes easily. Serve topped with the salsa.

Serves four or five

In 1993, under the direction of president Barbara Hill, Junior League members raised more than $400,000 to secure property, and began renovations of what would become "Children's Place South." That same year, members initiated a Done in a Day program for short-term, hands-on volunteer assistance for community projects. Done in a Day now accounts for approximately 1,500 hours of community service per year at various non-profit sites.

Grilled Tuna with Rosemary Butter

The rosemary butter adds a mouthwatering richness as it melts.

Rosemary Butter
1$\frac{1}{2}$ tablespoons butter,
   softened
1 teaspoon chopped fresh
   rosemary, or $\frac{1}{3}$ teaspoon
   dried rosemary
1 teaspoon finely chopped chives s
1 teaspoon grated lemon zest
salt and pepper to taste

Tuna
1 tablespoon fresh lemon juice
1 tablespoon olive oil
1 teaspoon chopped fresh
   rosemary, or $\frac{1}{3}$ teaspoon
   dried rosemary
2 (6-ounce, $\frac{3}{4}$- to 1-inch-thick)
   tuna steaks
salt and pepper to taste

For the butter, combine the butter, rosemary, chives and lemon zest in a small bowl. Season to taste with salt and pepper. Store, covered, in the refrigerator for up to 24 hours.

For the tuna, combine the lemon juice, olive oil and rosemary in a shallow dish. Sprinkle the tuna on both sides with salt and pepper. Add to the lemon juice mixture, turning to coat well. Marinate for 15 minutes, turning twice; drain.

Grill or broil the tuna for 4 minutes on each side or until it flakes easily. Serve topped with the butter.

Serves two

Classic Yellowtail

A year-round favorite at the Ocean Reef Club.

4 fresh yellowtail snapper fillets
salt and pepper to taste
flour
egg wash
1 ounce mixed clarified butter
   and oil

2 to 3 ounces sherry
$\frac{1}{4}$ cup capers
$\frac{1}{4}$ cup ($\frac{1}{2}$ stick) butter
chopped parsley

Sprinkle the fillets with salt and pepper. Coat with flour and dip into the egg wash. Sauté in the butter and oil in a heated ovenproof sauté pan until golden brown on both sides. Bake at 375 degrees for 3 to 4 minutes or until the fish flakes easily. Remove the fish to a serving platter.

Place the sauté pan on the stove top and add the wine, stirring to deglaze the pan. Cook until bubbly. Add the capers and butter and cook until smooth, stirring constantly. Stir in the parsley. Serve over the fish.

Serves two to four

Types of Tuna

Tuna is the largest member of the mackerel family. There are thirteen species, but only five are commercially harvested in the United States. Two of the most popular are albacore and yellowfin.

Albacore is often labeled white meat tuna. It is caught off the West Coast and around the Hawaiian Islands, and usually weighs between ten and thirty pounds. In Hawaii it is known as tombo.

Yellowfin, found off the coasts of California, Hawaii, and Florida, is named for its yellow dorsal fin and the yellow stripe on its sides. Hawaiians know it as ahi. Yellowfin can grow to four hundred pounds but is usually caught in the twenty- to one hundred-pound range.

Orange and Avocado Salsa

Peel and section 2 navel oranges. Combine with 1 chopped small red onion, 1 seeded and chopped tomato, 1 chopped avocado, $1/2$ jar seeded and minced jalapeños, 2 tablespoons chopped cilantro, 3 tablespoons orange juice, 2 tablespoons lime juice, $3/4$ teaspoon salt and $1/4$ teaspoon freshly ground pepper in a bowl. Mix well and chill until serving time.

Hawaiian Yellowtail Snapper with Orange Basil Beurre Blanc

The combination of nuts, fresh herbs, and citrus makes this an island standout. Perfect inspiration for a Hawaiian dinner party.

Yellowtail Snapper
$1/2$ cup heavy cream
1 cup macadamias, lightly toasted
2 tablespoons chopped parsley
2 tablespoons chopped basil
2 tablespoons chopped chives
2 ounces bread crumbs
2 tablespoons ($1/4$ stick) butter, softened
2 tablespoons virgin olive oil
2 tablespoons fresh lemon juice
4 (7- to 8-ounce) yellowtail snapper fillets
olive oil
$1/4$ cup chardonnay
salt and pepper to taste

Orange Basil Beurre Blanc
$1/2$ teaspoon chopped garlic
$1/2$ teaspoon chopped shallot
olive oil
$1/4$ cup chardonnay
$3/4$ cup orange juice
1 tablespoon lemon juice
2 tablespoons heavy cream
1 to $1^1/2$ cups (2 to 3 sticks) butter
$1/4$ bunch basil, cut into thin strips
salt and pepper to taste

For the fish, cook the cream in a saucepan until reduced by $1/3$. Grind the macadamias in a food processor until coarsely ground. Combine the cream with the macadamias, parsley, basil, chives, bread crumbs, butter, 2 tablespoons olive oil and lemon juice in a bowl and mix well.

For the beurre blanc, sauté the garlic and shallot in a small amount of olive oil in a skillet. Add the wine, stirring to deglaze the skillet. Stir in the orange juice, lemon juice and cream. Cook until reduced by $1/3$. Swirl in the butter. Strain into a bowl and fold in the basil, salt and pepper. Serve with the fish.

Brush the fish fillets with olive oil and arrange in an oiled baking pan. Pour the wine over the fillets and season with salt and pepper. Press the macadamia mixture over the fish. Bake at 400 degrees for 10 to 12 minutes or until the fish flakes easily.

Serves four

Baja Shrimp

Spice up your barbecue with this innovative way to serve shrimp.

juice of 1 lemon
2 cups loosely packed, finely
   chopped cilantro leaves
1 garlic clove, minced
1 large shallot, minced
1/4 cup olive oil
1 teaspoon coarse salt

1/2 teaspoon freshly ground
   pepper
16 jumbo shrimp, about
   1 1/4 pounds
4 teaspoons olive oil
1 lemon, cut into 8 wedges
1 cup dry white wine

Mix the lemon juice, cilantro, garlic, shallot, 1/4 cup olive oil, salt and pepper in a small bowl. Split each shrimp down the back, cutting just deep enough to expose the vein; remove the vein, leaving the shells and tails intact. Spoon the cilantro mixture into the spaces between the shells and shrimp.

Heat 2 teaspoons olive oil in a large skillet over medium-high heat. Arrange 8 shrimp and 4 lemon wedges in the skillet. Sauté for 3 to 4 minutes on each side or until the shrimp are opaque; remove to a platter. Repeat with the remaining olive oil, shrimp and lemon wedges.

Pour the wine into the skillet. Cook for 1 minute or until reduced by 1/2, stirring to deglaze the skillet. Pour over the shrimp.

Serves four

Shrimp Provençale

The flavors of France come alive in this blend of shrimp and rice.

1 1/2 pounds large uncooked
   shrimp, peeled, deveined
2 tablespoons olive oil
1 pound mushrooms, sliced
2 garlic cloves, minced
1 tablespoon olive oil

3 medium tomatoes, chopped
2 tablespoons lemon juice
3/4 teaspoon salt
1/8 teaspoon pepper
2 tablespoons minced parsley
3 cups hot cooked rice

Sauté the shrimp in 2 tablespoons olive oil in a 12-inch skillet over medium heat for 3 minutes or until opaque. Remove with a slotted spoon.

Sauté the mushrooms and garlic in 1 tablespoon olive oil in the same skillet for 3 minutes. Add the tomatoes, lemon juice, salt and pepper. Cook for 3 minutes longer. Return the shrimp to the skillet and cook until heated through. Sprinkle with parsley. Serve over the rice.

Serves six

Jalapeño Tartar Sauce

Combine 1 cup mayonnaise, 1/4 cup chopped fresh dill, 1 minced and seeded medium bottled jalapeño, 3 tablespoons chopped sweet pickle, 1 heaping tablespoon small capers and 1 tablespoon chopped chives in a bowl and mix well. Serve with seafood cakes.

Party-Pleasing Paella

A great one-dish meal for convenient entertaining.

1/2 medium Spanish onion,
   chopped
1 tablespoon olive oil
12 ounces hot Italian sausage,
   casings removed
16 ounces clams, scrubbed
4 (8-ounce) bottles clam juice
1 teaspoon saffron threads
2 cups uncooked arborio rice

1/2 cup dry white wine
8 ounces uncooked medium
   shrimp, peeled, deveined
8 ounces uncooked sea scallops
1 cup frozen tiny sweet peas,
   thawed, or fresh snow peas
3 large tomatoes, seeded, chopped
salt and pepper to taste
2 tablespoons chopped fresh parsley

Sauté the onion in the olive oil in a heavy large saucepan over medium heat for 5 minutes or until almost tender. Add the sausage. Cook for 5 minutes or until no longer pink, stirring with a fork to crumble. Add the clams and increase the heat to medium-high. Cook for 5 minutes or until the clam shells open. Remove the clams to a bowl, discarding any that do not open; keep warm.

Combine the clam juice and saffron in a small saucepan and bring to a simmer; keep warm over low heat.

Add the rice to the sausage mixture in the saucepan. Cook over medium heat for 2 minutes, stirring constantly. Stir in the wine. Cook for 3 minutes or until the wine is absorbed, stirring constantly. Add the clam juice mixture and simmer for 20 minutes or until the rice is tender and creamy, stirring constantly.

Stir in the shrimp, scallops, peas and tomatoes. Cook for 3 minutes or just until the shrimp and scallops are cooked through, stirring frequently. Season with salt and pepper. Top with the clams and parsley and serve immediately.

Serves four

Tropical Island Shrimp

A colorful, festive shrimp dish with a tropical taste.

1 cup uncooked basmati rice
1 avocado
1 mango
2 tablespoons lemon juice
1¼ pounds uncooked medium shrimp,
    peeled, deveined
2 tablespoons lemon juice
2 tablespoons chopped cilantro
1 jalapeño, seeded, finely chopped
salt and freshly ground pepper to taste
1 tablespoon butter
2 tablespoons olive oil
1 large red bell pepper, cut into ¼-inch strips
1 tablespoon finely chopped garlic

Garnish
2 tablespoons chopped cilantro

Cook the rice using the package directions; keep warm. Peel the avocado and mango and cut into ³/₄-inch slices. Combine with 2 tablespoons lemon juice in a bowl and mix gently.

Combine the shrimp with 2 tablespoons lemon juice, cilantro, jalapeño, salt and pepper in a bowl; cover with plastic wrap. Marinate for 15 minutes.

Melt the butter with the olive oil in a large skillet over high heat. Add the bell pepper and sauté for 30 seconds. Add the shrimp with the marinade. Cook for 2 minutes, stirring constantly. Add the avocado mixture and garlic. Season with salt and pepper. Cook for 1 to 2 minutes longer or just until the shrimp are cooked through; do not overcook. Serve over the rice. Garnish with cilantro.

Serves four

Pitting and Peeling Avocados

Cut the avocado in half lengthwise around the pit with a stainless steel knife. Carbon steel will discolor the fruit.

Rotate the two halves to separate them. The pit will stay in one half. If you are not using the whole fruit, set aside the half with the pit.

Remove the pit gently with a spoon or gently hit the pit with the blade of a chef's knife and, while grabbing hold of the fruit, gently rotate the pit out with the knife.

Place the avocado cut side down and peel the skin off with a knife or your fingers.

Sprinkle the cut surfaces with lemon or lime juice or white vinegar to keep it from darkening.

Pasta

Pastas del Sol—
Dining Al Fresco

Italy, Spain, Morocco or Greece; where will you dine today? It must be in the open air—a special place adorned with your favorite things. Whether at midday, sunset, or in the moonlight, the possibilities are endless. Pasta is the perfect choice for an informal gathering of family and friends.

Here the signs of Tuscany abound. The hostess took her inspiration from this dazzling tiled Spanish fountain. Brilliant Mediterranean colors and undulating lines amid a tropical sea of palms lend themselves to creating a mouthwatering array of robust pasta and side dishes.

What can you do to your garden to bring in the Old World, just for today? The feeling of tile can come from the tablecloth or serving pieces. Consider purchasing a special pitcher, a pedestal plate, and a platter. When grouped together, a trio like this Deruta "Arabesco" Italian china is enough to make a statement.

You can bring out a couple of glass jars of multi-colored, hand-made pasta and cruets for oil and vinegar. The sunlight will play wonderfully on the infused oils and vinegars. The dark wood of a cherry or mahogany dining table brought outside, against garden greens and sun drenched flowers, dresses up any backyard.

Before the guests leave, offer a hand-painted tile with raffia tied around it as a favor with an Italian flavor to take home the colors of the day. People will be sure to think of you each time these trivets are used. Or fill little tin buckets with all kinds of things from your country du jour. Biscotti for the women and cigars for the men are today's favor.

Mediterranean colors, textures, and lines dominate the South Florida landscape. Yet, to recreate the flavor of this pasta picnic does not require a mosaic of early 20th-century Spanish tiles, like the ones pictured here at The Boca Raton Resort & Club. Just let the colors of your outdoor setting inspire your passion for great entertaining.

The tins also would work as a novel invitation. And don't forget the children. They might take home a necklace of pasta, a mosaic design created at the craft table, or a tin of brightly wrapped candies.

On the Fast Track

Stop at the music store and pick up a CD of Andrea Bocelli's *Romanza,* Nino Rota's *La Dolce Vita* or *Carnival in Venice.* Next, run to the specialty market for the best pasta, bread, tomatoes, grapes, and cheese you can find. You'll need some flowers and Chianti bottles too.

When you get home, turn on the music, decant the wine, and light the candles to drip down the fiascos, or straw-covered Chianti bottles. Bring out the votives. You're in the mood to move fast now. After the entrée is in the oven, tie a different-colored ribbon around each wine glass so when guests set them down, they can find them later. Stuff the wine glasses with contrasting color napkins of thick cotton, and add the bread sticks. Display them all together. Chill the wine in a big garden pot. This creates instant ambiance in one corner.

Do you have the colors of Tuscany growing in your garden? Scour the yard for urns or pots with the patina that comes from being outside. Group a few together.

Borrow a child's chalk board. This one says "Buon Appetito" and spells out today's offerings—so easy, so memorable.

The checked tablecloth is key. Not the typical red and white picnic variety, this is really a shawl with checks that carry through the tile theme.

If you'll be dining in Italy tonight, then find a map of the boot from an old *National Geographic.* A small framed one here accents a spot for favors, as does the rooster.

You could also take a big map and place it on the diagonal to cover a table, leaving the ends of the wood to show.

Visit España and Be Back for Dessert

If you fancy a Spanish flavor, then point your compass west and sail the Mediterranean. Sausage and Pepper Paella (page 168), Cuban Pork Roast (page 158), and Havana Black Beans (page 159) served with Mojito Cocktail (page 159) will take the spotlight. Don't forget

to write "bienvenido" on the chalk board. Choose Ravel's *Bolero, Gypsy King,* or flamenco music for the CD player. There's nothing more romantic than the Spanish guitar.

Do you know anyone who can teach Greek dancing? Then switch the music to the sound track from *Zorba the Greek* or *Never on Sunday* and try Farfalle Olympus (page 194) or Shrimp and Feta Vermicelli (page 208).

What about Moroccan? Start with the sound track from *The English Patient* or Mozart's *Escape from the Seraglio.* Put Spicy Grilled Lamb Chops (page 157), Curried Couscous Salad (page 124), and Chick-Pea and Cucumber Salad (page 122) somewhere on the menu. The colors shift a bit with more browns and influences from the earth rather than the sky. Drape the fabric for a Middle Eastern feel. Perhaps a corner of the garden can be recreated to feel like the Casbah. Add leather. It's all an impression, a fantasy.

Switch the centerpiece to a bowl of the koi's cousins—pretty goldfish. Add chopsticks, colorful lacquer trays, and beautiful fans. Use lots of black for your backdrop. Set the CD player at Tchaikovsky's *Tea Dance* from *The Nutcracker Suite* or Puccini's *Turandot* while you create the perfect setting for a Chinese dinner of Asian Salad (page 121), Angel Hair Pasta with Oriental Sauce (page 194), and Banana Chocolate Won Tons (page 237).

The idea is to leave reality at the door. Whichever country's flavors you choose, this will be a destination of your own making.

R.S.V.P.

This is a great gathering that you can create at the spur of the moment with a few calls to family, friends, and neighbors. If you have more lead time, you could make the invitation up to look like a passport to Italy or the country of your choice.

The hearty food at this pasta party is as much of a visual treat as the fabulous tiles that surround it. The mood is alive and passionate to capture the imagination. Its beauty calms the spirit as it delights the eye. Blue and white "Arabesco" china from Deruta, Italy, and the menu written on the blackboard add to the charm.

Menu

*Pictured recipes

Uncanny Tomatoes

If tomatoes aren't in season when you need them for a recipe, choose imported canned plum tomatoes from the San Marzano region in Italy. If you can't find these, any good imported plum tomato will be much more delicious than a tasteless fresh tomato. Make sure to strain and chop or purée whole canned tomatoes before using them.

Bistro Pasta

Delights from the garden combine to round out this tasty eye-pleasing pasta.

1 leek
$^1\!/_2$ to 1 pound fresh asparagus
1 (16-ounce) package spaghetti or linguine
3 or 4 garlic cloves, chopped
hot pepper flakes to taste (optional)
olive oil
8 ounces mushrooms, sliced
1 red bell pepper, chopped
1 green bell pepper, chopped
1 pound shrimp, peeled, deveined
1 to 2 (14-ounce) cans chicken broth
salt and freshly ground pepper to taste
$^1\!/_2$ to $^3\!/_4$ cup chopped Italian parsley

Discard the green portion of the leek; cut 4 slits down the sides of the white portion and fan open. Rinse under running water and chop. Break the tough ends off the asparagus and cut the stalks into 1-inch pieces. Cook the pasta using the package directions; keep warm.

Sauté the leek and garlic with the pepper flakes in a small amount of olive oil in a skillet for 2 to 3 minutes. Add the mushrooms, bell peppers and asparagus. Sauté until the asparagus is tender-crisp. Add the shrimp and half the chicken broth. Cook just until the shrimp are opaque.

Add the pasta and remaining chicken broth if needed for the desired consistency. Cook until heated through. Season with salt and pepper. Stir in the parsley.

Note: You may substitute chopped grilled chicken or browned mild Italian sausage for the shrimp if preferred.

Serves eight

Nutty Fettuccine

You'll go nuts over the ease of preparation.

1 (9-ounce) package fresh
    fettuccine or linguine
3/4 cup chopped hazelnuts, pecans
    and/or pine nuts
1 tablespoon butter
1 tablespoon olive oil
1/4 cup grated Parmesan cheese

1/2 cup crumbled Gorgonzola or
    bleu cheese
2 tablespoons chopped fresh basil

Garnish
fresh basil

Cook the pasta using the package directions; drain and keep warm. Toast the hazelnuts in the butter and olive oil in a medium skillet until light brown, stirring frequently. Combine with the pasta, Parmesan cheese, Gorgonzola cheese and basil in a bowl and toss gently. Garnish with additional basil.

Serves two to four

Linguine with Asparagus and Prosciutto

An interesting way to include asparagus. Light and savory to the taste, delightful to the eye.

1 onion, finely chopped
1 1/2 teaspoons minced garlic
1/8 teaspoon dried thyme leaves,
    crumbled
2 tablespoons olive oil
1 tablespoon unsalted butter
12 ounces fresh asparagus,
    trimmed, peeled, sliced
    diagonally

2 ounces chopped prosciutto
8 ounces uncooked linguine
salt to taste
1 tablespoon water
1 tablespoon fresh lemon juice
2 tablespoons grated Parmesan
    cheese
pepper to taste

Sauté the onion, garlic and thyme in the olive oil and butter in a heavy skillet over medium heat until the onion is tender. Add the asparagus and prosciutto. Cook for 2 minutes, stirring constantly.

Cook the linguine in boiling salted water in a saucepan for 8 to 10 minutes or until al dente; drain. Combine with the asparagus mixture, water, lemon juice and cheese in a bowl. Season with salt and pepper and toss to coat well.

Serves two

Dried Pasta

How often does a recipe call for a pasta shape that you just don't have on hand? Not to worry, use any pasta of a similar size. Dried pasta has saved many a cook's life at the last minute. With hundreds of different shapes and flavors, pasta has become a necessary staple. Here are definitions of some of the more unusual pastas:

Conchigliette–little shells
Farfalle–butterflies or bow ties
Gemelli–twins; two short
    intertwinded strands
Penne–straight tubes cut
    on the diagonal
Orecchiette–little ears or
    thumbprints
Radiatore–radiators;
    small ridged shapes
Rotelle–wheels
Semi de Melone–melon seeds
Tortellini–pasta stuffed with
various fillings, folded over and
shaped into a ring or hat
Ziti–long thin tubes

Angel Hair Pasta with Oriental Sauce

Easy and delicious for shrimp or chicken.

1 tablespoon dry sherry
1 tablespoon sesame oil
1 tablespoon soy sauce
1 tablespoon ground ginger
8 ounces uncooked peeled shrimp
    or chopped chicken breasts
3 tablespoons lemon juice
3 tablespoons rice vinegar

2 tablespoons soy sauce
2 tablespoons sugar
$1/2$ teaspoon red pepper
2 garlic cloves, chopped
1 tablespoon ground ginger
2 tablespoons peanut oil
cornstarch (optional)
6 ounces angel hair pasta, cooked

Combine the sherry, sesame oil, 1 tablespoon soy sauce and
1 tablespoon ginger in a bowl and mix well. Add the shrimp. Marinate
in the refrigerator.

Combine the lemon juice, rice vinegar, 2 tablespoons soy sauce, sugar
and red pepper in a bowl and set aside.

Stir-fry the garlic with 1 tablespoon ginger in the peanut oil in a large
saucepan. Add the shrimp with the marinade. Stir fry until the shrimp are
cooked through. Stir in the lemon juice mixture. Cook until heated through.
Thicken with a paste of cornstarch and water if needed for the desired
consistency. Serve over the hot pasta.

Serves two

Golden Butternut Squash Lasagne

Comfort food, cheesy with an herbal bouquet.

3 pounds butternut squash
3 tablespoons vegetable oil
salt to taste
4 cups milk
2 tablespoons dried rosemary
    leaves, crumbled
1 tablespoon minced garlic
1/4 cup (1/2 stick) unsalted butter
1/4 cup flour
pepper to taste

9 uncooked lasagne noodles
8 ounces fontina cheese, thinly
    sliced
1 1/2 cups grated Parmesan cheese
1 cup whipping cream
1/2 teaspoon salt

Garnish
rosemary leaves

Cut the squash into quarters, discarding the seeds. Peel the squash and cut into 1/4-inch pieces. Toss with the oil. Spread in a single layer in 2 oiled shallow roasting pans. Roast at 450 degrees for 10 minutes. Sprinkle with salt to taste and roast for 10 to 15 minutes longer or until tender and light golden brown.

Combine the milk with the rosemary in a saucepan. Simmer for 10 minutes. Strain through a sieve into a pitcher and reserve.

Sauté the garlic in the butter in a heavy large saucepan over medium-low heat until tender. Stir in the flour. Cook for 3 minutes, stirring constantly. Remove from the heat and whisk in the milk. Simmer for 10 minutes or until thickened, whisking constantly. Stir in the squash and salt and pepper to taste.

Cook the lasagne noodles using the package directions. Drain and hold in cold water until needed. Spread 1 cup of the squash sauce in a buttered 9x13-inch baking dish. Layer 3 noodles over the sauce. Spread with half the remaining sauce, half the fontina cheese and 1/3 of the Parmesan cheese. Repeat the layers and top with a layer of noodles.

Beat the cream with 1/2 teaspoon salt in a mixing bowl until soft peaks form. Spread evenly over the layers, covering completely. Sprinkle with the remaining Parmesan cheese. Cover with foil tented so as not to touch the top layer.

Reduce the oven temperature to 375 degrees. Bake the lasagne on the center oven rack for 30 minutes. Remove the foil and bake for 10 minutes longer or until bubbly and golden brown. Garnish with rosemary.

Note: The squash mixture can be made up to 3 days in advance. Place plastic wrap directly on the surface and store in the refrigerator.

Serves six as a main dish or twelve as a side dish

Garlic Smell Be Gone

How do you get the smell of garlic off your fingers once you've peeled and chopped it? Rub your fingers on a stainless steel teaspoon. Voila!

Perfect Pasta

Fine ingredients and the right cooking tools make the perfect pasta. For the best results:

Use only the best-quality tomatoes, imported spaghetti, and Parmigiano-Reggiano cheese.

Cook pasta in a large saucepan, allowing six quarts of water for a pound of pasta.

Add 3^1/$_2$ tablespoons of kosher salt or coarse salt for six quarts of water.

Stir the pasta several times while cooking.

Do not rinse cooked pasta.

Serve pasta as soon as possible after cooking for it to be at its peak.

Thin sauce that is too thick with some of the water used to cook the pasta.

Mushroom Roll-Ups Fiorentina

Sent from heaven via East City Grill.

Béchamel Sauce
2 tablespoons butter
2 tablespoons flour
1 cup milk

Roll-Ups
2 cups drained ricotta cheese
1 cup mascarpone cheese
^{1}/$_2$ cup grated Parmigiano-Regianno cheese
3 eggs
4 cups sliced cooked portobello mushrooms
1 cup chopped basil
salt and pepper to taste
1 (16-ounce) package lasagne noodles
4 cups tomato sauce
1 (10-ounce) package fresh spinach, blanched
grated Parmigiano-Regianno cheese to taste

For the béchamel sauce, melt the butter in a saucepan. Stir in the flour and cook for several minutes, stirring constantly. Add the milk. Cook until thickened, stirring constantly. Remove from the heat and place plastic wrap directly on the surface to cover.

For the roll-ups, combine the ricotta cheese, mascarpone cheese, ^{1}/$_2$ cup Parmigiano-Regianno cheese and eggs in a large bowl and mix well. Add just enough of the mixture to the mushrooms to bind in a bowl. Stir in the basil, salt and pepper.

Cook the noodles using the package directions. Drain and rinse in ice water. Pat dry and arrange on a work surface. Place 2 to 3 tablespoons of the mushroom filling on 1 end of each noodle and roll to enclose the filling.

Spread the tomato sauce in a baking dish. Spread the spinach over the tomato sauce. Arrange the roll-ups seam side down in the prepared dish. Top with the béchamel sauce and sprinkle with Parmigiano-Regianno cheese to taste. Bake at 400 degrees for 15 minutes. Serve immediately.

Serves six

Wherever you are, reach for a look that sends the senses back in time, allowing the grace of the past to mingle with the convenience of the present. A jar of pickled apricots adds a bit of color. A head of kale and wildflowers add instant rustic charm. Party favors make a visual impact when grouped together. This hostess wrapped tile-designed trivets in raffia as a take-home memory for her guests. With a trusty glue gun, she embellished simple garden pots with moss and faux grapes to serve as containers for his and her treats—biscotti for the ladies and cigars for the men.

Soft Cheeses

Brie and Camembert are creamy French cheeses with a soft rind made from cows' milk. They are wonderful when melted. Camembert has more kick than Brie.

Feta is a crumbly Greek cheese made from goats' milk. It adds a great salty touch to salads. Gorgonzola is a semisoft Italian bleu cheese made from cows' milk. It is great melted on bread or on a salad.

Montrachet is a French cheese made from goats' milk. It is best when young and fresh.

Monterey Jack is a mild semisoft American cheese made from cows' milk. It is a must for nachos.

Roquefort is a French bleu cheese made from sheep's milk. It is great for salads.

Tomato Sausage Penne

Fancy, flavorful, and fulfilling.

3 medium onions, thinly sliced
9 garlic cloves, minced
3 tablespoons butter
3 tablespoons olive oil
2^1/$_4$ pounds sweet Italian sausage, casings removed
2 cups dry white wine
3 (28-ounce) cans stewed chopped Italian tomatoes
3 cups heavy cream
^{1}/$_4$ cup chopped fresh basil
oregano to taste
1 teaspoon crushed red pepper
2 (16-ounce) packages penne
2 cups grated Parmesan cheese

Sauté the onions and garlic in the butter and olive oil in a large saucepan over medium-high heat until tender and golden brown. Add the sausage and cook until brown, stirring to crumble; drain.

Add the wine and cook until most of the liquid has evaporated. Stir in the undrained tomatoes. Simmer for 5 minutes. Add the cream. Simmer until slightly thickened. Stir in the basil, oregano and red pepper.

Cook the pasta al dente using the package directions; drain. Add to the sauce with the cheese; toss to mix well. Serve with additional cheese.

Serves six to eight

Basil Cream Penne

Pine nuts enhance this classic Italian cream sauce.

1 cup dry-pack sun-dried tomatoes
4 teaspoons pine nuts
^{1}/$_2$ cup (1 stick) unsalted butter
4 cups heavy cream
1 teaspoon salt
1 teaspoon white pepper
16 ounces penne, cooked
2 cups chopped, loosely packed fresh basil
1 cup grated Parmesan cheese

Soak the sun-dried tomatoes in hot water in a bowl for 3 or 4 minutes. Drain, pat dry and mince. Toast the pine nuts in a skillet over medium heat just until lightly colored.

Combine the butter, cream, salt and white pepper in a large saucepan. Simmer for 10 minutes. Add the pasta, basil and sun-dried tomatoes and toss to coat well. Stir in the cheese. Cook for 4 to 5 minutes or just until heated through and creamy. Spoon into a serving bowl and top with the pine nuts.

Serves six

Penne with Capers and Sun-Dried Tomatoes

Savory, elegant and pleasing to the eye as well as to the palate.

15 dry-pack sun-dried tomatoes, minced
$1/2$ cup very hot water
3 tablespoons olive oil
2 medium onions, thinly sliced
6 garlic cloves, minced or pressed
3 tablespoons capers, drained, rinsed
$1^1/2$ teaspoons chopped fresh thyme, or
    $3/4$ teaspoon dried thyme
1 tablespoon minced fresh tarragon, or
    $1^1/2$ teaspoons dried tarragon
4 medium fresh tomatoes, chopped
1 cup fresh or frozen peas (optional)
salt and pepper to taste
16 ounces uncooked penne
$1/2$ cup chopped fresh parsley
grated Parmesan cheese

Soak the sun-dried tomatoes in $1/2$ cup very hot water in a small bowl. Drain, reserving the tomatoes and soaking liquid.

Heat the olive oil in a nonreactive skillet over medium heat. Add the onions and cook, covered, for 3 minutes. Add the sun-dried tomatoes. Stir in the garlic, capers, thyme, tarragon, fresh tomatoes, peas and reserved soaking liquid. Cook, covered, until the tomatoes are very tender. Season with salt and pepper.

Cook the pasta al dente in water to cover in a saucepan. Drain well. Combine with the tomato sauce in a large warm serving bowl and toss to mix well. Add the parsley and top with cheese. Serve immediately.

Serves four to six

Hard Cheeses

Cheshire is an English cheese made from cows' milk. It is an elegant relative of cheddar.

Parmigiano-Reggiano is an Italian cheese made from cows' milk. It a must with pasta and is great on its own, too.

Stilton is the sophisticated English version of bleu cheese made from cows' milk. It is best eaten with a full-bodied red wine or Port and fresh fruit.

Children's Herb Garden

To make all your dishes more wonderful, grow your own herbs. It's a fun family activity, and neighborhood kids love to taste the results. It also encourages kids to try more dishes if the herbs that they have grown are used.

Even a tiny space will accommodate an herb garden; a window box or the smallest yard will allow you to give your cooking that extra zing. Just remember that when cooking with fresh herbs, you should use three times as much as you would use if you were cooking with dried herbs.

Spaghetti with Magnifico Meatballs and Red Sauce

Size doesn't matter.

Red Sauce
1 pound lean ground beef
1 pound hot Italian pork or
    turkey sausage
1 (48-ounce) jar spaghetti sauce
    with fresh mushrooms
2 to 3 tablespoons oregano
2 to 3 tablespoons sweet basil
2 tablespoons Italian seasoning
1 teaspoon fennel seeds
1 bay leaf
1 teaspoon crushed red pepper

Meatballs and Spaghetti
1 pound hot Italian pork sausage
    or turkey sausage, crumbled
1 pound lean ground beef
3/4 cup Italian bread crumbs
2 eggs, beaten
12 parsley sprigs, finely chopped
1 large onion, finely chopped
1 garlic clove, minced (optional)
6 tablespoons grated Parmesan
    cheese
2 tablespoons chopped fresh
    oregano
2 tablespoons chopped fresh sweet
    basil
1 teaspoon salt
1 teaspoon pepper
olive oil
24 ounces spaghetti, cooked

For the sauce, brown the ground beef and sausage in a large saucepan, stirring until crumbly; drain. Add the spaghetti sauce, oregano, basil, Italian seasoning, fennel seeds, bay leaf and crushed red pepper. Rinse the spaghetti sauce jar with a small amount of water and add the water to the saucepan. Simmer for 1 1/2 hours; discard the bay leaf. Use immediately or store in the refrigerator for 8 hours or longer and reheat to improve the flavor.

For the meatballs and spaghetti, combine the sausage, ground beef, bread crumbs, eggs, parsley, onion, garlic, Parmesan cheese, oregano, basil, salt and pepper in a large bowl and mix well. Shape into balls.

Sauté in olive oil in a saucepan until dark brown on all sides, turning frequently. Combine with the red sauce in a saucepan and cook until heated through. Serve over the spaghetti.

Serves eight

Phenomenal Fettuccine

Rich alfredo-style pasta; throw out the scale.

8 ounces fresh mushrooms
1 tablespoon butter
2 tablespoons minced green
    onion tops
1 cup chicken broth
1/2 cup heavy cream

8 ounces bacon, crisp-fried,
    chopped
8 ounces fettuccine, cooked
1 cup sour cream
1 cup grated Parmesan cheese

Sauté the mushrooms in the butter in a very large skillet. Remove the mushrooms with a slotted spoon. Add the green onion tops to the skillet and sauté until tender. Stir in the chicken broth. Cook for 3 minutes; remove from the heat.

Stir in the cream gradually. Add the bacon and mushrooms. Add the pasta, sour cream and Parmesan cheese and toss to mix well. Simmer for 5 to 10 minutes or until heated through.

Serves three or four

Penne Cognac

You'll feel satisfied by the richness of this dish.

8 ounces uncooked penne
2 tablespoons chopped shallots
4 slices bacon
1/2 cup chopped prosciutto
1 ounce cognac
1 (8-ounce) can tomato sauce
Tabasco sauce to taste

1/4 cup (1/2 stick) butter
1/2 cup heavy cream
3 tablespoons grated Parmesan
    cheese
1 tablespoon chopped fresh
    parsley

Cook the pasta using the package directions. Keep warm.

Sauté the shallots with the bacon in a skillet until the shallots are golden brown. Add the prosciutto. Cook for 3 minutes. Remove the bacon.

Pour the cognac into the skillet and ignite. Cook until the flames die down. Stir in the tomato sauce, Tabasco sauce, butter and cream.

Drain the pasta and combine with the cognac sauce in a bowl. Add the Parmesan cheese and parsley; toss to mix well.

Serves three or four

Freezing Extra Tomato Paste

Inevitably, recipes call for only one or two tablespoons of tomato paste, and you're often left wondering what to do with the rest.

Here's one idea: use a can opener to open both ends of the can. Leave one metal top on one end and throw the other top out. Wrap the can with the tomato paste still inside it in plastic wrap and freeze. Once it's frozen, use the metal top to push the tomato paste out of the can, using just the amount needed.

Tomato paste can be frozen safely for several months.

Gorgonzola Sauce

Melt 3 tablespoons butter in a large saucepan over low heat and stir in 1 cup heavy cream. Cook until heated through. Stir in 8 ounces crumbled Gorgonzola cheese until melted. Add $^1/_3$ cup grated Parmesan cheese and mix well. Serve over 16 ounces of hot cooked pasta.

Penne alla Siciliana

So easy to prepare, so delicious to taste. This pasta can accompany meat or poultry or stand alone as a light supper.

16 ounces uncooked penne
4 ounces prosciutto, julienned
1 tablespoon olive oil
3 tablespoons butter
1 small onion, minced
1$^1/_2$ cups fresh or frozen peas
2 tablespoons chopped chives
salt and pepper to taste
$^1/_4$ cup beef stock
$^1/_4$ cup grated Parmesan cheese
1 tablespoon chopped Italian parsley

Cook the pasta al dente using the package directions; keep warm. Sauté the prosciutto in the olive oil and 1 tablespoon of the butter in a large skillet for 1 minute. Remove with a slotted spoon. Add the remaining 2 tablespoons butter, onion, peas, chives, salt and pepper. Sauté over medium heat until the onion is tender. Add the beef stock and prosciutto. Cook until heated through.

Drain the pasta and combine with the sauce in a bowl; toss gently to mix well. Top with the Parmesan cheese and parsley. Serve immediately.
Serves six

Farfalle Olympus

These flavors are the nectar of the gods.

1 cup dry-pack sun-dried tomatoes
3 large garlic cloves, minced
$^1/_3$ cup olive oil
10 kalamata olives, chopped
$^1/_4$ teaspoon red pepper
6 ounces farfalle, cooked
4 ounces goat cheese, crumbled
1 tablespoon pine nuts, toasted
salt and black pepper to taste

Soak the tomatoes in water to cover in a bowl to reconstitute. Drain and cut into $^1/_4$-inch strips. Sauté the garlic in the olive oil in a large skillet over medium heat for 1 minute. Add the tomatoes, olives and red pepper.

Combine with the pasta, goat cheese and pine nuts in a bowl. Season with salt and black pepper and toss to mix well.
Serves two

A bowl of fruit hints at the memory of the medieval hill town of Tuscany, which is covered in cypress trees, olive groves, and vineyards. While little has changed since the Renaissance artists painted there, you can change the mood to that of any port on the Mediterranean by switching the music, bringing out another map, and rewriting the menu.

The Right Sauce

For thin pasta, smooth sauces or simple sauces such as butter or olive oil and fresh Parmesan or Romano cheese with a bit of garlic work best. Thick sauces with chunks of meat or tomato stand up well to thick-shaped pastas.

Orecchiette with Broccoli Rabe and Sausage

Classically Italian!

16 ounces uncooked orecchiette or ziti
8 ounces sausage
2 medium onions, chopped
$1/3$ cup olive oil
1 pound broccoli rabe
2 large garlic cloves, minced
8 ounces carrots, julienned
2 small zucchini, chopped
$1/2$ teaspoon salt
$1/2$ teaspoon pepper
$1/2$ cup grated Parmesan cheese

Cook the pasta using the package directions. Remove 1 cup of the cooking liquid; keep the pasta warm.

Brown the sausage with the onions in the heated olive oil in a skillet over medium heat, stirring until the sausage is crumbly. Stir in the 1 cup reserved cooking liquid. Add the broccoli rabe and garlic and cook for 4 minutes. Add the carrots, zucchini, salt and pepper. Cook, covered, over high heat for 5 minutes.

Drain the pasta. Combine with the sausage mixture in a bowl and toss to mix well. Top with the cheese.

Serves six

Tortellini alla Prosciutto

A heady mix of sherry, cream, mushrooms, and prosciutto.

2 quarts water
1 teaspoon salt
2 pounds uncooked cheese-filled tortellini
4 ounces prosciutto, cut into thin strips
¼ cup (½ stick) butter
8 ounces assorted fresh mushrooms, sliced
¼ cup sherry
½ cup cream
¼ teaspoon freshly ground pepper
1 cup grated Parmesan cheese

Bring the water to a boil in a large saucepan. Add the salt and pasta and cook for 8 minutes or until tender; drain.

Sauté the prosciutto in the butter in a skillet for 2 minutes or until brown. Add the mushrooms and sauté for 2 minutes. Add the pasta and sherry. Cook over low heat for 2 minutes.

Stir in the cream and pepper. Cook until slightly thickened, stirring gently. Add the cheese and toss gently to mix. Serve immediately with additional cheese.

Serves eight

Spinach Flatbread

Sauté 5 ounces of sliced fresh spinach in 1 tablespoon olive oil in a large skillet over medium heat just until wilted. Remove the spinach from the skillet and add 2 cups sliced mushrooms, 1 thinly sliced onion and 1 tablespoon minced garlic and sauté until tender. Stir in the spinach. Spread 6 ounces goat cheese evenly over 4 flour tortillas. Top with the spinach mixture and place on a baking sheet. Bake at 350 degrees until heated through. Cut into wedges to serve.

Super Spaghetti Sauce

Brown 1 pound of ground beef
and 1 pound of ground veal in
2 tablespoons olive oil in a
saucepan. Add 4 cups canned
tomatoes, 1 cup tomato purée and
$^1/_2$ cup tomato paste. Combine
4 ounces fresh mushrooms,
1 medium onion, 3 garlic cloves,
$^1/_2$ teaspoon sweet basil,
$^1/_2$ teaspoon oregano,
1 tablespoon salt and $^1/_2$ teaspoon
pepper in a blender container and
process until smooth. Add to the
saucepan and mix well. Bring to a
boil, reduce the heat and simmer
for 30 minutes. Store in the
refrigerator or freezer.

Max's Radiatore

*The Mizner crowd lines up in droves to feast on this Boca favorite;
now you can prepare it in your own home!*

6 ounces uncooked radiatore
salt to taste
$^1/_2$ cup balsamic vinegar
$^3/_4$ cup dry-pack sun-dried tomatoes
$^1/_2$ cup olive oil
1 tablespoon minced shallots
3 garlic cloves, minced
2 teaspoons dried fines herbes
12 ounces boneless skinless chicken breasts, grilled or
    roasted, chopped
$1^1/_2$ cups reduced-sodium chicken stock
$^1/_4$ cup ($^1/_2$ stick) unsalted butter, cut into 4 pieces
pepper to taste
4 (or more) broccoli florets, steamed
2 ounces goat cheese
2 tablespoons pine nuts

Cook the pasta al dente in salted boiling water to cover in a saucepan, about 6 minutes. Drain and keep warm. Boil the vinegar in a small saucepan over high heat for 5 minutes or until reduced to $^1/_4$ cup. Soak the sun-dried tomatoes in water to cover in a bowl to reconstitute; drain and cut into thirds.

Heat the olive oil in a large skillet over medium heat. Add the shallots, garlic and fines herbes. Sauté for 1 to 2 minutes or until the shallots are tender but not brown. Stir in the sun-dried tomatoes, chicken, vinegar and chicken stock. Bring to a simmer. Add the butter. Cook until the butter melts, stirring to mix well. Season with salt and pepper.

Add the pasta and toss to mix well. Spoon into 2 pasta bowls. Top with the broccoli florets. Spoon the goat cheese into the center and sprinkle the pine nuts around the cheese.

Serves two

Classic Chicken Tetrazzini

This well-known Italian favorite is most satisfying and delicious.

4 ounces uncooked angel hair pasta
2 tablespoons olive oil
4 ounces whole button mushrooms
1/4 cup (1/2 stick) butter
1/3 cup flour
2 cups chicken broth
1/4 cup dry vermouth
1/2 cup heavy cream
2 cups chopped cooked chicken
nutmeg and salt to taste
1/4 cup grated Parmesan cheese

Cook the pasta using the package directions. Drain, rinse and combine with the olive oil and cold water to cover in the saucepan.

Sauté the mushrooms in the butter in a saucepan for 5 minutes. Remove the mushrooms with a slotted spoon. Sprinkle the flour over the butter remaining in the saucepan. Cook over low heat for 1 to 2 minutes, stirring constantly. Stir in the chicken broth gradually. Simmer until thickened and smooth, stirring constantly.

Remove from the heat. Add the vermouth, cream, chicken, mushrooms, nutmeg and salt to taste and mix well. Drain the pasta and add to the chicken mixture; mix gently. Spoon into a baking dish and sprinkle with the Parmesan cheese. Bake at 350 degrees for 30 minutes.

Serves four

Verde Cheese Sauce

Process 1 avocado, 3/4 cup Parmesan cheese and 2 tablespoons lemon juice with salt and freshly ground white pepper to taste in a food processor until smooth. Heat 3/4 cup heavy cream in a saucepan. Add the avocado mixture and mix gently. Cook for 3 to 5 minutes or just until heated through, stirring constantly. Serve over hot cooked cheese ravioli or lobster ravioli.

Shrimp and Feta Vermicelli

Elegant and tasteful, this light dish will satisfy the shrimp lovers in your dinner club.

1 pound medium shrimp, peeled, deveined
crushed red pepper to taste
2 tablespoons olive oil
²/₃ cup crumbled feta cheese
¹/₂ teaspoon crushed garlic
2 tablespoons olive oil
1 (14-ounce) can tomatoes
¹/₄ cup dry white wine

³/₄ teaspoon dried basil
¹/₂ teaspoon dried oregano
¹/₄ teaspoon salt
¹/₄ teaspoon pepper
8 ounces vermicelli, cooked

Garnish
fresh basil

Sauté the shrimp with the red pepper in 2 tablespoons olive oil in a skillet just until the shrimp are pink and opaque; do not overcook. Spoon into a 6x10-inch baking dish and sprinkle with the feta cheese.

Sauté the garlic in 2 tablespoons olive oil in the skillet until tender. Add the undrained tomatoes. Cook for 1 minute. Stir in the wine, basil, oregano, salt and pepper. Simmer until of the desired consistency. Pour over the shrimp.

Bake at 400 degrees for 10 minutes. Serve over the pasta. Garnish with fresh basil.

Serves three or four

In 1994, the Junior League of Boca Raton founded an all-women coalition to build a Habitat for Humanity house. Under the direction of president Jayne Malfitano, Junior League members and women representing fourteen other organizations staffed close to four months of volunteer shifts to construct the home for a single mother and her children to occupy. In addition, Children's Place South opened its doors and began caring for abused, abandoned, and neglected children in South Palm Beach County.

Frutti di Mare Coriander

Pleasures from the sea enveloped in a rich flavorful sauce.

1/2 cup finely chopped onion
3 to 5 garlic cloves, minced
3 tablespoons olive oil
2 tablespoons flour
1 teaspoon ground coriander
1/4 cup vermouth
1 cup heavy cream

8 ounces shrimp, peeled, deveined
8 ounces bay scallops
16 ounces fresh linguine, cooked

Garnish
1/4 cup chopped parsley

Sauté the onion and garlic in the heated olive oil in a heavy skillet over medium heat for 4 to 6 minutes or until light brown. Stir in the flour and coriander and cook for 1 minute.

Add the vermouth and cream. Bring to a simmer, stirring constantly. Add the shrimp and scallops. Cook for 5 minutes or just until the seafood is opaque; do not overcook.

Combine with the pasta in a bowl and toss gently to mix or spoon the sauce over the pasta to serve. Garnish with parsley.

Serves four

Sun-Dried Tomato Pesto

Rich and versatile. Serve it on pasta, fish, or Tuscan bread rounds.

4 garlic cloves, minced
2 1/2 tablespoons extra-virgin
　　olive oil
1 (28-ounce) can Italian plum
　　tomatoes in purée, crushed

1 cup oil-pack sun-dried tomatoes
1/4 cup finely chopped fresh basil
1/2 teaspoon salt
1/2 teaspoon freshly ground
　　pepper

Sauté the garlic in the heated olive oil in a saucepan over low heat for 3 minutes; do not brown. Add the undrained canned tomatoes. Simmer over low heat for 1 hour or until very thick. Remove from the heat.

Drain the sun-drained tomatoes, reserving 1/4 cup oil; chop the tomatoes. Stir the tomatoes into the sauce. Let stand for 5 minutes.

Process the mixture in a food processor until smooth, adding the reserved sun-dried tomato oil and processing constantly. Combine with the basil, salt and pepper in a bowl. Store, covered, in the refrigerator for up to 4 days.

Makes two and one-half cups

Cherry Tomato Sauce

Use red cherry tomatoes or tiny yellow pear tomatoes to make pasta sauce, tasting a couple of the tomatoes first to make sure they're sweet. Cook the little tomatoes just as you would the larger ones. For even more flavor, use a spoon to open and mash any that haven't broken up as they cook.

Vegetables ~ Side Dishes

Barefoot Elegance

As the days grow longer and stay warm into the night, *savor the moment* with friends at an elegant party under the gazebo. Here, sea breezes and salt air increase everyone's taste for fun. Calypso music and breaking waves provide a tropical rhythm. The setting begs for sun dresses and sandals and sips of chilled wine. Can't you just see everyone swaying to the beat?

Better still—while this Mediterranean pavilion promises the ultimate ocean view with its Gothic arches and Corinthian columns—you can make your own Neoclassical canopy to frame a beautiful lake, mountain, or meadow view.

This hostess took all of her cues from the sea, beginning with the invitation. Intrigued by the notion of finding a note in a bottle, she calligraphied her inviting messages atop copies of torn, faded treasure maps and rolled them inside clear plastic bottles. Sea shell-adorned address labels and collector's stamps allowed these messages to travel via the post office instead of out to sea.

A Mizner-era iron and copper chandelier is the focal point of the treasures under the gazebo. The hostess suspended it from a magnificent wood beam to enhance the Old-World theme of the party. Other objects reflecting the theme include a ram's-head urn, an Ionic capital, and burnished wood-carved candle sticks. To add more layers of detail, she gathered baskets, planters, chests, wooden boxes, and large flat stones from her home. All blend easily with native flowers and trinkets from the sea.

South Florida's sapphire blue ocean is the backdrop for this treasured gathering. The perfect setting for a casually elegant seaside party, this gazebo at Boca's South Inlet Park engages all of the senses. It's time to Savor the Moment.

She also looked beyond the traditional table linens and purchased bolts of fabric on sale, intertwining them to create a flowing three-dimensional look. Corsage straight pins and two-sided tape secure the fabrics and hide unfinished hems.

Setting the Stage

Displaying the dishes at varying heights enhances the architectural feel of the serving pieces. You can place boxes under one fabric to stage some of the dishes and drape a few yards of a coordinating fabric for drama and to fill in any gaps. This hostess turned one of the fabrics on the "wrong" side to get the right feel.

In the original message in a bottle, guests were asked to share in the feast by preparing a side dish to accompany her grilled entrée. The intrigue heightens on this treasure island afternoon as guests look for another corked bottle with their name on it to find their dining places.

The table is a visual feast with abalone shells, orchids, lanterns, gold coins, and jewels. During dinner, the hostess recommends that guests open the little bottles serving as their place cards and read their messages. Each contains a piece to a torn treasure map. Guests become better acquainted as they join forces to put the pieces of the puzzle together to decipher the map.

The Spirit of the Night

At twilight, with lanterns to guide them, all venture off through the sandy terrain on an odyssey quickly transformed by the moonlight. Signs hanging from trees request that a few treasure hunters sing a couple bars from pirate songs. Others are asked to twirl around three times with a partner. Each activity is supposed to be an effort to appease the spirits lurking in the night. Thwarting obstacles along the way requires the ingenuity of guests working as a team. A turtle nesting area requires a detour. Someone must pull clues from inside a fish skeleton. A "beware of alligators" sign causes guests to stay close together, moving quickly as they wonder if the hostess or the park service placed the sign.

Who will be brave enough to peer inside the native hut filled with more clues? And who can still use the rope like Tarzan to skirt the molten lava? The other choice is a tire swing, but it's next to a panther's den. (No one admits that the hut might be a boy scout tent covered in raffia or the lava really might be flashlights under red translucent fabric).

Soon, sharks' teeth arranged in arrows point the way to where "X" marks the spot. A resounding shout of glee shatters the stillness of the night as guests come upon a treasure trove of Magical Toffee (page 265) in jewel tone boxes, gold chocolate coins, and pearls waiting alongside Cappuccino Brownies (page 259) on the beach. A bit of brandy and port cap the finale.

Guests leave happy in the realization that the true treasure was discovered during the fantastic journey the hostess indulged them in—from the moment the invitations were opened, to their last moonlit walk with old and new-found friends

A Hunt for Great Ideas

A treasure hunt also works well as the theme for a child's birthday party. Add hermit crab races and a home-made water park made from a sprinkler in a roped off area with a water slide, and choose even more casual pirate and treasure decorations.

A day at the beach could easily become a day at the park with a majestic tree, secret waterfall, mountain cave, or pond. The last word: look for ideas from nature and magnify.

White-crackle, long-neck carafes are used unexpectedly at this buffet table, containing extra-virgin olive oil to drizzle over the vegetables. Not all serving pieces have to come from the china cabinet. And never hesitate to bring things from inside your home to your outdoor setting. This hostess strung a chandelier from the gazebo rafters and used items like the pictured antique Mizner-designed torchiere to create a special ambiance in her outdoor room.

Menu

*Spicy Grilled Shrimp**
(page 81)

*Beef Tenderloin with
Spicy Rub
and Barbecue Mop**
(page 150)

*Picnic Rice
with Cranberries**
(page 231)

Green Beans and Friends
(page 216)

*Marinated Tomatoes**
(page 131)

Cappuccino Brownies
(page 259)

Magical Toffee
(page 265)

*Pictured recipes

Grilled Asparagus with Roasted Peppers

Enjoy this tangy side dish creation from the chefs at 32 East.

1 pound large asparagus
salt to taste
1 red bell pepper
1 yellow bell pepper
1 bunch Italian parsley, chopped
1/3 cup balsamic vinegar

1 teaspoon Dijon mustard
1 cup extra-virgin olive oil
salt and pepper to taste
extra-virgin olive oil
shaved Parmesan cheese

Snap off the tough ends of the asparagus and peel any tough stems with a vegetable peeler. Simmer in a saucepan of salted boiling water for 8 minutes or until tender-crisp. Plunge into ice water to stop the cooking and drain.

Roast the bell peppers over a gas flame or under the broiler until charred on all sides. Place in a paper bag and let stand for 10 minutes. Remove the skins and seed the peppers over a bowl, reserving any juices. Chop the peppers and combine with the reserved juices, parsley, vinegar and Dijon mustard in a bowl. Stir in 1 cup olive oil and season with salt and pepper.

Brush olive oil lightly on the asparagus and season with salt and pepper. Grill until heated through. Remove to a serving plate. Spoon the pepper vinaigrette over the asparagus and top with Parmesan cheese.

Serves four

IN 1995, THE JUNIOR LEAGUE OF BOCA RATON INITIATED A PROJECT WITH LOCAL COMMUNICATIONS INDUSTRIES CALLED COMMUNITY CONNECTION. UNDER THE DIRECTION OF PRESIDENT BARBARA THOMPSON, JUNIOR LEAGUE MEMBERS WORKED DILIGENTLY ON THIS PROJECT PROVIDING VOICE MAIL TELEPHONE SERVICE TO HOMELESS PEOPLE, AS WELL AS PRE-PROGRAMMED 911 EMERGENCY CELLULAR PHONES TO AID VICTIMS OF DOMESTIC ASSAULT IN LIFE-THREATENING SITUATIONS.

Spicy Sesame Broccoli

A quick and easy dish with an oriental flair, this broccoli is crisp and flavorful.

1 large (1¹/2-pound) bunch broccoli	2 small garlic cloves, minced
salt to taste	4 teaspoons soy sauce
3 tablespoons sesame oil	2 teaspoons fresh lemon juice
	1 tablespoon sesame seeds, toasted

Cut the broccoli tops into florets. Trim the ends of the stalks and peel the tough outer layer. Cut the stalks into ¹/4-inch slices. Blanch the broccoli in salted boiling water in a saucepan for 5 minutes or until tender-crisp. Drain and rinse with cold water to stop the cooking.

Heat the sesame oil and garlic in a large skillet over low heat for 3 minutes. Stir in the soy sauce and lemon juice. Add the broccoli and toss to coat. Cook until heated through. Sprinkle with the sesame seeds.

Serves four

Ripley's Exceptional Brussels Sprouts

Believe it or not, your family will eat these.

2 pints brussels sprouts	¹/2 cup water
2 large yellow onions or Vidalia onions	2 tablespoons curry powder
4 garlic cloves, minced	1 tablespoon minced fresh thyme, or 1 teaspoon dried thyme
¹/4 cup (¹/2 stick) butter	

Trim the ends of the brussels sprouts and cut the sprouts into halves. Cut the onions into bite-size squares. Combine the brussels sprouts, onions, garlic, butter, water, curry powder and thyme in a large saucepan. Cook, covered, over high heat for 10 minutes, stirring occasionally. Reduce the heat to low and simmer for 12 to 15 minutes longer or until the brussels sprouts are tender. Serve immediately.

Serves four to six

Basic Basil Beurre Blanc

Combine ¹/2 cup dry white wine, 3 tablespoons white wine vinegar, 1 tablespoon minced shallot and 1 tablespoon minced garlic in a small saucepan and simmer until reduced by ¹/2. Stir in ¹/2 cup heavy cream and simmer until reduced by ¹/2. Whisk in ¹/2 cup (1 stick) chopped butter. Cook over medium-low heat until smooth and creamy, stirring constantly. Stir in ¹/4 cup chopped fresh basil. Cook for 1 minute longer. Drizzle over any steamed vegetable.

Green Beans and Friends

Bacon, shallots, and mushrooms round out this playful dish.

$1^1/4$ pounds fresh green beans,
    trimmed
salt to taste
4 slices bacon

2 shallots, minced
1 cup sliced mushrooms
$1/4$ teaspoon salt
$1/8$ teaspoon pepper

Blanch the green beans in salted boiling water for 5 minutes. Plunge into ice water to stop cooking and drain. Sauté the bacon in a skillet until crisp. Remove the bacon from the skillet, reserving the drippings. Drain the bacon and chop into small pieces.

Sauté the shallots in the bacon drippings until soft. Add the mushrooms and sauté until tender. Add the drained green beans and cook until done to taste. Season with $1/4$ teaspoon salt and pepper. Sprinkle with the chopped bacon.

Serves six

Artichokes and Spinach

Here's a great tradeoff: the iron in the spinach in this easily prepared dish surely outweighs the calories.

3 (10-ounce) packages frozen
    chopped spinach
$1/2$ cup (1 stick) butter
1 medium onion, chopped
8 ounces cream cheese, cubed

salt and pepper to taste
1 (14-ounce) can artichokes,
    drained and quartered
$1/2$ cup grated Parmesan cheese

Cook the spinach using the package directions and drain well. Melt the butter in a sauté pan. Add the onion and sauté until tender. Add the cream cheese and cook until melted, stirring constantly. Stir in the spinach and season with salt and pepper.

Alternate layers of the spinach mixture and artichokes in a greased 2-quart baking dish until all ingredients are used. Top with the Parmesan cheese. Bake at 350 degrees for 30 minutes.

Serves six

Baby Carrots with Brown Sugar and Mustard

When you need an easy last-minute vegetable but it has to be special, this is it!

1 pound baby carrots
3 tablespoons unsalted butter
2 tablespoons plus 1¹/₂ teaspoons
    light brown sugar

1 tablespoon grainy Dijon
    mustard

Blanch, steam or microwave the carrots for 8 to 10 minutes or until tender-crisp. Melt the butter in a skillet over medium heat. Add the brown sugar and mustard and stir until smooth. Add the cooked carrots and toss to coat. Cook over medium heat for 1 minute. Serve immediately.

Serves six

Carrots Marsala

These sweet buttery carrots make a colorful addition to any plate.

2 pounds medium carrots
3 tablespoons butter
³/₄ cup good-quality dry marsala

Garnish
2 tablespoons chopped fresh
    parsley

Peel the carrots and cut diagonally into ¹/₈-inch slices. Melt the butter in a large skillet. Add the carrots and sauté for 2 to 3 minutes or until the carrots are well coated with melted butter. Stir in the wine. Cook, covered, over low to medium heat for 8 to 10 minutes or until the carrots are tender and the liquid is reduced. Garnish with the parsley.

Serves six

Chiffonade

A French word meaning "made of rags," chiffonade refers to thin strips or shreds of vegetables–typically lettuce, cabbage, or basil–used as a garnish or ingredient. To make a chiffonade, stack 4 or 5 leaves on top of one another and roll into a tight cylinder. Using a chef's knife, make narrow parallel cuts to produce fine shreds.

Bouquet Garni

Place 1 small peeled and quartered onion, 1 garlic clove, 1 sprig thyme, 1 bay leaf, 4 sprigs of fresh parsley and 10 black peppercorns on a square of cheesecloth. Tie the packet with twine to enclose the ingredients. Use as a seasoning for the sauce in the Garlic Soufflé or other sauces or soups.

Garlic Soufflé

Delicate texture and flavor, melts in your mouth. Serve this at your fanciest dinner party to impress and delight your guests.

Garlic Purée
2 large garlic heads
1/2 cup olive oil
1/2 cup water
1 teaspoon minced fresh thyme, or 1/2 teaspoon dried thyme
2 bay leaves, crumbled
salt and pepper to taste

Béchamel Sauce
6 tablespoons (3/4 stick) butter
5 tablespoons flour
1 1/2 cups half-and-half
1 cup heavy cream
Bouquet Garni (at left)
salt to taste

Soufflé
5 egg yolks
3 ounces (3/4 cup) freshly shredded Gruyère cheese
5 ounces Parmesan cheese, grated
salt, cayenne and black pepper to taste
1 cup unbeaten egg whites (about 8 to 10)
1 tablespoon minced fresh thyme, or 1 1/2 teaspoons dried thyme

For the purée, break the garlic heads into cloves and place the unpeeled cloves in a small shallow baking dish. Add the olive oil and water. Stir in the thyme, bay leaves, salt and pepper. Cover with foil and bake at 250 degrees for 1 1/2 hours or until very tender. Squeeze the garlic from the skins and mash with a fork.

For the sauce, melt the butter in the top of a double boiler. Stir in the flour. Cook over simmering water for 5 to 8 minutes, stirring frequently. Scald the half-and-half and heavy cream in a saucepan. Remove the butter mixture from the heat and whisk in the hot cream. Add the bouquet garni, cover and cook over simmering water for 1 hour, stirring occasionally. Remove the bouquet garni and discard. Season with salt. Cool the sauce.

For the soufflé, stir the egg yolks 1 at a time into the sauce. Stir in the Gruyère cheese, 2 ounces of the Parmesan cheese and the garlic purée. Season with salt, cayenne and black pepper. Butter 6 shallow 6-inch gratin dishes or one 12-inch oval dish and lightly coat with some of the remaining Parmesan cheese.

Beat the egg whites until stiff and fold into the garlic mixture. Spoon into the prepared dishes and sprinkle with the thyme and the remaining Parmesan cheese. Bake on the top oven rack at 450 degrees for 20 to 25 minutes or until the tops are well browned. Serve immediately.

Serves six

*A*balone shell, copper-beaded napkin rings, orchids, and silk fabric are some of the natural elements used to dress the dinner tables. Sprinkle in some antiqued coins—the spray-painted loose change gives an Old World patina to the table. See the place cards in tiny bottles? They were the inspiration for this great party. Guests will remember their "message in a bottle" invitation that set the tone from the beginning. And the scented seashell sachets that mark each place are the perfect keepsake from this oceanfront afternoon.

Edible Mushrooms

Chanterelles are found in the Pacific Northwest. This wild trumpet-shaped mushroom is a real treat.

Enoki are pin-headed mushrooms often floated in clear soups, and are favored chiefly for their shape rather than their flavor.

Morels are highly prized wild mushrooms with black spongy heads. They are great in heavy cream sauces.

Porcini, usually sold dried, are native to Italy. Reconstitute them in hot soups, sauces, and stews.

Portobello mushrooms may measure up to six inches in diameter and are known for their flat open tops. Grill them whole, then cut into thick slices for sandwiches or salads.

Shiitake are dark-capped mushrooms that originated in Asia and are now grown in the United States. They can withstand longer cooking times.

Portobellos Stuffed with Spinach and Sun-Dried Tomatoes

For a different twist, try these on the grill at your next barbecue. The tantalizing aroma will have your guests hovering around the grill in anticipation of your delectable meal.

Vinaigrette Marinade
$1\frac{1}{2}$ teaspoons Dijon mustard
1 tablespoon red wine vinegar
$\frac{1}{4}$ teaspoon sugar
$\frac{1}{4}$ teaspoon salt
$\frac{1}{4}$ teaspoon freshly ground pepper
$\frac{1}{4}$ cup olive oil

Mushrooms
3 large portobello mushroom caps, gills removed
1 tablespoon olive oil
1 small onion, minced
1 garlic clove, minced
2 cups fresh spinach, washed, dried and stems removed
3 oil-pack sun-dried tomatoes, chopped
salt and pepper to taste
2 tablespoons grated Parmesan cheese

For the vinaigrette, combine the Dijon mustard, vinegar, sugar, salt and pepper in a small bowl. Add the olive oil gradually, whisking until the mixture thickens.

For the mushrooms, add the mushroom caps to the vinaigrette and marinate for 1 hour; drain. Broil or grill for 6 to 8 minutes per side. Set aside to cool.

Heat the olive oil in a large skillet. Add the onion and garlic and sauté for 3 to 5 minutes or until tender. Add the spinach and tomatoes and sauté for 3 to 4 minutes longer. Season with salt and pepper and remove from the heat.

Place the mushroom caps on a baking sheet and sprinkle with half the Parmesan cheese. Spoon the spinach mixture into the caps. Sprinkle with the remaining Parmesan cheese. Broil for 5 minutes or until hot and sizzling.

Serves three

Scalloped Potatoes and Butternut Squash with Leeks

Simple and delicious with a creamy onion flavor.

6 large leeks
1 pound butternut squash
3 tablespoons unsalted butter
3$\frac{1}{2}$ cups milk
5 tablespoons unsalted butter
6 tablespoons flour

salt and pepper to taste
1$\frac{1}{2}$ pounds baking potatoes
   (about 4 large)
1$\frac{1}{2}$ cups shredded Swiss cheese
   or fontina cheese

Wash the leeks well and drain. Slice the white and pale green part thinly and measure 3 cups. Peel, quarter and seed the butternut squash. Cut into $\frac{1}{8}$-inch-thick slices.

Melt 3 tablespoons butter in a skillet over medium-low heat. Add the sliced leeks and sauté until very tender. Heat the milk in a saucepan until almost boiling.

Melt 5 tablespoons butter in a heavy saucepan over medium-low heat. Whisk in the flour and cook for 3 minutes, whisking constantly. Add the milk in a stream , whisking constantly. Bring to a boil and reduce the heat. Cook for 1 minute or until thickened, whisking constantly. Season with salt and pepper. Spread $\frac{1}{3}$ of the sauce in a buttered 3-quart gratin dish at least 2 inches deep.

Peel the potatoes and slice $\frac{1}{8}$ inch thick. Layer $\frac{1}{3}$ of the potato and $\frac{1}{3}$ of the squash slices in an overlapping spiral over the sauce. Top with $\frac{1}{3}$ of the cooked leeks and sprinkle with $\frac{1}{3}$ of the cheese. Repeat the layers twice. Cover with foil and bake at 400 degrees for 30 minutes. Remove the foil and bake for 20 minutes longer or until the top is golden brown and the vegetables are tender.

Note: The dish can be baked 1 hour ahead and held at room temperature. Reheat at 350 degrees if needed.

Serves six

No More Tears

You can reduce your tears when cutting onions by using the following tips:

Wear safety goggles or contact lenses and work with lots of ventilation.

Immerse the onion in ice water or freeze for 30 minutes before cutting.

Rinse your hands often during the process.

Place the onion in boiling water for 30 seconds to slip off the skin.

Cut the stem end first and the root end last.

Potato and Wild Mushroom Galette

Outstanding; a perfect party item. You must try this!

5 to 6 baking potatoes
salt to taste
$1/4$ cup ($1/2$ stick) butter
6 ounces portobello mushrooms,
    sliced
6 ounces oyster mushrooms, sliced
6 ounces shiitake mushrooms,
    stemmed, sliced

pepper to taste
3 tablespoons chopped chives
6 tablespoons grated Parmesan
    cheese
$1/4$ cup olive oil

Peel the potatoes and cut into $1/8$-inch slices. Bring a large saucepan of salted water to a boil. Add the potatoes and blanch for 3 minutes. Drain and cool. Pat the slices dry with paper towels.

Melt half the butter in a skillet. Add the portobello mushrooms and sauté until tender. Remove the mushrooms to a bowl. Melt the remaining butter in the skillet and add the oyster and shiitake mushrooms. Sauté until tender. Add to the portobello mushrooms and let cool. Season with salt and pepper and stir in the chives.

Layer $1/4$ of the potatoes in an overlapping spiral in the bottom of a springform pan coated with nonstick cooking spray. Season generously with salt and pepper. Top with $1/3$ of the mushroom mixture and sprinkle with 2 tablespoons of the Parmesan cheese. Drizzle with 1 tablespoon of the olive oil. Repeat the layers twice. Top with the remaining potato slices and drizzle with the remaining olive oil. Season with salt and pepper. Cover with foil.

Bake at 400 degrees for 1 hour or until the potatoes are tender, pressing down on the foil with a spatula every 15 minutes to compress the potatoes. Remove the foil and brown the top of the potatoes under the broiler. Place on a heat-resistant serving plate. Loosen the galette from the side of the pan with a small sharp knife and carefully remove the side. Let stand for 10 minutes. Cut into wedges and serve.

Serves eight to ten

Potatoes Anna

You'll never go wrong with this elegant and classic dish.

$^{1}/_{4}$ to $^{1}/_{2}$ cup ($^{1}/_{2}$ to 1 stick) butter,
   clarified

$1^{1}/_{2}$ pounds russet potatoes
salt and pepper to taste

Melt the butter in a small saucepan and let stand for 10 minutes. Skim the clear butter from the cloudy sediment or remove the sediment by straining through 3 layers of cheesecloth.

Peel the potatoes and thinly slice in a food processor using the slicing blade, placing the slices in ice water until all of the potatoes are sliced. Drain and pat dry with paper towels. Brush the bottom and side of a heavy, nonstick 9-inch ovenproof skillet with some of the melted butter. Layer the potatoes in an overlapping spiral in the skillet, brushing each layer with butter and seasoning with salt and pepper. Cover with buttered foil and press firmly on the potatoes.

Bake at 425 degrees for 30 minutes, pressing firmly several times. Remove the foil and bake for 25 to 30 minutes longer or until the top is golden brown and the potatoes are tender. Place a cutting board over the skillet and invert the potatoes onto the board. Remove the skillet and cut the potatoes into wedges, draining excess butter.

Serves four

Parmesan Cheese-Crusted Zucchini

This is a simple, flavorful accompaniment for almost anything.

4 medium zucchini
2 tablespoons olive oil
$^{1}/_{4}$ cup sliced green onions
salt and pepper to taste

2 teaspoons minced garlic
$^{1}/_{4}$ cup coarsely chopped fresh
   basil
$^{1}/_{2}$ cup grated Parmesan cheese

Trim the zucchini and cut into $^{1}/_{4}$-inch slices. Heat the olive oil in a skillet over medium heat. Add the zucchini and green onions and season with salt and pepper. Sauté for 3 minutes. Add the garlic and basil and sauté for 10 minutes or until the garlic is tender but not brown.

Arrange the zucchini in a single layer in a baking dish. Sprinkle with the Parmesan cheese. Broil until the cheese is melted and golden brown.

Serves four

Clarified Butter

Also called "drawn butter," clarified butter is made by melting butter and allowing the milky particles which burn first in ordinary butter to fall to the bottom. The clarified butter is then drawn off the top after the surface foam is skimmed. Since it burns less easily, clarified butter works well in sauces.

Five-Vegetable Napoleons

These are colorful, delicious, and very appealing. They can also be served at room temperature, making them a convenient buffet dish.

$1/2$ cup olive oil
1 pound eggplant, cut into
   $1/3$-inch slices
$11/4$ pounds zucchini, cut into
   $1/3$-inch slices
2 red bell peppers, seeded and cut
   into bite-size squares
2 medium red onions, cut into
   $1/3$-inch slices
1 pound medium red potatoes, cut
   into $1/3$-inch slices
salt and pepper to taste
$3/4$ cup ricotta cheese
$11/2$ teaspoons chopped fresh
   thyme
8 ounces mozzarella cheese, cut
   into six $1/4$-inch slices
6 sprigs fresh rosemary

Brush 2 baking sheets with some of the olive oil. Arrange the vegetables in a single layer on the baking sheets. Brush the vegetables with oil and season with salt and pepper. Roast at 450 degrees on the middle and lower oven racks for 10 to 15 minutes or until the vegetables are tender and light brown, rearranging the positions of the baking sheets halfway through the roasting time. Transfer the vegetables to a single layer on a tray and repeat the roasting process with the remaining vegetables.

Combine the ricotta cheese and thyme in a small bowl. Season with salt and pepper. Place 1 eggplant slice on a baking sheet that has been lightly brushed with olive oil. Spread 1 tablespoon of the ricotta mixture on the eggplant. Layer with 2 potato slices, 2 zucchini slices, 1 onion slice, 1 mozzarella slice, 2 to 3 pepper pieces, 2 zucchini slices and 1 onion slice. Spread 1 tablespoon of the ricotta mixture on the onion slice and top with 1 eggplant slice. Make 5 more napoleons in the same manner.

Trim the rosemary sprigs to be 1 inch taller than the napoleons and remove the bottom leaves, leaving 1 inch of leaves at the top of the sprig. Make a hole through the center of each napoleon from top to bottom with a metal skewer or wooden pick and insert 1 rosemary sprig in each napoleon.

Bake the napoleons at 450 degrees for 5 minutes or until the mozzarella cheese is melted and the vegetables are heated through.

Note: The vegetables can be roasted 1 day ahead. Chill in layers between plastic wrap on trays. Let warm to room temperature before assembling the napoleons.

Serves six

What better way to make sure your guests get to know one another than by sending them on a group treasure hunt?
Hidden among the oceanside dunes, Cappuccino Brownies (page 259) are the favorite loot and the perfect accompaniment for a
toast to the winner's good fortune. The secret of a happy ending here is to make sure everyone gets a prize.

Vegetable Couscous

An international culinary cache of flavors.

2 cups water
1/4 teaspoon salt
1 1/3 cups uncooked couscous
2 tablespoons vegetable oil
3 onions, chopped
1 red bell pepper, julienned
4 garlic cloves, minced
2 1/4 teaspoons ground coriander
1 1/2 teaspoons ground cumin

3/4 teaspoon turmeric
1/8 teaspoon ground cloves
1/8 teaspoon cinnamon
2 teaspoons salt
1/4 teaspoon cayenne
2 1/3 cups chicken broth
4 plum tomatoes, chopped
3 tablespoons dried currants or
   raisins

Bring the water to a boil in a medium saucepan. Stir in 1/4 teaspoon salt and the couscous. Cover and remove from the heat. Let stand in a warm place.

Heat the oil in a medium skillet over medium-low heat. Add the onions and bell pepper and sauté for 5 minutes or until the onion is translucent. Increase the heat to medium and stir in the garlic, coriander, cumin, turmeric, cloves, cinnamon, 2 teaspoons salt and cayenne. Cook for 2 minutes, stirring constantly. Stir in the chicken broth and tomatoes and cook for 15 minutes or until the vegetables are very tender. Add the currants and cook for 3 minutes longer.

Spoon the couscous into a serving bowl. Top with the vegetable mixture.

Serves eight

Barley with Mushrooms and Onions

This healthy grain is a delicious alternative to rice.

8 ounces mushrooms
1/4 cup (1/2 stick) unsalted butter
1 large onion, finely chopped
1 cup uncooked pearl barley

1 teaspoon salt
1/2 teaspoon freshly ground
    pepper
2 cups chicken broth, heated

Slice the mushroom caps and chop the stems. Melt the butter in a large skillet. Add the onion and sauté for 3 to 4 minutes or until tender. Add the mushrooms and sauté for 4 to 5 minutes. Stir in the barley, salt and pepper and cook until light brown. Transfer the mixture to a buttered 1-quart casserole. Stir in the hot broth. Bake, covered, at 350 degrees for 50 minutes or until the barley is tender.

Serves six

Bulgur Wheat with Apricots

Freshly squeezed orange juice and apricots add a Florida flair.

1 tablespoon butter
1/2 cup finely chopped shallots
2 garlic cloves, minced
2 cups uncooked bulgur
1 (6-ounce) package dried
    apricots, sliced
1 teaspoon salt
1/4 teaspoon cinnamon

2 1/2 cups water
2/3 cup fresh orange juice
2 tablespoons olive oil
1/2 cup coarsely chopped
    pistachios (about 2 ounces)
1/2 cup chopped fresh Italian
    parsley
salt and pepper to taste

Melt the butter in a heavy medium saucepan over medium-high heat. Add the shallots and garlic and sauté for 3 minutes or until tender. Mix in the bulgur, apricots, salt and cinnamon. Stir in the water and bring to a boil. Reduce the heat to low and cover. Cook for 20 minutes or until the liquid is absorbed and the bulgur is tender, stirring frequently.

Spoon into a bowl and cool to room temperature. Add the orange juice and oil. Stir in the pistachios and parsley. Season with salt and pepper and serve at room temperature or chilled.

Note: The bulgur can be made 1 day ahead. Add the pistachios and parsley just before serving. Store in the refrigerator.

Serves eight

Parsley Pointers

Parsleys differ in appearance, taste, and use. Curly parsley is the most widely recognized and is used for culinary and medicinal purposes. Italian, or flat leaf, parsley has a much longer stalk and is used mostly as a culinary herb. Chervil has very lacy leaves and a delicate anise or tarragon taste. Parsley may be frozen and used in that form for soups and stew, etc. If used fresh, parsley should always be added during the last five minutes.

For Fried Parsley, *heat a small amount of oil until almost smoking in a skillet. Add 1 bunch of Italian or curly parsley a little at a time. Cook until the parsley turns a bright green; remove with a slotted spoon and drain on paper towels. Sprinkle with grated Parmesan cheese and serve at once. This makes a great hors d'oeuvre, garnish, or side dish.*

Cutting and Storing Garlic

Garlic is a surprisingly delicate ingredient and requires special care. The way it is cut and cooked will determine its flavor. To retain pungency, chop garlic with a stainless steel knife. Cutting into small bits will release a small amount of oil for a more delicate flavor. Use a garlic press to release a lot of oil for marinades or stews.

Use chopped garlic as soon as possible. If you have to store it, cover and refrigerate for use within a day, but the flavor will not be as fine. Store heads in a cool place with plenty of air circulation. Refrigeration is not recommended because the dampness invites mold. Sautéing garlic over low heat brings out its wonderfully strong flavor. Poaching in a liquid over low heat softens it and brings out its sweetness, so more can be used.

Roasting gives it that nutty, caramelized flavor everyone craves.

For a hint of garlic in a cream-based sauce, rub the wooden spoon and the pan itself with a cut clove.

Cheesy Polenta with Mushrooms

An aromatic combination; creamy, cheesy, and buttery.

Mushroom Filling
1 tablespoon olive oil
2 garlic cloves, minced
8 ounces button mushrooms, trimmed and sliced
8 ounces mixed portobello, oyster and/or cremini mushrooms, trimmed and sliced
salt and freshly ground pepper to taste
$1/2$ cup dry marsala
$1/4$ cup heavy cream
2 tablespoons chopped fresh parsley

Polenta
5 cups reduced-sodium chicken broth, vegetable broth or water
$1/2$ teaspoon salt
$1^1/2$ cups yellow cornmeal or polenta
2 tablespoons ($1/4$ stick) unsalted butter
$1/4$ cup grated Parmesan cheese
$1^1/4$ cups finely shredded mozzarella cheese
$1/2$ tablespoon unsalted butter, chopped
4 teaspoons freshly grated Parmesan cheese

For the mushroom filling, heat the oil in a heavy large skillet over medium-high heat until hot but not smoking. Add the garlic and sauté for 10 seconds or until fragrant but not brown. Add the mushrooms and season with salt and pepper. Sauté until the liquid from the mushrooms evaporates.

Add the marsala and boil until the liquid is reduced by half. Add the cream and parsley and boil for 3 to 5 minutes or until the mixture is thickened and reduced to a glaze, whisking constantly. Remove from the heat.

For the polenta, bring the broth and salt to a boil in a heavy 3- to 4-quart saucepan. Reduce the heat to simmer and add the cornmeal in a stream, whisking constantly. Cook for 3 to 4 minutes or until the mixture starts to pull away from the side of the pan, whisking constantly. Remove from the heat and whisk in 2 tablespoons butter, $1/4$ cup Parmesan cheese and mozzarella cheese.

Pour half the polenta into a lightly buttered 2- to $2^1/2$-quart shallow baking dish. Smooth the top and spread the mushroom filling over the polenta. Top with the remaining polenta and smooth the top. Dot with $1/2$ tablespoon butter and sprinkle with 4 teaspoons Parmesan cheese. Let stand for 15 minutes.

Bake at 400 degrees for 25 minutes. Broil for 1 minute to brown the top.

Note: The polenta can be assembled 4 hours before baking. Cover and chill.

Serves eight

White Truffle Polenta with Clams

An intriguing combination from Damiano's Restaurant.

Polenta
4 cups water
$^1/_2$ teaspoon salt
1$^1/_2$ cups polenta or cornmeal
1 tablespoon white truffle oil

Clams
3 tablespoons olive oil
18 littleneck clams, scrubbed and
    cleaned

2 teaspoons minced garlic
$^1/_2$ cup chopped red onion
$^3/4$ cup white wine
$^1/_2$ cup artichoke hearts,
    quartered
2 teaspoons chorizo sausage,
    chopped
12 ounces crushed tomatoes

For the polenta, bring the water and salt to a boil in a heavy large saucepan. Stir in the polenta gradually. Cook for 30 minutes or until thickened, stirring constantly. Remove from the heat and stir in the truffle oil. Cover and let stand for 5 minutes.

For the clams, heat the olive oil in a heavy large skillet over medium-high heat until hot but not smoking. Add the clams, garlic and onion and sauté until the onion is transparent. Pour in the wine and stir until the mixture stops sizzling. Stir in the artichoke hearts, sausage and tomatoes. Cook for 3 to 5 minutes or until the clams open. Serve over the polenta, discarding any clams that do not open.

Note: If white truffle oil is unavailable, substitute 3 ounces of finely chopped shiitake mushrooms and 1 tablespoon butter.

Serves four

Rice Remedies

To keep rice grains separate, add a tablespoon of butter or oil to the water.

To avoid gummy rice, do not stir simmering rice, as this mashes the grains.

To prevent scorching, simmer rice in a heavy pan.

To keep rice warm before serving, place it in a covered baking dish in a warm oven.

To add more flavor, simmer rice in broth or broth mixed with water.

To salvage watery rice, fluff it with a fork over low heat to evaporate the water.

Fragrant Oriental Rice

Snow peas give this colorful dish crispness; the sesame seeds add crunchiness.

1 tablespoon vegetable oil
1 cup finely chopped carrot
1 teaspoon finely chopped peeled
    fresh gingerroot
1 garlic clove, minced
1½ cups uncooked sushi rice or
    medium grain rice
2½ cups water

1 teaspoon salt
4 ounces (about 1 cup) snow
    peas, trimmed
1 tablespoon sesame seeds,
    lightly toasted
2 tablespoons seasoned rice
    vinegar, or to taste
salt and pepper to taste

Heat the oil in a large saucepan over medium heat until hot but not smoking. Add the carrot and stir-fry until it starts to brown. Add the gingerroot and garlic and stir-fry for 1 minute. Stir in the rice, water and salt and bring to a boil and reduce the heat. Simmer, covered, for 20 minutes.

Blanch the snow peas in boiling water for 15 seconds. Remove to ice water to stop cooking. Drain well and cut diagonally into thin slices. Combine with the cooked rice, sesame seeds and vinegar in a large bowl. Mix well and season with salt and pepper.

Note: Sushi rice and seasoned rice vinegar are available at Asian markets and some supermarkets.

Serve six

In 1996, the Junior League of Boca Raton celebrated its twenty-fifth anniversary under the direction of president Ellen Malone. It was also the year that the Junior League cemented a commitment to the Children's Science Explorium, a hands-on museum utilizing interactive exhibits and programs to awaken children's creative interests. The Explorium's new home at Sugar Sand Park provides a permanent space for the museum and houses a traveling exhibit for community outreach programming.

Picnic Rice with Cranberries

Don't wait for a tailgate party. This unique combination of colorful ingredients makes a delightful dish all year round.

1½ cups uncooked brown rice
½ cup uncooked wild rice
4 cups water
3 ounces dried cranberries
3 ounces pine nuts, toasted
½ yellow bell pepper, chopped

½ large red onion, chopped
3 tablespoons chopped fresh
    parsley
¼ cup balsamic vinegar
⅓ cup walnut oil
salt and pepper to taste

Combine the brown rice, wild rice and water in a medium saucepan. Bring to a boil over medium-high heat and reduce the heat. Simmer, covered, for 25 to 30 minutes or until the rice is tender and the liquid is absorbed. Cool to room temperature.

Combine with the cranberries, pine nuts, bell pepper, onion and parsley in a bowl. Add the vinegar and oil and toss gently to coat. Season with salt and pepper.

Serves eight

Cheese and Basil Risotto with White Wine

A versatile side dish, wonderful with chicken.

1 tablespoon olive oil
3 tablespoons butter
¾ cup finely chopped white
    onion
2 garlic cloves, minced
2 cups uncooked arborio rice

5½ cups chicken broth
¾ cup dry white wine, such as
    chardonnay
¾ cup grated Parmesan cheese
½ cup thinly sliced fresh basil
    (see Chiffonade, page 217)

Heat the oil and butter in a heavy medium saucepan. Add the onion and sauté until tender. Add the garlic and sauté for 1 minute. Add the rice and sauté for 3 minutes. Stir in ½ cup of the broth. Cook for 20 minutes or until the rice is tender and creamy, adding the remaining broth and then the wine gradually and cooking until each addition of liquid is absorbed, stirring constantly. Add the cheese and basil and stir until the cheese melts.

Serves six

Ravishing Rice

Long grain rice is four to five times as long as it is wide. The grains stay separate when cooked, so they are light and fluffy. It is recommended for curries, pilafs, and paella.

Short grain rice is almost round. The grains are softer and stick together, so it's great for sushi and rice pudding.

Arborio rice is a short pearly grain from Italy's Po Valley. It gradually absorbs hot broth when cooked and patiently stirred for 45 minutes. This superior variety is used for making risotto.

Basmati rice is a long, tender, and aromatic grain from India and Pakistan. It is also grown in Texas. Its distinctive nutty taste makes it a perfect choice for curries and pilafs.

Brown rice is the unpolished grain. It takes longer to cook than white and has a dense, nutty flavor. It is valued for the nutritious bran it retains. Look for quick-cooking forms, which are becoming more readily available.

Desserts

East Meets West

There's something enchanting about drinking tea under a canopy of trees at the water's edge. Here a gentle breeze carries the fragrance of night jasmine ready to open. The mist from a nearby waterfall sparkles like a bejeweled bridal veil draped over the rocks. Its beauty is a natural complement to the antique lace handkerchiefs brought out of the armoire to act as today's serviettes.

This might be the very special occasion of your best friend's birthday. Or perhaps you and another dear friend are lucky enough to have your mothers in town on the same weekend. What a perfect setting to trade childhood stories with child-rearing ones. Today could also be the day your daughter is telling the family of her engagement. Or maybe it's a bridal shower for your favorite niece. You can count a lifetime of these special moments on your fingers, so why not make them as lovely as possible? Guests will delight in the daydream that they, too, could make this a tradition.

You could be on the veranda or under a canopy on the terrace. Even a small balcony overlooking the river would assure that the flavor of this peaceful setting came through if you brought out your best collections.

A must for tea time is a three-tiered caddy. This one is filled with Celestial Sugar Cookies (page 48) with edible flowers and Chocolate Mint Melt-Aways (page 255). You could buy chocolate and pastel-colored petits fours or other delicacies from a wonderful little pastry shop if your time is at a premium. A bowl of strawberries adds balance and color. Pedestal cake plates are also a regal touch for any dessert table. The Toasted Coconut Cake (page 251)

Morikami Park, a Japanese garden and museum in neighboring Delray Beach, is the setting for this enchanting tea party under the trees. Upon her guests' arrival, this hostess thought to offer them a scroll that details the ritual of the Japanese Tea Ceremony. She attached the scroll to a special packet of Japanese teas and pampered her guests with delicacies displayed on the finest tableware.

seems to float on its candlewick Depression glass stand, while the Chocolate Turtle Tart (page 271) is in the center of things resting on a silver pedestal. Little cookie sticks and sugar cubes are placed in crystal glasses.

A Room with a View

Since the party is outside, look to nature for embellishment ideas, and decorate with leaves and flowers. They are the perfect transition from indoors to out.

East meets West on the table not only in the orchids atop the botanical-patterned, soft mint floral fabric, but also in the choice of the ivory and sterling cake serving set. To accent the eclectic mixing of East and West, add CDs of Japanese music and gradually switch over to Renaissance melodies.

This hostess collects beautiful teacups from all over the world. Today she can use them all. Not only can people enjoy looking at the different colors and shapes of the top-drawer china all at once, but everyone can remember whose cup is whose, since no two are alike.

Fruit Tea (page 262) is a treat to lavish on your guests. The pitcher can be kept cool with a ring of ice-covered roses. Just fill the mold with distilled water one-third of the way up, add the flowers, and freeze. With the first layer frozen, add cold water and flowers to form the second layer, allow to freeze, and repeat the process a third time. If you try to freeze the mold all at once, the flowers will float to the top, rather than being scattered throughout.

Edible flowers, pears, and peaches garnish each glass. Watch the flowers blossom as the ice melts. Sticks of crystallized sugar in a silver creamer are a delightful way to sweeten any glass.

Perhaps this tea was set for the ballet company's costume preview, or it's a thank-you tea for a gala fund-raiser. Either way, it may be an ideal time to ask children twelve and older to help serve. Participating even at a young age builds social graces and fosters creativity and confidence. Smaller children can be asked to help hand out the favors. Ten-year-olds may not be old enough to pour, but might pass a tray of scones or dish of straw-berries as the grownups are visiting. Just practice with them in advance. You can also involve the children in filling a dish of mints and arranging the lemons and flower petals. The older ones can help arrange the desserts and tea sandwiches.

As the time to say good-bye nears, favor your guests with real silver spoons dipped in chocolate by the best chocolatier (pages 244 and 245). For an intimate gathering, place them on a beautiful china plate sprinkled with rose petals; if the gathering is large, keep them in a spooner.

With an Artful Hand

Once you choose a theme, try to read everything about the era that you can find. This will help inspire a truly original invitation that will capture the recipient's imagination so guests look forward to your special day. If you can offer the promise of transporting them back to a magical point in time, guests will find a way to get there.

This hostess tried her hand at Japanese haiku, verse that uses five syllables on the first line, seven on the second, and five again on the third. She penned the Japanese symbol for, "o cha," meaning "tea" on the front of cream parchment paper in thick black ink, and inside she included a story on the origins of tea.

What Else Is Brewing?

If this is a Fall day, consider a tea-tasting using Majolica-style teapots. Earl Grey, English Breakfast, Orange Pekoe, and Celyon are the tried and true teas. First-Flush Darjeeling, grown high in the Himalayas, is often referred to as the champagne of teas. Keemun teas from China are dramatic for their red color. Formosa Oolong and Lapsang Souchong, also from China, round out the selection for a small gathering. Let each guest take a card and rate the tea. Then ask each to turn over their saucer. The person with the winning tea labeled on the back will receive a basket of teas from around the world. All guests also could go home with a special tea cup.

Raise the dessert offerings on pedestals of different heights. You can then tuck little extras underneath for interest and still have some space to see the tabletop. Ivory-accented serving pieces and beautiful orchids gently remind guests of their Eastern-inspired setting.

Menu

Apple Cinnamon Cannoli

Italy's answer to America's apple pie.

Vanilla Crème Anglaise
1½ cups heavy cream
1 vanilla bean, split lengthwise
3 egg yolks
3 tablespoons sugar

Cannoli
½ cup raisins
½ cup dark rum
3 tablespoons butter

4 Granny Smith apples, peeled,
    cored, cut into ½-inch pieces
    or sliced
¼ cup packed dark brown sugar
3 tablespoons lemon juice
½ teaspoon cinnamon
½ teaspoon allspice
6 sheets phyllo dough
3 tablespoons butter, melted
2 tablespoons confectioners' sugar

For the vanilla crème, scald the cream with the vanilla bean in a saucepan. Remove from the heat, cover and let stand for 20 minutes. Remove the vanilla bean, rinse and save for another use.

Beat the egg yolks and sugar in a medium bowl until pale yellow. Whisk ¼ cup of the hot cream into the egg yolks; whisk the egg yolks into the hot cream. Cook over medium heat for 10 minutes or until the mixture coats a wooden spoon, stirring constantly. Pour through a fine strainer into a bowl. Whisk for 1 minute. Chill for 3 hours or longer.

For the cannoli, combine the raisins and rum in a small bowl. Let stand for 30 minutes or longer. Drain, discarding the rum.

Melt 3 tablespoons butter in a large sauté pan. Add the apples and sauté for 5 to 7 minutes or until tender. Add the brown sugar, lemon juice, cinnamon, allspice and raisins. Cook until the apples are tender. Transfer the mixture to a bowl and cool for 1 hour or longer.

Place 3 sheets of the phyllo on a work surface, leaving the remaining sheets covered with a dampened towel. Brush melted butter on the first sheet. Spread about ½ cup of the apple mixture along the short side of the sheet, starting 2 inches in from the edge. Roll up tightly. Brush melted butter on the second sheet. Place the filled roll on the edge of the second buttered sheet and roll them together. Brush melted butter on the third sheet. Place the filled roll on the edge of the third buttered sheet and roll them together. Repeat the procedure with the remaining ingredients. Place both rolls on a nonstick baking sheet and brush the tops with melted butter.

Bake at 375 degrees for 7 to 10 minutes or until golden brown. Cool for 5 minutes. Sift the confectioners' sugar on top of each cannoli and slice with a serrated knife. Serve hot with the vanilla crème .

Note: Purchased cannoli shells can be used instead of phyllo.

Serves four

Banana Chocolate Won Tons

Take the Red Bowl's slow boat to China with these favorites.

2 ripe bananas
8 ounces white chocolate, chopped
1 egg
1 tablespoon water

24 won ton wrappers
2 cups vegetable oil
3 tablespoons sugar
1 teaspoon cinnamon

Mash the bananas in a bowl with a fork. Add the chopped white chocolate and stir to combine.

Beat the egg with the water in a small bowl. Brush the edges of the won ton wrappers with the egg mixture. Place the banana mixture on each wrapper. Fold into halves diagonally to enclose the filling and press the edges to seal. Deep-fry the won tons in the heated oil until crisp and golden brown. Drain on paper towels.

Combine the sugar and cinnamon in a small bowl. Toss the warm won tons in the cinnamon sugar to coat. Serve warm with vanilla ice cream and caramel sauce.

Serves six

Praline Bananas Foster

The only sound you'll hear after serving this dessert is the sound of spoons scraping the bottoms of the bowls!

$1/4$ cup packed dark brown sugar
$1^1/2$ teaspoons cornstarch
$1/2$ cup evaporated skim milk
2 tablespoons chopped pecans, toasted
$1/4$ cup praline liqueur or dark rum

2 teaspoons reduced-calorie margarine
1 teaspoon vanilla extract
2 medium firm ripe bananas
2 cups low-fat vanilla frozen yogurt

Combine the brown sugar and cornstarch in a medium saucepan. Stir in the milk gradually. Cook over medium heat until the mixture comes to a boil and thickens slightly, stirring constantly. Remove from the heat and add the pecans, liqueur, margarine and vanilla. Stir until the margarine melts.

Cut each banana into halves crosswise and then lengthwise. Place the bananas in a heavy skillet and add the praline mixture. Carefully flambé the bananas.

Spoon $1/2$ cup frozen yogurt into each of 4 dessert dishes. Top each with 2 banana slices and 3 tablespoons of praline sauce.

Serves four

To Flambé

Flambéing a dish with brandy or liqueur must be done with great care. Always remove the dish from the heat source before lighting. It is best to use long matches and to take care not to lean over the dish while igniting.

Brownie-Bottom Crème Brûlée

Your guests will be pleasantly surprised when they discover the fudge brownie bottom to this classic vanilla bean crème brûlée. It satisfies all your dessert cravings in one bite!

Brownies

4^1/2 ounces bittersweet or
    semisweet chocolate
^{1}/4 cup (^{1}/2 stick) unsalted butter
^{1}/2 cup sugar
^{1}/2 teaspoon vanilla extract
^{1}/4 teaspoon salt
1 large egg
^{1}/4 cup flour
^{3}/4 cup chopped pecans

Custard

3 cups whipping cream
^{1}/2 vanilla bean, split lengthwise
6 large egg yolks
6 tablespoons sugar
8 teaspoons sugar

For the brownies, melt the chocolate and butter in a small saucepan over low heat. Stir until smooth and transfer to a large bowl. Cool for 10 minutes.

Whisk the sugar, vanilla and salt into the chocolate mixture. Whisk in the egg. Add the flour and stir just until blended. Fold in the pecans. Pour into a greased and floured 8-inch square baking pan. Smooth the top.

Bake at 350 degrees for 20 minutes or until the brownie layer is set and pulls away from the edges of the pan. Cool on a wire rack. Cut into 9 squares.

For the custard, pour the cream into a medium saucepan. Scrape the seeds from the vanilla bean into the cream and add the bean. Bring to a simmer and remove from the heat. Discard the vanilla bean. Whisk the egg yolks and the 6 tablespoons of sugar in a large bowl. Whisk a small amount of the hot mixture into the egg yolks; whisk the egg yolks into the hot mixture. Cook over medium-low heat for 2 minutes or until the mixture coats the spoon, stirring constantly; do not boil. Pour through a fine strainer into a bowl.

Press 1 brownie square into the bottom of each of eight ^{3}/4-cup custard cups; there will be 1 brownie left over. Pour the custard into the cups.

Arrange the custard cups in a large baking pan. Add enough hot water to the pan to come halfway up the custard cups. Cover the pan loosely with foil. Bake at 325 degrees for 35 minutes or until the custard is softly set. Remove the custards to a wire rack to cool. Chill for 3 hours or longer.

Arrange the custards on a heavy large baking sheet. Sprinkle 1 teaspoon of sugar on top of each custard. Broil for 2 minutes or until golden brown, watching closely to avoid burning. Chill for 3 to 6 hours.

Serves eight

Pear Napoleon with Apple Cider Cream

They wouldn't have run him out of France if this had been served–a favorite from Gigi's.

Pastry Cream
2 cups milk
1 vanilla bean, split
6 egg yolks
¼ cup cornstarch

Red Wine Poached Pears
2 cups water
2 cups cabernet sauvignon or
other dry red wine

2 lemons, cut into halves
¼ cup sugar
2 pears, peeled, cut into halves,
cored

Pear Napoleons
4 (4-inch) squares puff pastry
1 cup whipping cream, whipped
confectioners' sugar
Apple Cider Cream (at right)

For the pastry cream, scald the milk with the vanilla bean in a saucepan. Remove the vanilla bean. Beat the egg yolks and cornstarch in a medium bowl until pale yellow. Whisk half the hot milk into the egg yolks; whisk the egg yolks into the hot milk in the saucepan. Cook over medium heat until thickened in the center, whisking constantly. Pour into a bowl. Cover and chill until serving time.

For the pears, heat the water, wine, lemons and sugar in a large deep saucepan. Add the pears. Place a heavy plate on top of the pears to keep them submerged in the poaching liquid. Poach the pears until slightly softened, piercing frequently with a fork to test for doneness. Remove pears and chill until serving time. Discard the poaching liquid.

For the Napoleons, bake the puff pastry squares using the package directions. Remove to a wire rack to cool. Split the squares into halves and spread the bottoms with the pastry cream. Slice the chilled poached pears and arrange on top. Cover with whipped cream and the pastry top halves. Sprinkle with confectioners' sugar.

Spoon Apple Cider Cream onto 4 dessert plates. Place the Napoleons in the cream.

Serves four

Apple Cider Cream

Boil 1 cup apple cider in a saucepan over medium heat until reduced to ¼ cup. Combine with ¼ cup sugar and 4 egg yolks in a double boiler. Cook over simmering water for 4 to 5 minutes or until slightly thickened, whisking constantly. Cool and stir in ¾ cup sour cream.

Sugar Cookie Crust

Mix $3/4$ cup flour with $2^1/2$ tablespoons sugar in a bowl. Add 1 lightly beaten egg, $1/4$ cup softened butter and $1/2$ teaspoon vanilla extract and mix well to form a dough. Press evenly into the bottom of a greased 9-inch springform pan. Bake at 350 degrees for 12 to 15 minutes or until light browned. Cool on a wire rack.

Caramel-Drenched Cheesecake

This is a classic cheesecake covered in a buttery caramel sauce.

Graham Cracker Crust
$1^1/2$ cups graham cracker crumbs
6 tablespoons ($3/4$ stick) unsalted
  butter, melted
$1/4$ cup packed dark brown sugar

Cheesecake Filling
32 ounces cream cheese, softened
$1^1/2$ cups sugar
5 large eggs, at room temperature
$2^1/2$ teaspoons vanilla extract
2 teaspoons fresh lemon juice

Caramel Sauce
$1^1/4$ cups sugar
$1/3$ cup water
1 cup heavy cream
$1/2$ cup (1 stick) unsalted butter,
  softened
1 teaspoon vanilla extract
$3/4$ cup whipping cream
2 tablespoons sugar
3 (1.4-ounce) toffee candy bars,
  broken into pieces

For the crust, combine the graham cracker crumbs, butter and brown sugar in a medium bowl. Press the mixture over the bottom and 1 inch up the side of a lightly buttered 9-inch springform pan. Chill for 1 hour.

For the filling, beat the cream cheese in a large mixing bowl until light. Add the sugar and beat until smooth. Beat in the eggs 1 at a time. Add the vanilla and lemon juice and beat until blended. Pour into the chilled crust. Bake at 350 degrees for $1^1/4$ hours or until cheesecake has risen $1/2$ inch over the rim and the center is nearly set when the pan is shaken. Remove to a wire rack to cool; the cheesecake will fall as it cools and sink in the center. Cover and chill for 6 to 24 hours.

For the sauce, heat $1^1/4$ cups sugar and water in a heavy medium saucepan over low heat, stirring until the sugar dissolves. Increase the heat and boil without stirring for 8 minutes or until the mixture is a rich caramel color, swirling the pan occasionally and washing down the sides with a brush dipped in cold water. Reduce the heat to very low and add 1 cup heavy cream. Stir until smooth. Cut the butter into small pieces and stir into the mixture. Let cool slightly and stir in the vanilla.

Loosen the cheesecake from the side of the springform pan with a small sharp knife. Place on a serving plate and remove the side of the pan. Pour $2/3$ cup of caramel sauce on the center of the cheesecake. Chill the cheesecake for 2 to 8 hours. Cover the remaining caramel sauce and reserve at room temperature.

Whip $3/4$ cup whipping cream with 2 tablespoons sugar in a medium mixing bowl until firm peaks form. Spoon the whipped cream into a pastry bag fitted with a star tip. Pipe the cream around the edge of the cheesecake. Arrange the toffee pieces in the whipped cream. Chill until serving time. Serve with the remaining caramel sauce.

Serves eight

Cinderella Cheesecake

Peanut buttery cream cheese on a fudge brownie crust—
guaranteed to disappear before midnight!

Brownie Crust
3 (1-ounce) squares unsweetened
    chocolate, chopped
$1/4$ cup ($1/2$ stick) unsalted butter
$1/2$ cup sifted flour
$1/8$ teaspoon salt
$1/8$ teaspoon baking powder
2 large eggs
1 cup packed brown sugar
$1 1/2$ teaspoons vanilla extract
$1/2$ ounce bittersweet or semisweet
    chocolate, finely chopped

Peanut Butter Filling
12 ounces cream cheese, softened
1 cup packed brown sugar
3 large eggs
$1/2$ cup sour cream
$1 1/3$ cups creamy peanut butter

Peanut Butter Topping
$3/4$ cup sour cream
2 teaspoons sugar
$1/2$ cup creamy peanut butter

For the crust, melt the unsweetened chocolate and butter in a small heavy saucepan over low heat. Remove from the heat and cool. Combine the flour, salt and baking powder in a small bowl. Beat the eggs and brown sugar in a medium mixing bowl for 4 minutes or until the batter forms thin ribbons when beaters are lifted. Beat in the melted chocolate, vanilla and chopped chocolate. Add the dry ingredients and mix until just blended.

Spread 1 cup of the brownie batter over the bottom of a greased and floured 9-inch springform pan. Bake at 350 degrees on the center oven rack for 17 minutes or until firm. Cool in the freezer for 15 minutes. Spread the remaining brownie batter evenly around the side of the springform pan with a knife, sealing it to the baked bottom crust.

For the filling, process the cream cheese and brown sugar in a food processor until smooth. Add the eggs and sour cream and pulse until smooth, scraping the sides as needed. Add the peanut butter and pulse until smooth. Pour in to the prepared springform pan; the filling will not be as high as the brownie batter. Bake at 350 degrees for 30 minutes or until the center is nearly set and the brownie forms a 1-inch ring around the filling.

For the topping, mix the sour cream and sugar in a small bowl. Spread to within $3/4$ inch of the edge of the hot cheesecake. Bake for 1 minute longer. Place on a wire rack and loosen from the side of the pan with a small sharp knife. Cool completely. Spoon the peanut butter into a pastry bag fitted with a star tip. Pipe tiny rosettes around the edge of the sour cream. Chill for 30 minutes or until the rosettes are firm. Chill, covered with foil, for 8 to 24 hours. Place on a serving plate and remove the side of the pan.

Note: Do not use old-fashioned or freshly ground peanut butter.
Serves twelve

Shortcut Crusts

Crusts for cheesecakes can be made the easy way. Just slice an 8-ounce tube of refrigerated cookie dough using the package directions and arrange the slices in the springform pan, starting at the outer edge and working toward the center. Press the dough to cover evenly and bake at 350 degrees for 12 to 15 minutes or until light brown. A chocolate crust can be made by crushing 11 chocolate sandwich cream cookies and mixing the crumbs with 3 tablespoons melted butter or margarine. Press the mixture firmly over the bottom of a greased 9-inch springform pan.

White Chocolate Macadamia Cheesecake

Prepare 1 of the crusts suggested on pages 240 and 241. Press into a 9-inch springform pan and bake as suggested. Prepare the Key Lime Filling (at right), omitting the rum and Key lime juice and bake as directed. Cool completely. For Macadamia Caramel Topping, combine 3 cups sugar, 1 cup water and $1/2$ cup (1 stick) butter in a heavy saucepan. Cook over low heat until golden brown. Add $1^1/2$ cups heavy cream and bring to a boil. Remove from the heat and stir in 1 cup toasted chopped macadamias. Cool for 5 minutes and pour over the cheesecake.

Key Lime White Chocolate Cheesecake

If you can't be in Key West, travel there with this tart cheesecake.

Chocolate Crust
$1^1/2$ cups finely crushed chocolate wafer cookies
5 tablespoon unsalted butter, melted

Key Lime Filling
8 ounces white chocolate, finely chopped
$1/2$ cup heavy cream
24 ounces cream cheese, softened
$1^1/2$ cups sugar
4 large eggs, at room temperature
$1/3$ cup fresh Key lime juice
1 teaspoon vanilla extract
$1/4$ cup white rum (optional)

For the crust, combine the cookie wafer crumbs and butter in a medium bowl until well mixed. Press the crumbs evenly into the bottom and up the side of a lightly buttered 10-inch springform pan. Chill for 1 hour.

For the filling, combine the white chocolate and cream in the top of a double boiler. Heat over hot water until the chocolate melts, stirring frequently. Cool for 10 minutes, stirring occasionally.

Beat the cream cheese and sugar at high speed in a large mixing bowl for 1 minute or until light and fluffy. Add the cooled white chocolate mixture and beat until well blended. Beat in the eggs 1 at a time. Add the lime juice, vanilla and rum and beat until blended.

Pour into the chilled crust. Bake at 350 degrees on the center oven rack for 45 to 50 minutes or until barely set in the center. Place on a wire rack and loosen from the side of the pan with a small sharp knife. Cool completely. Chill the cheesecake for 8 hours or longer. Place on a serving plate and remove the side of the pan.

Serves ten

Peanut Butter Mousse Torte

A chocolate cake base spread with creamy peanut butter mousse and served with a rich toffee sauce . . . true decadence from Café Maxx.

Chocolate Cake Base
10$\frac{1}{2}$ ounces semisweet
    chocolate
11 tablespoons unsalted butter
$\frac{1}{4}$ cup sugar
4 large eggs

Peanut Crunch
10 ounces milk chocolate
1 cup creamy peanut butter
2 tablespoons vegetable oil
1 package Pirouline cookies,
    crushed

Peanut Butter Mousse Filling
1$\frac{1}{2}$ cups packed brown sugar
1 cup (2 sticks) unsalted butter,
    softened
2 cups creamy peanut butter
3 large eggs

Peanut Butter Toffee Sauce
$\frac{3}{4}$ cup packed brown sugar
$\frac{1}{2}$ cup (1 stick) butter
1 cup creamy peanut butter
1$\frac{1}{2}$ cups plus 1 tablespoon heavy
    cream

For the cake, melt the chocolate and butter in a saucepan over very low heat, stirring until the chocolate is melted and the mixture is smooth. Remove from the heat and set aside to cool.

Beat the sugar and eggs in a bowl at high speed for 8 minutes or until very stiff and more than tripled in volume. Fold in the chocolate mixture gently until well combined. Pour into a 9-inch springform pan that has been coated with nonstick cooking spray. Bake at 325 degrees on the center oven rack for 30 to 35 minutes or until firm in the center. Set on a wire rack and cool completely; the cake will sink as it cools.

For the peanut crunch, combine the chocolate, peanut butter and oil in a saucepan. Cook over low heat until the chocolate and peanut butter melt, stirring to mix well. Stir in the cookie crumbs. Spread over the cooled cake base, covering completely.

For the filling, beat the brown sugar in a bowl until smooth. Add the eggs 1 at a time, beating for 5 minutes or until doubled in volume. Add the butter and peanut butter and beat at low speed until well mixed. Pour over the crunch layer. Chill, covered, in the refrigerator for 8 hours or longer.

For the sauce, combine the brown sugar, butter, peanut butter and cream in a large saucepan. Cook over low heat until the mixture begins to bubble, stirring constantly to blend well.

To serve, loosen the side of the pan with a small sharp knife and remove the side. Cut the torte with a sharp knife rinsed in warm water. Spoon the sauce onto dessert plates. Top with a slice of the torte.

Note: The torte may be frozen if your prefer. Allow it to stand in the refrigerator before serving. The sauce can be made in advance and reheated to serve.

Serves twelve

White Chocolate Sauce

Bring 2 cups heavy cream to a boil in a 2$\frac{1}{2}$-quart saucepan. Pour over 8 ounces broken white chocolate in a stainless steel bowl. Cover tightly with plastic wrap and let stand for 5 minutes. Whisk until smooth. Cool in an ice water bath for 15 minutes or to 40 to 45 degrees. Stir in $\frac{1}{2}$ teaspoon vanilla extract. Store, covered, in the refrigerator for up to 5 days.

Chocolate

When you buy chocolate, you are paying for the quality of the beans from which it was made and the texture of the finished product. Look for chocolate that is shiny on the outside. It should have a good snap when you break it and uniform color and texture throughout. It should melt like butter on the tongue and have a pleasant lingering flavor.

Because of its high fat content, chocolate picks up odors easily. It should be stored in a cool dry place away from anything with a strong odor, such as onions.

It is best to find a favorite brand of chocolate that is consistent in quality and stick with it. Different brands of chocolate vary considerably in taste and texture.

White chocolate is not true chocolate. It is usually a mixture of sugar, cocoa butter, milk solids, lecithin, and vanilla. If cocoa butter is not on the label, the product is confectionery coating, not white chocolate.

White Chocolate Mousse Torte

A sophisticated, yet easy-to-make, dessert with a delicious Oreo cookie crust. Sweet dreams!

Oreo Crust
24 Oreo cookies
$1/4$ cup ($1/2$ stick) unsalted butter, melted
$3/4$ cup heavy cream
8 (1-ounce) squares semisweet chocolate, chopped

White Chocolate Filling
1 pound imported white chocolate, chopped
1 cup heavy cream
1 tablespoon unflavored gelatin
$1/4$ cup water
2 cups whipping cream, chilled
1 teaspoon vanilla extract

Garnish
chopped Oreo cookies

For the crust, crush the Oreo cookies to fine crumbs in a food processor. Add the melted butter and process to combine. Press the crumb mixture over the bottom of a buttered 10-inch springform pan.

Bring the cream to a simmer in a medium heavy saucepan. Reduce the heat to low and add the chocolate. Heat until the chocolate is melted, whisking until the mixture is smooth. Pour over the crust. Chill in the refrigerator.

For the filling, combine the white chocolate and 1 cup cream in the top of a double boiler. Heat over simmering water until the chocolate is melted, stirring until the mixture is smooth. Cool to lukewarm.

Sprinkle the gelatin over $1/4$ cup water in a small heavy saucepan and let stand for 10 minutes to soften. Heat over low heat until the gelatin dissolves, stirring to mix well. Combine with 2 cups cream and vanilla in a large mixing bowl. Beat until soft peaks form. Fold in the white chocolate mixture and pour into the crust. Chill for 6 hours or until set.

Place on a serving plate and loosen from the side of the pan with a small sharp knife; remove the side of the pan. Garnish the top with chopped Oreo cookies.

Serves ten

Bow-tied with dainty silver tea roses, these silver spoons dipped in chocolate make for a memorable party favor. (See page 248.)
Look for odd lots of spoons at antique shows and flea markets. Scalloped and violin-shaped spoons are wonderful finds.
Add rose petals for color on any English bone china plate. This Spode plate is bordered in silver, but you could set
yours atop a silver tray or charger. Just keep the chocolate chilled until your guests' departure.

Frozen Lemon Mousse

The perfect dessert that can be stored in the freezer for up to two weeks.

4 egg yolks
$^1/_2$ cup fresh lemon juice
$^1/_4$ cup sugar
$1^1/_2$ tablespoons grated lemon
    zest
4 egg whites
$^1/_8$ teaspoon cream of tartar

$^1/_8$ teaspoon salt
$^3/_4$ cup sugar
$1^1/_2$ cups whipping cream

Garnish
fresh raspberries or blueberries
sprigs of fresh mint

Combine the egg yolks, lemon juice, $^1/_4$ cup sugar and lemon zest in a large bowl and mix well.

Beat the egg whites in a medium mixing bowl until foamy. Add the cream of tartar and salt and beat until soft peaks form. Add $^3/_4$ cup sugar gradually and beat until stiff and glossy. Whip the cream in a bowl until stiff. Fold the egg whites and whipped cream gently into the egg yolk mixture. Spoon into a bowl. Freeze, covered with foil, for 8 hours or longer.

Let the mousse stand in the refrigerator for 1 or 2 hours before serving. Spoon into 12 dessert dishes and garnish with fresh raspberries or blueberries and a sprig of mint.

Serves twelve

Macadamia Nut Crunch Torte

As the saying goes: "Life is uncertain, eat dessert first!"
Make sure this is the one!

2 cups crushed chocolate wafer cookies
6 tablespoons (3/4 stick) unsalted butter, melted
7 ounces macadamias
1 1/2 cups (3 sticks) unsalted butter
1 cup packed brown sugar
11 ounces cream cheese, softened
3/4 cup confectioners' sugar
1/4 cup packed brown sugar
1 cup heavy cream
1 1/3 cups semisweet chocolate chips
1 teaspoon vanilla extract

Mix the cookie wafer crumbs and melted butter in a medium bowl. Press the crumbs evenly over the bottom of an ungreased 9-inch springform pan. Sprinkle with the macadamias.

Melt 1 1/2 cups butter and 1 cup brown sugar in a saucepan. Cook over medium heat until bubbles form. Pour into the prepared springform pan. Bake at 350 degrees for 15 to 20 minutes or until golden brown. Cool in the refrigerator.

Combine the cream cheese, confectioners' sugar and 1/4 cup brown sugar in a bowl. Beat until smooth. Spread in cooled crust; chill in the refrigerator.

Scald the cream in a saucepan. Add the chocolate chips and vanilla; stir until the chocolate is melted and the mixture is smooth. Chill until thick enough to spread.

Place the torte on a serving plate and loosen from the side of the pan with a small sharp knife; remove the side of the pan. Spread the top with the chocolate cream mixture. Chill until serving time.

Serves eight to ten

White Trash

Mix 1/2 package Crispix cereal, 5 ounces pretzel twists, 1/2 can salted peanuts, 1/2 pound "M & M's" Chocolate Candies, 1/4 cup pecans and 1/4 cup raisins in a large bowl. Melt 1 pound white chocolate in a double boiler or microwave (see page 249). Add to the cereal mixture and mix carefully. Spread on waxed paper and let stand until firm.

Chocolate-Covered Spoons

Place 12 ounces semisweet chocolate chips in a microwave-safe bowl. Microwave on High for 1 minute. Whisk until melted and smooth. If not warm enough to melt completely, microwave in 30-second intervals, just until the chocolate is smooth. Immediately dip the bowls of the spoons tip down into the chocolate and place on a waxed paper-lined tray. Let stand at room temperature until firm. (See photograph on page 245.)

Cappuccino Sundaes

Serve these sundaes in edible chocolate bowls for a special presentation!

1/2 cup strong brewed coffee
1/2 cup heavy cream
1/4 cup plus 2 tablespoons packed brown sugar
1/4 teaspoon cinnamon

8 1/2 ounces semisweet chocolate, chopped
3 pints coffee ice cream
3/4 cup chopped Heath bar candy (about 4 1/4 ounces)

Combine the coffee, cream, brown sugar and cinnamon in a small heavy saucepan. Cook over low heat until the sugar dissolves and the mixture comes to a simmer, stirring constantly. Remove from the heat and add the chocolate. Stir until melted and smooth.

Spoon the ice cream into 10 dessert dishes. Spoon the sauce over the top and sprinkle with the candy.

Note: The sauce can be made 1 day ahead. Store, covered, in the refrigerator and rewarm over low heat before serving.

Serves ten

Decadent Ice Cream Cake Dessert

The devil made me eat it!

2 1/4 cups crumbled macaroons
3 cups chocolate ice cream, slightly softened
5 Heath bars, coarsely chopped

4 tablespoons chocolate syrup
3 tablespoons Kahlúa
3 cups vanilla ice cream, slightly softened

Spread 1 1/4 cups of the macaroons in the bottom of an 8-inch springform pan. Spread the chocolate ice cream evenly over the macaroons and sprinkle with 4 of the candy bars. Drizzle with 3 tablespoons of the chocolate syrup and 2 tablespoons of the Kahlúa.

Spread the remaining 1 cup macaroons over the top. Layer the vanilla ice cream, the remaining candy bar, tablespoon of chocolate syrup and tablespoon Kahlúa over the crumbs. Cover and freeze for 8 hours or longer.

Place on a serving plate and remove the side of the springform pan.

Note: Freeze the Heath bars to break easily with a mallet. Substitute chocolate or vanilla wafers for the macaroons or use other flavors of ice cream if preferred.

Serves six

Warm Lemon Pudding Cakes with Marbled Berry Cream

Warning! These are addictive. Serve at your own risk! No one can eat just one of these individually baked cakes with a pudding-like center.

Pudding Cakes
3/4 cup plus 2 tablespoons
    sugar
6 tablespoons (3/4 stick) unsalted
    butter, softened
1 tablespoon grated
    lemon zest
3 large egg yolks
1/3 cup flour
1/3 cup fresh lemon juice
1 1/2 cups whole milk
3 large egg whites
2 tablespoons sugar

Garnish
confectioners' sugar

Marbled Berry Cream
1/2 cup thawed frozen raspberries
    in syrup
3/4 cup chilled whipping cream
2 tablespoons sugar

For the cakes, beat 3/4 cup plus 2 tablespoons sugar, butter and zest in a medium mixing bowl until well blended. Beat in the egg yolks 1 at a time. Beat in the flour and then the lemon juice. Add the milk gradually, beating to form a thin batter; the mixture may appear curdled.

Beat the egg whites in a mixing bowl until soft peaks form. Add 2 tablespoons sugar and beat until stiff but not dry peaks form. Fold into the yolk mixture 1/3 at a time; the mixture will be thin. Spoon into 6 buttered 3/4-cup soufflé dishes or custard cups. Arrange the dishes in a large baking pan. Add enough hot water to the pan to come halfway up the dishes.

Bake at 350 degrees for 25 minutes or until the cakes are puffed and firm to the touch. Transfer the dishes to serving plates and let stand at room temperature for up to 8 hours. Garnish with confectioners' sugar.

For the berry cream, purée the undrained raspberries in a food processor or blender. Strain the purée and discard the seeds. Beat the cream and sugar in a medium bowl until soft peaks form. Drizzle the raspberry purée over the cream and swirl gently into the cream with a knife to form a marbled design. Serve immediately with the pudding cakes or store, covered, in the refrigerator for up to 4 hours.

Serves six

Melting Chocolate

Because it scorches easily, chocolate should be melted slowly over low heat. If using a double boiler, remove the pan from the heat when the chocolate is melted slightly more than halfway and stir until completely smooth. If using a microwave, heat at 50% power. Timing will vary based on wattage and type of chocolate.

If your chocolate begins to clump or harden when mixed with liquid, it can sometimes be corrected by immediately stirring in a little vegetable oil, using a ratio of 1 tablespoon oil to 6 ounces of chocolate.

Designs on Dessert

Sift confectioners' sugar or cocoa onto dessert plates and place the desserts on top. Surround with fresh raspberries.

Arrange mint leaves around the dessert and top with strawberries.

Top a frosted cake with untreated rose petals or pansies and garnish the dessert plates with the same flower.

Use long thin twists of fresh orange or lemon peel made with a vegetable peeler or lemon stripper as a dessert garnish.

Use a squeeze bottle to make a design with liquid chocolate or sauces.

Bourbon Butter-Glazed Cake

Baked in a sheet cake pan and served in squares, this rich, velvety cake, brushed with a buttery bourbon glaze is reminiscent of a rum cake.

Cake
3^1/4 cups flour
^{1}/2 teaspoon baking soda
1 teaspoon salt
1 teaspoon nutmeg
1 cup (2 sticks) unsalted butter, softened
^{1}/4 cup shortening
2^1/4 cups sugar
4 large eggs
1 tablespoon vanilla extract
1 cup milk

Bourbon Butter Glaze
7 tablespoons unsalted butter, cut into pieces
^{1}/2 cup sugar
^{1}/4 teaspoon nutmeg
7 tablespoons bourbon
1^1/2 teaspoons vanilla extract

For the cake, sift the flour, baking soda, salt and nutmeg into a bowl. Cream the butter and shortening at medium speed in a large mixing bowl for 4 to 5 minutes or until light. Add the sugar ^{1}/3 at a time, beating for 1 minute after each addition Add the eggs 1 at a time, beating for 1 minute after each addition. Beat in the vanilla.

Add the dry ingredients alternately with the milk, beginning and ending with the dry ingredients and adding them ^{1}/3 at a time; scrape down the side of the bowl as needed. Spread the batter into a 9x13-inch pan sprayed with nonstick cooking spray; smooth the top of the batter with a spatula. Bake at 350 degrees for 50 minutes or until a wooden pick inserted in the center comes out clean. Cool on a wire rack for 5 minutes.

For the glaze, combine the butter, sugar, nutmeg and bourbon in a small nonreactive saucepan. Cook over medium heat for 10 minutes or until the butter is melted and the sugar is dissolved, stirring frequently. Increase the heat to high and bring the mixture to a boil. Reduce the heat and simmer for 4 to 5 minutes or until the mixture is reduced by ^{1}/4. Strain into a bowl and stir in the vanilla. Spoon over the hot cake gradually, allowing the mixture to be absorbed before adding more. Cool the cake completely and cut into squares.

Serves twenty

Toasted Coconut Cake

An impressive cake—as beautiful as it is delicious—and surprisingly easy.

Cake
2¹/₂ cups flour
1 tablespoon baking powder
¹/₂ teaspoon salt
¹/₂ cup (1 stick) butter, softened
1²/₃ cups sugar
2 teaspoons vanilla extract
3 egg yolks
1¹/₄ cups milk

Coconut Filling
¹/₂ cup sugar
2 tablespoons flour
¹/₄ teaspoon salt
¹/₂ cup water
1 tablespoon butter
1 cup flaked coconut
1 teaspoon vanilla extract

Fluffy White Frosting
1¹/₂ cups sugar
¹/₄ teaspoon cream of tartar
¹/₃ cup water
3 egg whites
1 cup flaked coconut, toasted

For the cake, combine the flour, baking powder and salt in a small bowl. Cream the butter for 30 seconds in a large mixing bowl until light. Add the sugar and vanilla; beat until fluffy. Beat in the egg yolks 1 at a time. Add the dry ingredients alternately with the milk, beating well after each addition. Pour the batter into 2 greased and floured 9-inch round cake pans.

Bake at 350 degrees for 30 to 35 minutes or until a wooden pick inserted in the center comes out clean. Cool in the pans for 10 minutes. Invert onto wire racks to cool completely.

For the filling, combine the sugar, flour and salt in a saucepan. Stir in the water slowly. Cook over medium heat until the mixture is bubbly, stirring constantly. Cook for 1 minute longer. Remove from the heat and stir in the butter, coconut and vanilla. Cool to room temperature.

For the frosting, combine the sugar, cream of tartar and water in a saucepan. Cook over medium heat until the sugar dissolves, stirring constantly. Cook to 242 degrees on a candy thermometer; do not stir.

Beat the egg whites in a bowl until stiff peaks form. Pour the hot syrup gradually into the beaten egg whites, beating constantly at high speed until stiff peaks form.

Spread the filling between the layers of the cake. Spread the frosting over the top and side and sprinkle with the toasted coconut.

Serves twelve

Cutting a Cake

For a clean well-defined cut, heat the blade of a thin sharp knife—either serrated or straight-edged—by running it under hot water and drying it before cutting. A serrated edge with small compact teeth produces cleaner cuts. Serrated edges work well with angel food cakes and dental floss works well with cheesecakes.

Fabulous Fudge Cake

Sophisticated, yet unpretentious; rich, moist and delicious.

Cake
2 cups flour
2 cups sugar
$^1/_2$ teaspoon salt
1 cup (2 sticks) margarine
1 cup water
1 tablespoon baking cocoa
2 eggs
1 teaspoon baking soda
$^1/_2$ cup buttermilk
1 teaspoon vanilla extract

Marshmallow Fudge Frosting
$^1/_2$ cup (1 stick) margarine
1 tablespoon baking cocoa
1 cup miniature marshmallows
6 tablespoons milk
1 (1-pound) package
    confectioners' sugar
salt to taste
1 teaspoon vanilla extract

For the cake, sift the flour, sugar and salt into a large bowl. Combine the margarine, water and cocoa in a saucepan. Bring to a boil over medium heat, stirring to mix well. Pour over the dry ingredients and mix well. Beat the eggs in a small bowl and stir in the baking soda, buttermilk and vanilla. Add to the cocoa mixture and mix well. Pour into a 9x13-inch cake pan. Bake at 350 degrees for 25 minutes.

For the frosting, melt the margarine and cocoa in a saucepan over low heat. Add the marshmallows and heat until melted, stirring to blend well. Remove from the heat and stir in the milk, confectioners' sugar, salt and vanilla. Pour over the warm cake.

Note: You may add nuts to the frosting if desired.

Serves twelve

IN 1997, IN THE PINES AND THE JUNIOR LEAGUE OF BOCA RATON CONTINUED THEIR PARTNERSHIP TO IMPROVE THE LIVES OF FARMWORKER FAMILIES IN OUR COMMUNITY. UNDER THE DIRECTION OF PRESIDENT LISA MULHALL, THE JUNIOR LEAGUE RECEIVED THE ASSOCIATION OF JUNIOR LEAGUES INTERNATIONAL'S BMW COMMUNITY IMPACT MERIT AWARD— RECOGNIZING OUR MEMBERSHIP FOR BEST FULFILLING THE AJLI MISSION OF EFFECTIVE COMMUNITY IMPROVEMENT THROUGH VOLUNTEER LEADERSHIP.

Deep Chocolate Raspberry Cake

The natural affinity of chocolate for raspberry is a sumptuous combination.

Cake
6 (1-ounce) squares semisweet chocolate, chopped
6 (1-ounce) squares unsweetened chocolate, chopped
$^1/_4$ cup water
7 egg yolks
1 cup (2 sticks) butter, softened
$1^1/_2$ cups sugar
$1^1/_2$ teaspoons vanilla extract
1 cup flour, sifted
7 egg whites
$^1/_2$ cup sugar

Chocolate Frosting
$^3/_4$ cup heavy cream
6 (1-ounce) squares semisweet chocolate, chopped

Raspberry Filling
4 ounces frozen raspberries, thawed, drained
3 tablespoons seedless raspberry jam

Garnish
fresh raspberries

For the cake, line the bottoms of two 9-inch cake pans with waxed paper. Combine the semisweet and unsweetened chocolate with the water in a heatproof bowl. Place in a 300-degree oven until the chocolate melts, stirring frequently to blend well. Cool to room temperature. Stir in the egg yolks.

Cream the butter, $1^1/_2$ cups sugar and vanilla at medium speed in a mixing bowl until light and fluffy. Beat in the chocolate mixture. Add the flour and beat at low speed just until moistened.

Beat the egg whites until foamy. Add $^1/_2$ cup sugar and beat until soft peaks form. Fold into the chocolate mixture. Spoon into the prepared cake pans and smooth the tops.

Bake at 300 degrees for 45 minutes or until a wooden pick inserted in the center comes out with moist crumbs. Cool in the pans on wire racks. Remove from the pans.

For the frosting, bring the cream just to a simmer in a saucepan. Stir in the chocolate and remove from the heat. Stir until mixture is smooth. Place plastic wrap directly on the surface. Chill until thick enough to spread.

For the filling, mix the thawed raspberries and raspberry jam in a bowl. Spread between the cake layers. Spread the frosting over the top and side. Garnish with fresh raspberries.

Serves twelve to sixteen

Cocoa Creations

Dust the greased cake pan with cocoa powder instead of flour to bake a dark-colored cake. This eliminates the hazy white film of flour on the cake and provides a dark uniform color. For a decorative touch, sift a generous amount of confectioners' sugar over the top of a cake. Place a stencil on top and redust with unsweetened baking cocoa.

Raspberry Sauce

Combine 12 ounces thawed dry-pack frozen raspberries, $^1/_3$ cup sugar, $^1/_4$ cup raspberry liqueur and 1 teaspoon fresh lemon juice in a food processor container and process for 30 to 45 seconds or until smooth. Strain into a small nonreactive bowl. Chill, covered, for 1 hour or longer. Store in the refrigerator for up to 2 weeks.

Grilled Pound Cake

Cut a pound cake into $1/2$-inch slices and brush both sides with melted butter. Grill for 30 seconds on each side or until lightly toasted. Serve with sliced fresh fruit and chocolate sauce, white chocolate sauce (page 243), or raspberry sauce (page 253).

Fallen Chocolate Soufflé Cakes

These soufflés are a favorite at Café Maxx.

1 cup (2 sticks) butter
8 (1-ounce) squares ounces bittersweet chocolate
6 eggs

10 ounces packed light brown sugar
3 ounces baking cocoa

Melt the butter and chocolate in a double boiler over hot water. Beat the eggs in a large mixing bowl until pale yellow and foamy. Sift in the brown sugar and baking cocoa. Add the chocolate mixture and stir until thickened. Spoon into 6 buttered and sugared 1-cup ramekins.

Bake at 300 degrees for 20 to 25 minutes or until the edges are dry but the centers are still soft. Let cool for 20 to 30 minutes; the centers will fall. Unmold from the ramekins or serve in the ramekins. Serve warm with vanilla ice cream and chocolate or raspberry sauce.

Note: The cakes can be made up to 12 hours ahead and chilled. Reheat in a 300-degree oven for 5 to 8 minutes or microwave for 1 to 2 minutes or until warm.

Serves six

Sour Cream Pound Cake

Simple yet satisfying, this traditional cake is still a great favorite.

1 cup (2 sticks) butter, softened
3 cups sugar
6 egg yolks
2 teaspoons vanilla extract
3 cups minus 2 tablespoons flour

$1/4$ teaspoon baking soda
salt to taste
1 cup sour cream
6 egg whites

Cream the butter in a large mixing bowl until light. Add the sugar and beat until fluffy. Beat in the egg yolks 1 at a time. Beat in the vanilla. Sift the flour, baking soda and salt into a small bowl. Add $1/4$ of the dry ingredients alternately with $1/3$ of the sour cream, mixing well after each addition and beginning and ending with the dry ingredients. Beat the egg whites until stiff in a small bowl. Fold into the batter.

Spoon into a greased tube pan. Bake at 300 degrees for 2 hours or until a wooden pick inserted in the center comes out clean. Cool in the pan for 10 minutes. Invert onto a wire rack to cool completely.

Serves twelve

Chocolate Mint Melt Aways

Watch out Girl Scouts! These cookies are outrageously delicious and available all year long.

Cookies
1 cup (2 sticks) butter, softened
2 teaspoons vanilla extract
1/2 teaspoon peppermint extract
1/2 cup plus 2 tablespoons
    confectioners' sugar
2 cups flour

White Chocolate Ganache
1/4 cup plus 2 tablespoons
    heavy cream
2 tablespoons (1/4 stick) unsalted
    butter
9 ounces imported white
    chocolate, chopped
1/4 teaspoon peppermint extract

Chocolate Coating
9 (1-ounce) squares bittersweet
    or semisweet chocolate,
    chopped
1 tablespoon shortening

For the cookies, cream the butter, vanilla and peppermint extract in a mixing bowl until light. Beat in the confectioners' sugar. Beat in half of the flour. Stir in the remaining flour. Spoon into a pastry bag fitted with a large rosette tip or a sealable plastic bag with a 1-inch opening snipped off 1 corner. Squeeze into 2-inch logs on buttered heavy cookie sheets. Bake at 350 degrees for 12 minutes or until the edges are golden brown. Remove to paper towels to cool.

For the ganache, bring the cream and butter to a simmer in a small heavy saucepan over low heat. Add the chocolate and stir until smooth. Stir in the peppermint extract. Chill for 30 minutes or until just firm enough to spread, stirring occasionally. Spread 1 teaspoon of ganache on the flat bottom side of each cookie. Place the cookies ganache side up on foil-lined cookie sheets. Chill for 30 minutes or until the ganache is firm.

For the coating, melt the chocolate and shortening in the top of a double boiler over simmering water, stirring occasionally until smooth. Remove from the heat. Spread 1 teaspoon of the coating on top of the ganache. Place chocolate side up on the foil-lined cookie sheet Repeat with the remaining cookies. Chill for 30 minutes or until the chocolate sets.

Note: These can be made up to 2 weeks ahead. Store in single layers in an airtight container in the refrigerator. Let stand at room temperature for 10 minutes before serving.

Makes three to four dozen

The Ultimate Chocolate Ganache

Break 12 ounces semisweet chocolate, 6 ounces unsweetened chocolate and 4 ounces white chocolate into a stainless steel bowl. Combine 2 cups heavy cream, 1/4 cup unsalted butter and 1/4 cup sugar in a 2 1/2 quart saucepan. Bring to a boil over medium-high heat, stirring to dissolve the sugar. Pour over the chocolates and let stand for 5 minutes. Stir until smooth and cool to room temperature.

Chocolate Snappers

Crunchy chocolate cookies with a snappy hint of cinnamon.

1 cup sugar
³/4 cup shortening
1 egg
¹/4 cup corn syrup
2 (1-ounce) squares unsweetened
   chocolate, melted

1³/4 cups flour
2 teaspoons baking soda
1 teaspoon cinnamon
¹/4 teaspoon salt
sugar

Combine 1 cup sugar, shortening and egg in a large bowl and beat until creamy. Stir in the corn syrup and melted chocolate. Sift the flour, baking soda, cinnamon and salt into a bowl. Add the dry ingredients gradually to the chocolate mixture and mix well. Shape by tablespoonfuls into 1-inch balls. Roll in additional sugar and place on ungreased cookie sheets.

Bake at 350 degrees for 15 minutes. Cool on the cookie sheets for a few minutes. Remove to a wire rack to cool completely.

Makes three dozen

Crunchy Key Lime Cookies

Mouth-watering cookies with a tropical flair, made with the juice and rind of the Key lime–a small yellow lime native to Florida.

¹/2 cup (1 stick) butter or
   margarine, softened
1¹/2 cups confectioners' sugar
1 egg
1 tablespoon Key lime juice

2 teaspoons grated Key lime zest
1 cup flour
1 teaspoon baking powder
¹/4 teaspoon salt
2 cups cornflakes, crushed

Cream the butter and confectioners' sugar in a mixing bowl until light and fluffy. Stir in the egg, Key lime juice and zest; the mixture may appear curdled. Add the flour, baking powder and salt and mix well.

Drop the dough by teaspoonfuls into the cornflakes and turn to coat. Place on ungreased cookie sheets. Bake at 350 degrees for 16 minutes. Remove to a wire rack to cool.

Makes two dozen

Oatmeal Cookies with Chocolate-Covered Raisins

Not just raisins, but CHOCOLATE-covered raisins . . . oh my!

1¼ cups (2½ sticks) margarine,
    softened
¾ cup packed brown sugar
½ cup sugar
1 large egg
1 teaspoon vanilla extract

1½ cups flour
1 teaspoon baking soda
3 cups oats (quick or old-
    fashioned)
1 cup chocolate-covered raisins

Cream the margarine, brown sugar and sugar in a mixing bowl until light and fluffy. Beat in the egg and vanilla. Add the flour and baking soda and mix well. Stir in the oats and raisins. Drop by rounded tablespoonfuls onto ungreased cookie sheets.

Bake at 375 degrees for 8 to 9 minutes for a chewy texture or 10 to 11 minutes for a crisp cookie. Cool on the cookie sheets for 1 minute. Remove to a wire rack to cool. Store in an airtight container.

Makes four dozen

Peanut Butter Chocolate Chipperoos

This is one smart cookie.

6 ounces semisweet chocolate
    chips
1 cup (2 sticks) butter, softened
1 cup sugar
1 cup packed dark brown sugar
½ cup creamy peanut butter
2 eggs, at room temperature

1 teaspoon vanilla extract
2½ cups flour
1 teaspoon baking soda
¼ teaspoon salt
4 ounces white chocolate chips
4 ounces toffee chips

Melt the semisweet chocolate in a double boiler or in the microwave; stir until smooth. Cream the butter in a large mixing bowl until light. Add the sugar, brown sugar and peanut butter gradually and beat until smooth. Beat in the eggs and vanilla. Mix in the flour, baking soda and salt. Stir in the white chocolate chips and toffee chips. Add the melted chocolate and swirl with a spatula to marbleize.

Drop by teaspoonfuls 1 inch apart onto ungreased cookie sheets. Bake at 350 degrees for 10 to 12 minutes. Remove to a wire rack to cool.

Note: Add unmelted chocolate chips with the white chocolate chips for bites instead of stripes of chocolate.

Makes four to five dozen

Freezing Cookie Dough

Form cookie dough into cylinders and wrap well in plastic wrap and foil before freezing. The dough will keep its round form if placed in a glass or plastic tumbler until frozen. Frozen dough will keep up to three months. If cookie dough has been cut into shapes, place in layers separated by wax paper, and store in an airtight container. Cut dough will keep for up to one month.

Designated Brownies

You don't need a "designated driver" after eating these spirited brownies; they just taste like you do!

Triple Chocolate Brownies

6 (1-ounce) squares bittersweet
  chocolate, chopped
2 (1-ounce) squares unsweetened
  chocolate, chopped
3/4 cup (1 1/2 sticks) unsalted
  butter
1 1/2 cups sugar
2 teaspoons vanilla extract
4 eggs
1 cup flour
1 teaspoon salt
6 ounces semisweet chocolate chips
1/4 cup bourbon

Rum Topping

1 cup (2 sticks) butter or
  margarine, softened
3 tablespoons rum
2 cups confectioners' sugar
6 ounces semisweet chocolate
  chips
1 tablespoon shortening

For the brownies, melt the bittersweet chocolate, unsweetened chocolate and butter in a double boiler or in the microwave, stirring until smooth. Cool to lukewarm. Stir in the sugar and vanilla. Stir in the eggs 1 at a time. Add the flour and salt and stir just until combined. Stir in the chocolate chips.

Pour into a greased and floured 9x13-inch baking pan. Bake at 350 degrees for 25 to 30 minutes or until a wooden pick inserted in the center comes out with moist crumbs. Drizzle with the bourbon. Chill in the refrigerator.

For the topping, cream the butter, rum and confectioners' sugar in a bowl until light. Spread on the cooled brownies and chill until firm. Melt the chocolate and shortening in a sealable plastic bag in the microwave. Knead the bag to mix the chocolate. Cut a small hole in the corner and drizzle the chocolate over the brownies. Chill until serving time and cut into bars.

Makes two dozen

IN 1998, UNDER THE DIRECTION OF MICHELLE RUBIN, THE JUNIOR LEAGUE OF BOCA RATON PLANNED, DEVELOPED, AND OPENED THE DOORS TO A FAMILY VISITATION CENTER TO CREATE A HOMELIKE ENVIRONMENT FOR VISITATION OF FAMILY MEMBERS WITH CHILDREN IN FOSTER CARE. FURTHER, THE JUNIOR LEAGUE CONTINUED ITS WORK AT DIXIE MANOR TO ASSIST WITH A SUMMER AND AFTER-SCHOOL PROGRAM FOR SIXTY-FIVE CHILDREN.

Cappuccino Brownies

Brownies all dressed up in their Sunday best! A chocolate and coffee brownie frosted with cream cheese and topped with a mocha glaze.

Brownies

2 tablespoons instant espresso
   powder
1 teaspoon boiling water
8 ounces fine-quality bittersweet
   chocolate, chopped
3/4 cup (1 1/2 sticks) unsalted
   butter, cut into pieces
1 1/2 cups sugar
2 teaspoons vanilla extract
4 large eggs
1 cup flour
1/2 teaspoon salt
1 cup chopped walnuts

Cream Cheese Frosting

8 ounces cream cheese, softened
6 tablespoons (3/4 stick) unsalted
   butter, softened
1 1/2 cups sifted confectioners'
   sugar
1 teaspoon vanilla extract
1 teaspoon cinnamon

Mocha Glaze

1 tablespoon plus 1 1/2 teaspoons
   instant espresso powder
1 tablespoon boiling water
6 ounces fine-quality bittersweet
   chocolate
2 tablespoons (1/4 stick) unsalted
   butter
1/2 cup heavy cream

For the brownies, dissolve the espresso powder in the boiling water in a small cup. Melt the chocolate and butter with the dissolved espresso in a metal bowl set over a pan of barely simmering water, stirring until smooth. Cool to lukewarm. Stir in the sugar and vanilla. Stir in the eggs 1 at a time. Add the flour and salt and stir just until combined. Stir in the walnuts. Pour into a greased and floured 9x13-inch baking pan; smooth the top of the batter.

Bake at 350 degrees for 22 to 25 minutes or until a wooden pick inserted in the center comes out with moist crumbs. Cool in the pan on a wire rack.

For the frosting, beat the cream cheese and butter in a mixing bowl until light and fluffy. Add the confectioners' sugar, vanilla and cinnamon and beat until smooth. Spread evenly over the brownies and chill for 1 hour or until firm.

For the glaze, dissolve the espresso powder in the boiling water in a small cup. Melt the chocolate and butter with the dissolved espresso and the cream in a metal bowl set over a pan of barely simmering water, stirring until smooth. Cool to room temperature. Spread carefully over the frosting layer. Chill, covered, for 3 hours or longer. Cut into bars.

Makes two dozen

Flour Facts

It is important to use the correct form of flour for baking. If you substitute one flour for another, you could significantly change the texture of a dessert. Flour should be stored in an airtight container in a cool dry place.

All-purpose flour is a blend of wheats and can be used for both bread and cakes, although it gives cakes a coarser and heavier texture than cake flour. It has the perfect protein content for pie doughs, making them easy to roll without crumbling or getting tough. Bleached and unbleached flours may be used interchangeably.

Bread flour has the highest protein content of any flour. It is best suited for bread doughs because the extra protein supports the dough as it rises and gives it better texture and shape.

Cake flour has the lowest protein content of any flour and is milled the finest. Very light and soft, it makes light tender cakes and cookies.

Chocolate Bundles

Thaw a sheet of frozen puff pastry for 30 minutes. Roll to a 12-inch square on a lightly floured surface and cut into four 6-inch squares. Place $^1/_4$ cup chocolate chips and 1 tablespoon walnuts in the center of each square. Bring the corners up to enclose the chocolate and walnuts and twist to seal; fan out the corners. Place on an ungreased baking sheet and bake at 425 degrees for 10 to 15 minutes or until golden brown. Let stand for 10 minutes or longer and sprinkle with confectioners' sugar.

Bodacious Bars

Your friends will hoot and holler over this heavenly mixture—no baking required.

Coconut Bars
$^1/_2$ cup (1 stick) butter
$^1/_4$ cup sugar
2 tablespoons baking cocoa
2 teaspoons vanilla extract
$^1/_4$ teaspoon salt
1 egg, lightly beaten
1 cup sliced almonds, toasted, chopped
1$^3/_4$ cups crushed vanilla wafers
$^1/_2$ cup flaked coconut

Chocolate Topping
$^1/_3$ cup butter, softened
egg substitute to equal 1 egg
$^1/_2$ teaspoon vanilla extract
2$^1/_3$ to 3 cups sifted confectioners' sugar
2 (1-ounce) squares milk chocolate

For the bars, combine the butter, sugar, baking cocoa, vanilla, salt and egg in a saucepan. Cook over low heat until the butter melts and the mixture thickens, stirring to mix well. Remove from the heat and stir in the almonds, cookie crumbs and coconut. Press into an ungreased 9-inch square pan. Chill, covered, in the refrigerator.

For the topping, cream the butter at high speed in a medium mixing bowl. Beat in the egg substitute and vanilla. Add the confectioners' sugar gradually and beat until smooth. Spread over the bars. Cover and chill.

Place the chocolate in a sealable plastic bag. Set the bag in hot water until the chocolate melts. Cut a small hole in the corner of the bag and drizzle the chocolate over the bars. Chill until serving time. Cut into bars to serve.

Makes two dozen

Road to Riches Fudge Bars

Your search for a decadently rich dessert is over! Bake these and experience heaven on earth!

Fudge Bars
1/2 cup (1 stick) butter
1 (1-ounce) square unsweetened
    chocolate
1 cup sugar
2 eggs
1 teaspoon vanilla extract
1 cup flour
1 teaspoon baking powder
1/2 to 1 cup chopped nuts

Chocolate Filling
6 ounces cream cheese, softened
1/4 cup (1/2 stick) butter, softened
1/2 cup sugar
2 tablespoons flour
1 egg

1/2 teaspoon vanilla extract
1/4 cup chopped nuts
6 ounces semisweet chocolate
    chips

Marshmallow Topping
2 cups miniature marshmallows
1/4 cup (1/2 stick) butter
1 (1-ounce) square unsweetened
    chocolate
2 ounces cream cheese, softened
1/2 cup milk
1 (1-pound) package
    confectioners' sugar
1 teaspoon vanilla extract

For the bars, melt the butter and chocolate in a large saucepan over low heat. Stir in the sugar, eggs, vanilla, flour, baking powder and nuts and mix well. Spread into a greased and floured 9x13-inch baking pan.

For the filling, beat the cream cheese, butter and sugar in a medium bowl. Add the flour, egg and vanilla and beat until smooth and fluffy. Stir in the nuts. Spread over the chocolate layer. Sprinkle with the chocolate chips. Bake at 350 degrees for 25 to 30 minutes or until a wooden pick inserted in the center comes out clean.

For the topping, sprinkle the marshmallows on the hot baked layer. Bake for 2 minutes longer. Combine the butter, chocolate, cream cheese and milk in a large saucepan over low heat. Cook until smooth, stirring to mix well. Add the confectioners' sugar and vanilla and mix well. Pour over the marshmallows and swirl together with a spatula. Cool on a wire rack and cut into bars.

Makes two dozen

Decorating with Chocolate

To make chocolate curls, allow a bar or block of chocolate to warm slightly by placing it near an oven pilot or in a barely warm oven. Peel curls from the chocolate with a vegetable peeler and chill them until firm. Larger curls can be made by spreading melted chocolate on a smooth flat surface and allowing to stand until firm. Scrape a metal spatula across the chocolate in a smooth slow motion.

For drizzles, pour melted chocolate into a pastry bag or sealable plastic bag; snip a small corner off the bottom of the plastic bag. Drizzle the chocolate on the dessert or serving plate for a dramatic effect.

For chocolate leaves, brush melted chocolate on the backs of clean lemon leaves or other nonpoisonous leaves, and allow to harden. Peel the leaves gently from the chocolate.

Fruit Tea

Simmer 2 cups sugar in $^3/_4$ cup water in a saucepan until the sugar dissolves; cool. Combine 1 quart freshly brewed tea with 3 cups fresh pineapple juice, 2 cups fresh orange juice and $^1/_2$ cup fresh lemon juice in a 1-gallon container. Add the sugar syrup and mix well. Add $^1/_2$ large bottle of ginger ale just before serving. Serve over ice in tall glasses and garnish with fresh mint.

Oatmeal Carmelitas

These drive Boca absolutely loca!

$1^1/_2$ cups flour
$1^1/_2$ cups quick-cooking oats
1 cup packed brown sugar
$^3/_4$ teaspoon baking soda
$^1/_2$ teaspoon salt
1 cup (2 sticks) margarine, melted
6 ounces semisweet chocolate chips
$^1/_2$ cup chopped walnuts
$^3/_4$ cup caramel topping
$^1/_4$ cup flour

Combine $1^1/_2$ cups flour, oats, brown sugar, baking soda and salt in a bowl. Add the melted margarine and stir until crumbly. Press half of the crumb mixture into a 9-inch square baking pan coated with nonstick cooking spray.

Bake at 350 degrees for 10 minutes. Sprinkle with the chocolate chips and walnuts. Combine the caramel topping and $^1/_4$ cup flour in a small bowl. Drizzle over the chocolate and walnuts. Crumble the remaining oats mixture over the top. Bake at 350 degrees for 15 to 20 minutes or until golden brown. Cool on a wire rack. Chill for 4 hours. Cut into 1x2-inch bars to serve.

Makes three dozen

Pretty flowers set the tone for this ultra-feminine tea party. Crystal and silver glimmer in the sunshine as a rose-petal ice ring adds height while cooling the fruit tea. Edible flowers and fruits are frozen inside the ice cubes for a colorful accent. Even the hostess' collection of antique handkerchiefs are individually tied with a grapevine napkin ring and crowned with a delicate flower.

Raspberry Lemon Shortbread Squares

A hint of Spring awaits you in the lemony flavor of this dessert, beautifully accented with fresh raspberries.

Butter Crust
1 cup flour
1/4 cup confectioners' sugar
1/8 teaspoon salt
1/2 cup (1 stick) unsalted
    butter, chilled, cut into
    8 pieces

Raspberry Lemon Filling
1 1/4 cups sugar
3 tablespoons flour
3 large eggs
1/4 cup fresh lemon juice
2 teaspoons grated lemon zest
1/4 cup heavy cream
1 cup fresh raspberries
confectioners' sugar

For the crust, line a 9-inch square baking pan with heavy-duty foil, extending the foil over the sides of the pan; butter the foil. Mix the flour, confectioners' sugar and salt at low speed in a mixing bowl just until blended. Add the butter and mix for 1 minute or until it has the texture of fine crumbs. Press the mixture over the bottom of the prepared pan. Bake at 325 degrees for 25 minutes or until golden brown.

For the filling, whisk the sugar and flour in a large bowl. Add the eggs and whisk until smooth. Stir in the lemon juice and zest. Add the cream and stir until blended. Pour into the crust and arrange the raspberries evenly on top.

Bake at 300 degrees for 45 minutes or until the filling is set. Remove to a wire rack. Loosen the foil from the edge with a small sharp knife. Cool in the pan on a wire rack. Dust with confectioners' sugar when cool. Lift the foil and shortbread out of the pan. Cut into squares and use a wide spatula to slide the squares off the foil. Wrap tightly and chill for up to 3 days. Serve cold.

Makes sixteen squares

IN 1999, THE JUNIOR LEAGUE OF BOCA RATON PUBLISHED *Savor the Moment* WITH PROCEEDS BENEFITING JUNIOR LEAGUE COMMUNITY PROJECTS. UNDER THE DIRECTION OF PRESIDENT DEBBIE ABRAMS, JUNIOR LEAGUE MEMBERS ALSO WORKED TOWARD ESTABLISHING A HOMELESS SHELTER IN SOUTH PALM BEACH COUNTY.

Toffee Cheesecake Temptations

Creamy and rich bite-size cheesecakes. Ideal to serve on a buffet.

$2/3$ cup butter or margarine,
   softened
$3/4$ cup packed brown sugar
2 cups flour
$1/2$ cup chopped pecans
16 ounces cream cheese, softened

$3/4$ cup sugar
2 large eggs
1 tablespoon lemon juice
2 teaspoons vanilla extract
1 (7-ounce) Heath Bar, crushed

Beat the butter at medium speed in a mixing bowl until light. Add the brown sugar gradually, beating until fluffy. Add the flour and mix well. Stir in the pecans. Set aside 1 cup of the mixture. Press the remaining mixture over the bottom of a greased 9x13-inch baking pan. Bake at 350 degrees for 14 to15 minutes or until light brown.

Beat the cream cheese at medium speed in a mixing bowl until smooth. Add the sugar gradually, beating until light and fluffy. Beat in the eggs 1 at a time. Stir in the lemon juice and vanilla. Pour over the hot crust. Sprinkle the reserved crumb mixture evenly over the batter. Bake at 350 degrees for 25 minutes or until nearly set; cheesecake will firm when chilled. Sprinkle the candy over the hot cheesecake. Cool on a wire rack. Chill, covered, for 8 hours. Cut into bars to serve.

Makes three dozen

Magical Toffee

Arrange 40 saltine crackers on a foil-lined 11x17-inch baking pan. Bring 1 cup butter or margarine and 1 cup packed brown sugar to a boil in a saucepan and boil for 3 minutes. Pour over the crackers. Bake at 400 degrees for 6 minutes. Sprinkle with 12 ounces chocolate chips and let stand until softened. Spread over the top and sprinkle with $1/2$ cup nuts. Place in the freezer to cool. Break into pieces and store in an airtight container.

Macadamia Nut Bars

Macadamias and coconut make this easy bar cookie recipe extra special.

$\frac{1}{2}$ cup (1 stick) butter, softened
$\frac{1}{4}$ cup sugar
1 cup flour
2 eggs, lightly beaten
$1\frac{1}{2}$ cups packed brown sugar
$1\frac{1}{2}$ teaspoons vanilla extract
2 tablespoons flour
$\frac{1}{2}$ teaspoon baking powder
$\frac{1}{2}$ cup flaked coconut
1 to $1\frac{1}{2}$ cups halved macadamias

Cream the butter and sugar in a small mixing bowl until light and fluffy. Add 1 cup flour and mix well. Press over the bottom of a 9-inch square baking pan. Bake at 350 degrees for 20 minutes.

Mix the eggs, brown sugar, vanilla, 2 tablespoons flour, baking powder, coconut and macadamias in a medium bowl. Pour over the hot crust. Bake at 350 degrees for 20 minutes. Cool in the pan on a wire rack. Cut into bars.

Makes twenty bars

IN 2000, THE JUNIOR LEAGUE OF BOCA RATON REPRINTED A SECOND EDITION OF *Savor the Moment* AFTER RAPIDLY SELLING THROUGH THE COOKBOOK'S VERY SUCCESSFUL FIRST PRINTING. IN ADDITION, UNDER THE DIRECTION OF JUNIOR LEAGUE PRESIDENT SUSAN DIENER, MEMBERS KICKED OFF A CAPITAL CAMPAIGN TO ACQUIRE A NEW HEADQUARTERS FOR THEIR OFFICES AS WELL AS SPACE TO SERVE AS A COMMUNITY VOLUNTEER RESOURCE AND DEVELOPMENT CENTER.

Deep-Dish Caramel Apple Pie

Keep this away from your denture-wearing Grandma!

Oil Pastry

2¹/₂ cups flour
¹/₄ cup sugar
1 teaspoon salt
¹/₂ cup (1 stick) butter or
    margarine
¹/₄ cup vegetable oil
¹/₄ cup water
1 egg

Apple Filling

6 medium apples, peeled, sliced
1 cup sugar
¹/₃ cup flour
2 teaspoons fresh lemon juice
2 teaspoons grated lemon zest
1¹/₂ teaspoons cinnamon
8 ounces (about 28) caramels,
    unwrapped
¹/₂ cup half-and-half or
    evaporated milk
8 ounces cream cheese, softened
¹/₃ cup sugar
1 egg
¹/₃ cup chopped walnuts

For the pastry, combine the flour, sugar and salt in a large bowl. Cut in the butter until the mixture is crumbly. Combine the oil, water and egg in a small bowl and beat until smooth and creamy. Add to the flour mixture and mix to form a smooth dough. Press over the bottom and up the side of a 10-inch pie pan or 10-inch springform pan.

For the filling, combine the apples, 1 cup sugar, flour, lemon juice, zest and cinnamon in a large bowl. Toss lightly to coat the apples. Spoon into the prepared pie pan.

Combine the caramels and half-and-half in a medium saucepan. Stir over low heat until melted and smooth. Drizzle over the apple mixture.

Combine the cream cheese, ¹/₃ cup sugar and egg in a medium saucepan. Melt over low heat, stirring until smooth. Spoon over the apple mixture. Sprinkle with the walnuts.

Bake at 375 degrees for 35 to 40 minutes or until golden brown. Cool on a wire rack. Serve at room temperature. Store leftovers in the refrigerator.

Serves eight

Freezing Pie Pastry

Shape pie dough into a disk and wrap in plastic wrap and foil. It can also be rolled and fitted into a pie pan or tart pan and wrapped in plastic wrap. To thaw, leave wrapped and let stand at room temperature for 2 hours or longer.

Food Processor Pastry

Combine 3 cups flour, ¹/₂ teaspoon salt and 1 cup plus 2 tablespoons shortening in a food processor container and pulse until the mixture resembles coarse crumbs. Add about 6 tablespoons ice water 1 tablespoon at a time and mixing until the mixture holds together. Shape into 2 balls. The recipe will make 2 pastry crusts. Use in your favorite recipes. For filled crusts, fit the pastry into a pie plate and prick bottom and side with a fork. Bake at 475 degrees for 8 to 10 minutes or until light brown.

Cut It Out

Use your favorite cookie cutter to add seasonal fun shapes as garnishes for your desserts. If you don't have extra pie pastry, commercial refrigerated pastry can be used. Brush the cutouts with beaten egg and bake according to directions.

Raspberry Cream Pie

A luscious berry pie topped with a buttery pecan praline garnish.

1 cup sugar
$1/3$ cup flour
2 large eggs, lightly beaten
$1^1/3$ cups sour cream
1 teaspoon vanilla extract
3 cups fresh raspberries or frozen raspberries, thawed
1 unbaked (9-inch) pie shell
$1/3$ cup flour
$1/3$ cup packed brown sugar
$1/3$ cup chopped pecans
3 tablespoons butter, softened

Garnish
whipped cream
fresh raspberries

Combine 1 cup sugar, $1/3$ cup flour, eggs, sour cream and vanilla in a large bowl and mix well. Fold in the raspberries gradually. Spoon into the pie shell. Bake at 400 degrees for 30 to 35 minutes or until the center is set.

Mix $1/3$ cup flour, brown sugar, pecans and butter in a small bowl. Sprinkle over the hot pie. Bake for 10 minutes longer or until golden brown. Cool on a wire rack. Garnish with whipped cream and fresh raspberries.

Serves six

Luscious Lime Tart with Glazed Berries

Luscious? Oh my, yes, and it looks as great as it tastes!

Lime Crust
1$\frac{1}{4}$ cups unbleached flour
2 tablespoons sugar
$\frac{1}{2}$ teaspoon grated lime zest
$\frac{1}{4}$ teaspoon salt
$\frac{1}{2}$ cup (1 stick) unsalted butter,
    chilled, cut into pieces
1 large egg yolk
1 tablespoon cold water

Lime Filling
1$\frac{1}{4}$ cups plus 2 tablespoons
    sugar
1 cup heavy cream
$\frac{1}{2}$ cup dry white wine
3 large eggs
2 large egg yolks
1 tablespoon grated lime zest
$\frac{3}{4}$ cup fresh lime juice
1 tablespoon cornstarch
1 large egg
Glazed Berries (at right)

Garnish
fresh mint leaves

For the crust, combine the flour, sugar, zest and salt in a large bowl. Cut in the chilled butter until the mixture has the texture of coarse crumbs. Beat the egg yolk with the cold water in a small bowl. Add to the flour mixture and stir with a fork just until the mixture forms a dough. Shape into a ball and flatten into a disk. Wrap in plastic wrap and chill for 30 minutes or until firm.

Roll the dough to a 13-inch circle on a lightly floured surface. Fit into an 11-inch tart pan with a removable bottom, pressing over the bottom and side of the pan; trim the edge. Freeze for 1 hour or until very firm.

Line the frozen crust with foil. Fill with dried beans or pie weights. Bake at 400 degrees for 12 minutes or until the edge is set. Remove the beans and foil. Bake at 400 degrees for 14 minutes longer or until golden brown. Cool on a wire rack.

For the filling, combine the sugar, cream and wine in a medium heavy saucepan. Whisk in the 3 eggs, egg yolks and zest. Whisk the lime juice gradually into the cornstarch in a small bowl. Add to the saucepan. Bring to a boil over medium-high heat, stirring constantly. Cook for 1 minute, stirring constantly. Pour into a medium bowl and cool to room temperature.

Beat 1 egg into the cooled filling. Pour into the baked crust. Bake at 350 degrees for 40 minutes or until the filling is set and beginning to bubble around the edges. Cool on a wire rack. Chill for 6 to 24 hours. Top with the Glazed Berries and garnish with mint leaves.

Note: The prepared crust can be covered and frozen for up to 3 days before baking.

Serves eight

Glazed Berries

Combine 2 tablespoons fruit-flavored liqueur, such as crème de cassis, framboise or Grand Marnier, with 2 tablespoons sugar and $\frac{1}{2}$ teaspoon grated lime zest in a small saucepan. Bring to a boil over medium-high heat, stirring constantly. Boil for 1 minute or until syrupy. Cool slightly. Pour over 2 cups assorted fresh berries and toss gently to coat well.

Tarte Tatin with Oatmeal Crust

This classic French dessert is an unbelievably scrumptious delight!

Oatmeal Crust
$1/3$ cup rolled oats
2 tablespoons sugar
$1^1/4$ cups unbleached flour
$1/8$ teaspoon salt
$1/2$ cup (1 stick) unsalted butter, chilled, cut into $1/2$-inch pieces
$1/4$ cup (about) ice water

Apple Filling
$2^1/2$ pounds medium Golden Delicious apples
6 tablespoons ($3/4$ stick) unsalted butter
$1/3$ cup sugar
$1/3$ cup packed light brown sugar
$1^3/4$ teaspoons grated lemon zest

For the crust, mix the oats and sugar in a food processor until the oats are finely ground. Mix in the flour and salt. Add the butter and pulse until the mixture has the texture of coarse crumbs. Mix in the ice water by tablespoons until a dough forms. Mold the dough into a ball and flatten into a disk. Wrap in plastic wrap and chill for 1 hour.

For the filling, peel the apples and cut each into 6 wedges, discarding the cores. Melt the butter in a 10-inch cast-iron skillet over medium heat. Stir in the sugar and brown sugar gradually. Cook for 2 minutes or until the sugar is dissolved and the mixture begins to bubble, stirring constantly. Stir in the zest and remove from the heat.

Arrange the apple wedges on their sides in a tight circle around the edge of the skillet. Fit several apple wedges tightly in the center. Cut any remaining apple into $1/2$-inch pieces and scatter over the wedges, mounding slightly in the center. Cook over medium heat for 3 minutes. Cover the skillet and cook for 5 minutes. Uncover and cook for 10 minutes longer or until a syrup has formed but the apples are still firm. Remove from the heat.

Roll the dough to a 12-inch circle between sheets of floured waxed paper. Peel off the top sheet and invert the dough over the apples in the skillet. Remove the paper. Press the pastry down and inside the skillet around the apples. Bake at 425 degrees for 40 minutes or until the crust is golden brown. Loosen the crust from the side of the skillet with a small sharp knife. Let stand for 1 minute.

Place a large serving plate over the skillet. Hold the skillet and plate together tightly using oven mitts and invert the tart onto the plate. Rearrange any apples that may have become dislodged. Cool for 30 minutes. Serve lukewarm or at room temperature cut into wedges.

Note: The dough can be chilled for up to 2 days. Let stand at room temperature before rolling.

Serves eight

Chocolate Turtle Tart

Be sure to try this one! With a shortbread crust, caramel pecan filling, and semisweet chocolate topping, you'll think you just came from the candy store.

Shortbread Crust
1$\frac{1}{2}$ cups sifted flour
$\frac{1}{4}$ teaspoon salt
$\frac{1}{4}$ teaspoon baking powder
6 tablespoons ($\frac{3}{4}$ stick) unsalted
    butter, softened
3 tablespoons sugar
1 large egg
$\frac{1}{4}$ teaspoon vanilla extract

Honey Pecan Filling
$\frac{1}{2}$ cup (1 stick) unsalted butter,
    cut into tablespoons
2 tablespoons honey
2 tablespoons sugar
$\frac{1}{2}$ cup packed light brown sugar
1 cup pecan halves
2 tablespoons heavy cream

Chocolate Topping
$\frac{1}{2}$ cup heavy cream
1 tablespoon sugar
$\frac{2}{3}$ cup semisweet chocolate chips
1 ounce white chocolate, coarsely
    chopped

For the crust, sift the flour, salt and baking powder into a medium bowl. Cream the butter and sugar in a medium mixing bowl until light and fluffy. Add the egg and vanilla and beat at low speed until blended. Beat in the dry ingredients $\frac{1}{3}$ at a time and mix to form a dough. Press evenly over the bottom and up the side of a 9$\frac{1}{2}$-inch fluted tart pan with a removable bottom.

For the filling, combine the butter, honey, sugar and brown sugar in a small saucepan. Bring to a boil over medium-high heat, stirring to mix well. Boil for 3 minutes. Remove from the heat and stir in the pecans and cream. Pour into the prepared tart shell. Bake at 350 degrees for 30 minutes. Cool on a wire rack for 1 hour.

For the topping, combine the cream and sugar in a small saucepan. Bring to a boil over medium-high heat. Remove from the heat and whisk in the chocolate chips until smooth. Reserve $\frac{1}{3}$ cup of the mixture. Pour over the filling and spread evenly with a spatula. Chill the tart for 15 minutes or until the chocolate topping is set.

Melt the white chocolate in a sealable plastic bag in the microwave. Cut a small hole in the corner and drizzle over the tart. Drizzle with the reserved chocolate mixture.

Serves eight

Storing Chocolate

Chocolate should be tightly wrapped and stored in a 60- to 70-degree dry place. If chocolate is too warm, it develops pale gray streaks. If too damp, tiny gray sugar crystals form. It can, however, still be used. Chocolate and white chocolate should be stored no longer than nine months. Dark chocolate can be stored longer under the correct conditions.

Acknowledgments

The Junior League of Boca Raton, Inc. thanks our generous members and friends who helped sponsor *Savor the Moment.*

Exceptional Guests
Banfi Chianti Classico Riserva
Clos du Bois "Alexander Valley" Cabernet
    Sauvignon
Gallo of Sonoma "Laguna Ranch"
    Chardonnay
Mezza Corona Pinot Grigio
Mr. and Mrs. Scott R. Morrison, Jr.
Publix Super Markets, Inc.
Toppel Family Foundation
    (Patricia Toppel, Kimberlee Toppel,
    Brooke Toppel and
    Jennifer Sawyer)

Featured Guests
Aucamp, Dellenback & Whitney
Marta Batmasian
Mr. and Mrs. Edward L. Diener
Mr. and Mrs. Louis B. Green
Peggy Henry
Ben S. Kennedy, Jr. P.A.
Dr. and Mrs. Michael Krebsbach
Mr. and Mrs. Richard C. Rochon
Mr. and Mrs. Henry Talerico III
Eleanor Zaccagnini

Celebrated Guests
Mr. and Mrs. Steven L. Abrams
Pam and Mark Begelman
Mr. and Mrs. James. E. Chaney
Mr. and Mrs. David Feder
Barbara Fox
Mr. and Mrs. Bernard Godin
Mr. and Mrs. John U. Harrold
Mr. and Mrs. Keith Holcomb
Mr. and Mrs. Douglas Ingalls
Mr. and Mrs. Eddie Kinsel
Mr. and Mrs. Paul M. Lawless
Mr. and Mrs. Christopher Malfitano
Mr. and Mrs. Richard H. Malone
Mr. and Mrs. John T. Mulhall III
Mr. and Mrs. Ron Qualk
Mr. and Mrs. Steven Sarka
Mr. and Mrs. Richard Thompson
Mr. and Mrs. Peter Vegso

Treasured Guests
Mr. and Mrs. Eugene Baur
Mr. and Mrs. Richard Critchfield
Mr. and Mrs. Frank J. Csar
Mr. and Mrs. Richard Damron Jr.
Mr. and Mrs. David B. Dickenson
Mr. and Mrs. D. Douglas Hill
Mr. and Mrs. Donald C. Hilsmier
Mr. and Mrs. Thomas P. Husak
Marsha L. Love
Mr. and Mrs. Charles Putman
Mr. and Mrs. Robert Rubin
Mr. and Mrs. Joseph Saxton
Mr. and Mrs. Edward W. Toomey

Preferred Guests
Mr. and Mrs. Thomas E. Buser
Mr. and Mrs. Thomas DeVita
Mr. and Mrs. Robert Dockerty
Mr. and Mrs. James A. Moseley
Robin C. Muir
Petal's Restaurant
Mr. and Mrs. Ronald Qualk
Mr. and Mrs. Charles Rutherford
Mr. and Mrs. Randall R. Weller

Outstanding Guests
Dr. and Mrs. Steven R. Alman
Dr. and Mrs. James R. Barron
Michele C. Broadfoot
Mr. and Mrs. Colin W. Brown
Mr. and Mrs. Timothy J. Bull
Susan L. Cavalear
Dr. and Mrs. James R. Cook
Mr. and Mrs. Mario Crespo
Mr. and Mrs. Scott Disher
Mr. and Mrs. Craig Edwards
Mr. and Mrs. Craig Evans
Mr. and Mrs. Scott Hedge
Renee A. Holmes
Diane S. Hopkins
James A. Krumholtz, D.D.S., P.A..
Wendy T. Kulberg
Mr. and Mrs. Lawrence L. Lavalle
Mr. and Mrs. Michael Lawrence
Janie Lott
Jane A. Lyons

Mr. and Mrs. Randy B. Nobles
Mr. and Mrs. John L. Page
Dr. Sandra Katz Porterfield
Mr. and Mrs. Densel L. Raines
Mr. and Mrs. Kenneth H. Robertson
Mr. and Mrs. Stephen J. Ruzika
Mr. and Mrs. Stephen F. Snyder
Mr. and Mrs. Thomas Ternus

Notable Guests
Paula E. Cochran
Mr. and Mrs. Gary S. Dunay
Jane Hoffstetter
Mr. and Mrs. Andrew L. Kirsch
Mary O. Mowry
Marian Norton
Mr. and Mrs. Karl E. Preusse
Mr. and Mrs. Gregory C. Ryder
Janice T. Scott
Dr. Michele Weizer Simon
Mr. and Mrs. Robert L. Walker
Mr. and Mrs. Christopher Warren
Mr. and Mrs. Allen W. Whittemore
Susan Whelchel

Highly Regarded Past President Guests
Debbie Abrams
Jeanne Baur
Christine Critchfield
Mary Csar
Pattie Damron
Katharine Dickenson
Barbara W. Hill
Judy Hilsmier
Mary C. Lavalle
Marsha L. Love
Jayne Malfitano
Ellen D. Malone
Joan Moseley
Lisa N. Mulhall
Carole Putman
Michelle Rubin
Susan Saxton
Barbara Thompson
Catherine C. Toomey

Cookbook Committee

Original Committee

Steering Committee
Cookbook Chairperson: Cynthia Krebsbach
Cookbook Assistant Chairperson: Wanda Harrold
Marketing Chairperson: Kelly Husak
Assistant Marketing Chairperson: Victoria Taylor
Recipe Chairperson: Julie Talerico
Sales Chairperson: Lisa Mulhall
Finance Chairperson: Marti Kinsel
Assistant Finance Chairperson: Michele Ferrara

Chapter Chairs

Sheila Aucamp	Martha Lawrence
Laura Cohen-Bull	Laurie Mattioli
Joyce DeVita	Dotty McGowan
Cindy Dunay	Diane Nestor
Mary Lou Eastham	Pamela Pierce
Julia Finnigan	Suzanne Puchaty
Joni Goldberg	Cathie Smaga
Adrienne Haag	Brenda Sulmonetti
Katy Hayes	Kimball Tenser
Katrina Holcomb	Alison Trout
Sandy Kipp	Liz Zucker
Carol Lawley	

Photography Coordinator
Lynn Holcomb

Table and Set Designers

Stacy Bruder	Lynn Holcomb
Patsy Burke	Christine Jarjura
Cindy Crespo	Mary Meloy
Linda Dragin	Brooke Qualk
Mary Lou Eastham	Kay Sarka
Sylvie Godin	Kathleen Smith
Adrienne Haag	Cristina Vazquez
Rita Haskins	Dale Workman
Katy Hayes	

Marketing
Kathleen Altizer
Tina Brennan
Stacy Bruder
Kristin Butcher Calder
Amy Coxhead
Anne-Randolph Davis
Amy Elofson
Sarah Flynn
Dana Goldberg
Chris Heathcott
Lynn Holcomb
Emily Kingston-Smith
Christine Kraft
Kathleen Levinson
Christine Najac
Diane Nestor
Donna Seffer
Kimball Tenser
Tricia Ternus
Julia Trevarthen
Gail Weller

Legal Advisor
Pam Wirt

Finance and Operations
Suzanne Federico
Kristin Foret
Adrienne Haag
Sandra Kipp
Sharon McGuire
Lisa Panik
Michele Weizer-Simon

Sustainer Liaisons
Pattie Damron
Jane DeBoe
Susan Saxton
Liz Zucker

Sales
Rhonda Brent
Marina Chaney
Jill Conrad
Cindy Crespo
Susan Diener
Cindy Dunay
Karen Edwards
Ellen Elam
Kathy Ferguson
Diane Fox
Julie Halvorsen
Katrina Holcomb
Teri Kennedy
Lynn Lawless
Marnie Lezark
Sandra Maier
Rebecca Marciniak
Jean McGhee
Susan Mersch
Dina Misemer
Hetty Nerod
Laurel Salsberry
Debbie Stine
Christina Stutman
Alison Trout

CD-Rom
Karen Edwards
Carolyn Miller
Kim Wheeler
Adrienne Haag

CD-Rom Photographer
Darcy Plimpton-Sims

Advisors
Laurie Applewhite
Sheila Aucamp
Linda Davidson

Non-Committee Active and Sustaining Junior League Members who loaned treasures and talents:
Debbie Abrams
Carol Bedotto
Pam Begelman
The Binnie Family
Michele Broadfoot
Cynthia Brown
Colette Clark
Linda Deery
Robin Deyo
Katharine Dickenson
Linda Effinger
Renee Feder
Cristy Fimiani
Jen Gulden
Shelly Hedge
Cibi Hoffman
Betsy Hvide
Nancy Ingalls
Barbara Kac
Kris Killip
Patty Kirsch
Mary Lavalle
Kathleen Levinson
Janie Lott
Brenda Lusher
Ellen Malone
Emily McMullin
Camille Mohaupt
Christine Najac
Janet Nodine
Barbara O'Connell
Robin Philpit
Sharon Raines
Michelle Rubin
Susan Saxton
Jackie Slatkow
Patricia Ternus
Angela Wagenti
Susan Whelchel

Post Publication Committee

Cookbook Committee
Cookbook Chairperson: Wanda Harrold
Marketing Chairperson: Victoria Taylor
Sales Chairperson: Karen Edwards
Assistant Sales Chairperson: DeeDee Borden
Finance Chairperson: Michele Ferrara
Assistant Finance Chairperson: Michele Weizer-Simon

Kathleen Altizer
Dina Barganier
Dianne Black
Tina Brennan
Jennifer Carretta
Laura Cohen-Bull
Anne-Randolph Davis
Robin Deyo
Kathy Ferguson

Rhoni Harding
Sarah Hole
Emily McMullin
Jill Nickell
Megan O'Connell
Anna Olsen
Heather Preusse
Jenni Travasos

Sustainer Liaisons
Kelly Husak
Lynn Lawless
Julie Talerico

Advisor
Janet Lano

Recipe Contributors and Testers

More than two years prior to the publication of *Savor the Moment,* The Junior League of Boca Raton cookbook committee put the word out. Send us your family's, your best friend's, your favorite chef's and your very own special recipes. The response was overwhelming! We received more than 3,250 time-honored treasures from the great cooks listed below. In addition, so many of these women spent countless hours in their kitchens testing and retesting our recipes. Thank you all for your help in making it possible to *Savor the Moment!*

Debbie Abrams	Kecia Bosworth	Anne Destout	Kristin Foret	Cibi Hoffman
Kathryn Adkins	Kimberly Bottomley	Joyce DeVita	Kay Forrest	Katrina Holcomb
Roberto Adurie	Tina Brennan	Patricia Dias	Patty Forrestel	Lynn Holcomb
Brenda Alber	Kim Brewer	Katharine Dickenson	Cricket French-Wright	Renee Holmes
Diana Alesi	Janet Bridges	Susan Diener	Juliette Fuller	Jay Holsinger
Eileen Alford	Michele Broadfoot	Pamela Disher	Kimberly Galeota	David Holtquist
Eunice Allen	Cynthia Brown	Caron Dockerty	Jennifer Gardner	Diane Hopkins
Lisa Allen	Kelley Brown	Jennifer Doerr	Joan Genest	Leslie Hoy
Denise Alman	Becky Brubaker	Linda Dolan	Meg Gerdes	Blair Hull
Kathleen Altizer	Ellen Bruno	Cathy Donnellan	Bette Ghysels	Kelly Husak
Debbie Anderson	Sharon Budd	Ellen Donoho	Jeanne Gifford	Susan Hutchens
Mert Anderson	Carolyn Burie	Nancy Doyal	Sann Godin	Patty Iacobelli
Susan Anderson	Julie Buser	Sandra Doyle	Sylvie Godin	Nancy Ingalls
Laurie Applewhite	Kristin Butcher Calder	Mary Doyle-Kimball	Dana Goldberg	Polly Jackson
Elena Armburst	Anne Cairncross	Sandra Dreker	Joni Goldberg	Bobbie Jameson
Carolyn Arnold	Vickie Capitena	Cindy Dunay	Barb Goodman	Christine Jarjura
A. J. Aucamp	Madelyn Caple	Janine Duval	Beth Goodman	Susan Jasinski
Jody Aucamp	Meg Carey	Lindsay Duval	Cynthia Goodman	Pamela Jaworski
Sheila Aucamp	Mary Carlson	Mary Lou Eastham	Samantha Goodman	Wendy Johnson
Tara Auclair	Sherry Carusillo	Linda Eckelson	Joanne Gordon	Angela Jones
Karina Bahr	Susan Casserly	Karen Edwards	Cheryl Gorman	Barbara Jones
Lois Baker	Marina Chaney	Linda Effinger	Beth Grossman	Miryana Juvan
Karen Bandy	Cheryl Cleary	Lisa Egan	Elise Guidos	Christina Karas
Emily Baratta	Patricia Clenzi	Kelli Eich	Jennifer Gulden	Debora Kellogg
Allyn Barghini	Polly Cochran	Ellen Elam	Linda Gunn	Julie Kendig-Schrader
Lisa Bariso	Laura Cohen-Bull	Denise Elia	Adrienne Haag	Lisa Kennedy
Anne Barron	Jill Conrad	Amy Elofson	Gayl Hackett	Sally Kennedy
Katie Bartlett	Tami Constantine	Anna Embree	Lesley Hackett	Teri Kennedy
Peggy Bartzokis	Kay Cook	Nancy Engh	Julie Halvorsen	Ingrid Kennemer
Jeanne Baur	Shani Cook	Chantell Euteneuer	Virginia Harrold	Kimberly Kenney
Terry Bayt	Tammie Cook	Robin Evans	Wanda Harrold	Janis Keyser
Lorraie Becker	Amy Coxhead	Binky Fash	Lindy Harvey	Lisa Kiefer
Linda Bell	Mary Csar	Renee Feder	Bonnie Haschke	Kris Killip
Stephanie Berens	Jeanne Cummins	Suzanne Federico	Kristen Hay	Beth King
Chrissy Biagiotti	Carolyn Cunningham	Johanna Felberbaum	Katy Hayes	Emily Kingston-Smith
Mary Ann Billings	Barbara Dale	Kathy Ferguson	Lisa Hays	Marti Kinsel
Joanne Bingo	Pattie Damron	Michele Ferrara	Chris Heathcott	Barbara Kipp
Mary Birnbaum	Laurie Dankowski	Cristy Fimiani	Shelly-Marie Hedge	Sandra Kipp
Betsy Bleich	Linda Davidson	Rosanne Fimini	Anne Henderson	Patty Kirsch
Debbie Blum	Jane DeBoe	Janann Fine	Cathy Heutmaker	Ellen Knudsen
Vanessa Boltz	Linda Deery	Julie Finnigan	Candy Heydt	Jacqueline Kozarsky
Gail Bonani	Cherié Dees	Michele Fisher	Barbara Hill	Christine Kraft
DeeDee Borden	Patricia DeLay	Elizabeth Fletcher	Judith Hilsmier	Cindy Krebsbach
Jill Borsky	Maryann DeShields	Sarah Flynn	Bob Hofacker	Elizabeth Krebsbach

Monica Krebsbach
Marilyn Langholtz
Liska Langston
Janet Lano
Susan Lapham
Mary Lavalle
Lynn Lawless
Carol Lawley
Martha Lawrence
Diane Laws
Kathy Laws
Chris Leavitt
Susan Lebrun
Janice Lempereur
Thomas Leone
Lillian LePree
Martha Lezark
Tina Lindsley
Kathy Linus
Janet Little
Veronica Little
Elizabeth Locke
Beth Logullo
Paula Long
Janie Lott
Marsha Love
Raye Lubin
Ricki Luciani
Paola Luptak
Brenda Lusher
Linda Lyman
Christine Lyons
Missy Lyons
Sandra Maier
Daphne Maingot
Ellen Malone
Caroline Mancini
Juliet Mandel
Rebecca Marciniak
Janelle Mariani
Rani Mathura
Katie Matthews
Laurie Mattioli
Jule Mattson
Sue McDonald
Jean McGhee
Jennifer McGlinn
Dotty McGowan
Sharon McGuire
Megan McKinney
Shannon McKnight

Jocelyn McNulty
Carol McPhee
Carol Mears
Frank Melillo
Louise Melillo
Mary Meloy
Astra Merck
Anne Merrell
Susan Mersch
Heidi Michitsch
Marian Michitsch
Carolyn Miller
Jane Miller
Tracy Mischler
Camille Mohaupt
Kimberly Monroy
Jeanne Monte
Judy Moore
Maria Moraitis
Anna Morgan
Lisa Morgan
Norma Morrison
Scott Morrison
Ellen Mouw
Mary Mowry
Nicole Mugavero
Lisa Mulhall
Kathy Murdoch
Barbara Murphy
Pauline Murphy
Laura Myers
Eileen Nagy
Christine Najac
Sara Nakashian
Cynthia Neeves
Hetty Nerod
Diane Nestor
Jill Nickell
Martha Nicoli
Allene Niemiec
Mary Jo Nobles
Janet Nodine
Paula Nylen
Megan O'Connell
M. E. O'Connor
Kristen Oliver
Cinnamin O'Shell
Janet Page
Sharon Paggi
Elizabeth Pankey-Warren
Donna Patrick

Peggy Patterson
Donna Pelstring
Robin Philpit
Pamela Pierce
Darcy Plimpton-Sims
Kathy Pordon
Sue Posey
Barbara Presley
Heather Preusse
Tracey Pribsco
Clare Puchaty
Suzanne Puchaty
Carole Putman
Janet Queally
Sharon Raines
Edie Marie Rattner
Jane Rea
James Reaux
Janie Reed
Joan Reiling
Anne Reynolds
Sharon Rinehimer
Lisa Ring
Marcella Roberts
Joan Robertson
Terri Robinson
Shelby Rogerson
Evelyn Ross
Tracey Rossi
Marylou Rouelle
Michelle Rubin
Jamie Russo
Peggy Ruzika
LeeAnn Ryan
Elisabeth Salvadore
Barbara Sanford
Donna Saxenmeyer
Susan Saxton
Cheryl Scardina
Ann Schauer
Leslie Schnake
Jody Schoen
Carmelita Schultz
Nancy Schwaderer
Donna Seffer
Judy Segesta
Sandy Sexton
Sherry Shaffer
Jill Sheahan
Jana Shiffert
Elyse Sims

Shelly Sipp
Liz Slaven
Cathie Smaga
Virginia Smith
Gayle Songy
Lynn Speedy
Sarah Spence
Deana Spurgeon
Maria Sterrenberg
Kimberlee Stiles
Debbie Stine
Laura Stoltz
Diana Strickland
Scarlette Studdard
Christina Stutman
Lou Ann Such
Brenda Sulmonetti
Julie Talerico
Carol Taylor
Heide Taylor
Jeanette Taylor
Kimball Tenser
Tricia Ternus
Teresa Testa
Lisagay Thomlinson
Barbara Thompson
Catherine Toomey
Karen Travis
Shelly Treadwell
Julia Trevarthen
Alison Trout
Tibisay Vasile
Anne Vegso
Quincie Velie
Nancy Wade
Angela Wagenti
Marc Walker
Cori Walker-Ginsburg
Mary Jo Walsh
Amy Warfield
Sandy Wargo
LuAnn Warner-Prokos
Lisa Weinert
Louise Weir
Shari Wekk
Shari Welch
Gail Weller
Barbara Wentel
Laura West
Linda Westphal
Kim Wheeler

Barbara Williams
Pamela Wirt
Karen Wollowick
Dale Workman
Evan Wright
Phyllis Wright
Brenda Zebarth-Solomon
Darrah Zehring
Elizabeth Ziegler
Lisa Ziels
Dawn Zook
Liz Zucker

Restaurant Contributors
Damiano's
 Tony Damiano,
 Owner/Chef
East City Grill
 Giani Respinto,
 Executive Chef/Partner
Red Bowl
 Kenny Guy,
 Executive Chef
Gigi's
 Bobby Lane,
 Executive Chef
Boca Raton Resort and Club
 James Reaux,
 Executive Chef
Darrel & Oliver's Café Maxx
 Oliver Saucy,
 Owner/Chef
32 East
 Wayne Alcaide,
 Executive Chef
Hillsboro Club
 Kurt Franklin,
 Executive Chef
Nick & Max's
 Nick Morforgan,
 Executive Chef
Dakotah 624
 Ron Radabaugh,
 Owner/Chef

275

Resources

Food and Spirits

American Spoon Foods
P. O. Box 566
Petoskey, MI 49770
Phone (800) 222-5886
Facsimile (800) 647-2512
   Jams, jellies, dried cranberries, dried
   cherries and other fruits

Best of Luck
Hunt Country Foods, Inc.
P.O. Box 876
Middleburg, VA 20118
Phone (540) 364-2622
Facsimile (540) 364-3112
   Horseshoe cookies and chocolates

Comeaux's Inc.
118 Canaan Drive
Lafayette, LA 70508
Phone (800) 323-2492
Facsimile (318) 989-8925
   Andouille sausages, crawfish and seafood

The Chocolate Truffle
1297 West Palmetto Park Road
Boca Raton, FL 33486
Phone (561) 395-8402
Facsimile (561) 395-8407
E-mail: choctruffle@msn.com
   Gourmet chocolates and fine gifts

Diamond Organics Catalog
Phone (888) 674-2642
Website: www.diamondorganics.com
   Fresh organic edible flowers, fruits and vegetables

Emil's Sausage
1384 South Federal Highway
Pompano Beach, FL 33062
Phone (954) 942-3944
   Andouille, German, Polish and Italian
   sausage and patés

Farmer's Market
505 South Cypress Road
Pompano Beach, FL 33060
Phone (954) 785-5075
Facsimile (954) 785-5075
   Edible flowers

Meadowsweets
RD#1 Box 371
Middleburgh, NY 12122
Phone (888) 827-6477
Facsimile (518) 827-8277
   Edible flowers

National Distributing Company, Inc.
441 SW 12th Avenue
Deerfield Beach, FL 33442
Phone (954) 421-9990
Facsimile (954) 425-7777
   Distributors of fine wines

New York Cake and Baking Distributor
56 West 22nd Street
New York, NY 10010
Phone (800) 942-2539
Facsimile (212) 675-7099
   Cake decorations, supplies and cocoa powder

Phillip's Exotic Mushrooms
909 East Baltimore Pike
Kennett Square, PA 19348
Phone (800) 243-8644
Facsimile (610) 388-3985
   Fresh and dried exotic mushrooms

Sweet Celebration
P.O. Box 39426
Edina, MN 55439
Phone (800) 328-6722
Facsimile (612) 943-1688
   Cake and candy supplies including candied
   violets and rose petals

Vermont Butter and Cheese Company
P.O. Box 95, Pitman Road
Websterville, VT 05678
Phone (800) 884-6287
Facsimile (802) 479-3674
   Specialty European style cheeses

Vermont Only
Mile Square Farm
P.O. Box 60873
Longmeadow, MA 01116
Phone (888) 868-6659
Facsimile (413) 567-0245
   Maple syrups of all grades and sizes

Walter's Caviar
P.O. Box 263
Boone Dock Road
Darien, GA 31305
Phone (912) 265-4269
Facsimile (912) 437-6560
   Caviar and Georgia shrimp

Williams-Sonoma
6000 Glades Road
Boca Raton, FL 33431
Phone (561) 620-0245
   Gourmet cooking supplies

For the Home

ABC Carpet & Home, the outlet
777 South Congress Avenue
Delray Beach, FL 33445
Phone (561) 279-7777
Facsimile (561) 279-8408
   Home furnishings

Atlantic Silver & China
7471 Northwest 57th Street
Tamarac, FL 33319
Phone (954) 720-4559
Facsimile (954) 720-4577
   Hard to find silver, crystal and china

Bloomingdale's
5840 Glades Road
Boca Raton, FL 33431
Phone (561) 394-2000
Facsimile (561) 394-2258
*A full line department store offering
merchandise like no other in the world*

Boca Bargoons
190 Northwest 20th Street
Boca Raton, FL 33431 and
910 U.S. Highway 1
Lake Park, FL 33403
Phone (561) 392-5700
Facsimile (561) 393-7321
Decorative fabric outlet

Boca Raton Historical Society
Fire Bay Gift Shop
71 North Federal Highway
Boca Raton, FL 33432
Phone (561) 395-6766
Facsimile (561) 395-4049
Gifts, home accessories, florals and more

Botanica of Boca
7050-40 West Palmetto Park Road
Boca Raton, FL 33433
Phone (561) 392-0053
Facsimile (561) 392-4052
Unique accessories for home and garden

Bow Baskets by M. Lew
Delray Beach, FL
Phone (561) 276-3779
Basket centerpieces

C'Trois & Co.
2831 North Federal Highway
Boca Raton, FL 33431
Phone (561) 347-1169
Facsimile (561) 347-1169
Antiques, gifts and home furnishings

Calico Corners
170 NW 20th Street
Boca Raton, FL 33431
Phone (561) 395-4244
Fabrics for your home

Carls Furniture
6650 North Federal Highway
Boca Raton, FL 33487
Phone (561) 994-8228
Facsimile (561) 226-1497
Everything you love about home

Crate and Barrel
192 Town Center
Boca Raton, FL 33431
Phone (561) 395-1060
Facsimile (561) 395-0630
Home accessories

Cynthia's Gifts
22191 Powerline Road
Boca Raton, FL 33433
Phone (561) 392-3222
Gifts and home accessories

Scalamandre
DCOTA
Suite A150
1855 Griffin Road
Dania, FL 33004
Phone (954) 929-4900
Facsimile (954) 923-3444
*Fabrics, wallcoverings, trimmings
and carpets*

The Elegant Trunk, Inc.
1051 East Atlantic Avenue
Delray Beach, FL 33483
Phone (561) 274-GIFT
Facsimile (561) 274-6822
Gifts and home accessories

Fabriko
2610 South Federal Highway
Fort Lauderdale, FL 33316
Phone (954) 462-8103
Facsimile (954) 462-8104
Draperies, cushions and upholstery

Farber Antiques, Inc.
187 Northeast 2nd Avenue
Delray Beach, FL 33444
Phone (561) 274-6418
Facsimile (561) 274-6419
Trading in the old and peculiar since 1957

Hermès
255 Worth Avenue
Palm Beach, FL 33480
Phone (561) 655-6655
Facsimile (561) 655-4778
*Leather goods, silks, fragrances, jewelry,
ready-to-wear and home furnishings*

Levengers
420 South Congress Avenue
Delray Beach, FL 33445
Phone (561) 276-4141
Facsimile (561) 544-6910
Tools for the serious reader

Mizner's Provisions
Boca Raton Resort & Club
501 East Camino Real
Boca Raton, FL 33432
Phone (561) 447-3000
Facsimile (561) 447-3183
*The finest in gourmet and specialty items;
Italian pottery*

Nu-turf of Pompano Beach, Inc.
2801 North Dixie Highway
Pompano Beach, FL 33064
Phone (954) 942-8409
Facsimile (954) 942-9156
Complete garden center

The Perfect Setting of Boca Raton
5050 Town Center Circle
Boca Raton, FL 33486
Phone (561) 338-8292
Facsimile (561) 368-1359
  *Fine china, crystal, silver, bridal registry
  and corporate gifts*

Pier One Imports
2975 South Federal Highway
Delray Beach, FL 33483
Phone (561) 265-2978
Facsimile (561) 278-2795
  *Furniture, candles, dinnerware, decorative
  accessories and so much more*

Pierre Deux
330 Worth Avenue
Palm Beach, FL 33480
Phone (561) 655-6810
Facsimile (561) 832-4096
  *French country home furnishings, linens
  and accessories*

Polo Ralph Lauren
446 Boca Town Center
Boca Raton, FL 33431
Phone (561) 395-7656
Facsimile (561) 395-7922
  Mens, ladies and home collection

Pottery Barn
3101 PGA Boulevard
Suite N213
Palm Beach Gardens, FL 33410
Phone (561) 626-9700
Facsimile (561) 622-6498
  Home furnishings

Royce Industries
3100 Boca Raton Boulevard #101-105
Boca Raton, FL 33431
Phone (561) 750-9002
Facsimile (561) 750-9796
  Custom iron furnishings

Saks Fifth Avenue
5820 Glades Road
Boca Raton, FL 33431
Phone (561) 393-9100

Treasures & Antiques
640 East Ocean Avenue
Boynton Beach, FL 33435
Phone (561) 364-1272
  Buy, sell and trade

Vignettes
Rita Haskins
1401 Tamarind Way
Boca Raton, FL 33486
Phone (561) 392-3859
  Decorative designs and interiors

Vilda B. de Porro
211 Worth Avenue
Palm Beach, FL 33480
Phone (561) 655-3147
Facsimile (561) 833-9549
  European and Oriental art for the collector

Services

Aldrich Party Rental
2744 Hillsboro Road
West Palm Beach, FL 33405
Phone (561) 394-3233
Facsimile (561) 833-8954
  Party rental service

Boca by Design
1500 Northwest 1st Court
Boca Raton, FL 33431
Phone (561) 447-5444
Facsimile (561) 447-5445
  Floral designs and event planning

Butterfly Mystique of Miami
10755 Southwest 34th Street
Miami, FL 33165
Phone (305) 207-8448
E-mail: bflynmiami@aol.com
Website: www.butterflyinmiami.com
  *Butterfly farm, consulting and
  releasing of butterflies for all occasions*

Central Dynamics Corporation
1515 North Federal Highway
Boca Raton, FL 33432
Phone (561) 750-3173
Facsimile (561) 750-6795
Website: www.cendyn.com
  Customized CD-ROM production

Linda Dragin Interiors, Inc.
Linda Dragin – Designer
Cristina Vazquez – Designer
P.O. Box 3411
Boynton Beach, FL 33424
Phone (561) 738-0357
Facsimile (561) 738-7758
  Creating for you a look that lasts

Foreign Car Engineering
75 North Congress Avenue
Delray Beach, FL 33445
Phone (561) 276-0114
Facsimile (561) 274-9127
  *Certified engineers and foreign trained
  mechanics*

Jacalyn Slatkow & Associates
29 Northeast Fourth Avenue
Delray Beach, FL 33483
Phone (561) 278-0850
Facsimile (561) 278-2955
  *Public relations, media relations, marketing
  support and special events*

Photography

Child of Mine
Photography and Design
Darcy Plimpton-Sims
  Photography and design

Dan Forer, Inc.
6815 Southwest 81st Terrace
Miami, FL 33143
Phone (305) 667-3646
Facsimile (305) 667-4733
  Photography

Invitations

Janie's Pen and Paper
2249 East Maya Palm Drive
Boca Raton, FL 33432
Phone (561) 391-8638
   Fine paper and calligraphy

Post-A-Gram
P.O. Box 2130
Hamilton, MT 59840
Phone (800) 866-5214
Facsimile (406) 363-1880
   Invitations are…better in a bottle!

Resorts, Hotels and Clubs

Boca Raton Resort & Club
501 East Camino Real
Boca Raton, FL 33432
Phone (561) 447-3000
Facsimile (561) 447-3183
   The elegant place to play

Hillsboro Club
901 Hillsboro Mile (A1A)
Hillsboro Beach, FL 33062
Phone (954) 941-2220
Facsimile (954) 785-4425
   Available for catered parties and events

Groups and Organizations

Boca Raton Chamber of Commerce
1800 North Dixie Highway
Boca Raton, FL 33432-1892
Phone (561) 395-4433
Facsimile (561) 392-3780
Website: bocaratonchamber.com
E-mail: chamber@bocaratonchamber.com

Junior League of Boca Raton, Inc.
261 N.W. 13th Street
Boca Raton, FL 33432
Phone (561) 620-2553
Facsimile (561) 620-2554
Website: www.jlbr.org
E-mail: cookbook@jlbr.org

Other Sponsors

Aim Riverside Press
2300 West Copans Road
Pompano Beach, FL 33069-1230
Phone (954) 960-4912
Facsimile (954) 960-1657
   Printing and ad specialties

Allied Domecq Spirits USA, Inc.
5100 Town Center Circle, Suite 550
Boca Raton, FL 33486
Phone (561) 368-5010
Facsimile (561) 368-2559

David W. Roberts
Arvida Realty Services
555 South Federal Highway
Boca Raton, FL 33432
Phone (561) 368-6200
Facsimile (561) 368-7020
   *Presenting properties exclusively in Royal
   Palm Yacht & Country Club*

Arvida Realty Services
2301 Glades Road
Boca Raton, FL 33431
Phone (561) 994-8886
Facsimile (561) 997-9129
   For every real estate reason

*Aucamp, Dellenback & Whitney
Appraisers & Consultants*
4700 Northwest Boca Raton Boulevard
Suite 102
Boca Raton, FL 33431
Phone (561) 998-9326
   Appraisers and Consultants

Bacardi Martini USA, Inc.
2075 Biscayne Boulevard
Miami, FL 33137
Phone (305) 573-8600

Boca Raton Community Hospital
800 Meadows Road
Boca Raton, FL 33486
Phone (561) 395-7100
Facsimile (561) 362-5040
   One of the nation's top 100 hospitals

Boca Raton Magazine
6413 Congress Avenue
Suite 100
Boca Raton, FL 33487
Phone (561) 997-8683
Facsimile (561) 997-8909
   Florida at its best

Digital City South Florida
200 East Las Olas Boulevard
Fort Lauderdale, FL 33301
Phone (954) 459-2267
Facsimile (954) 459-2288
Website: http://southflorida.digitalcity.com
AOL keyword: South Florida
   *Digital City South Florida is your online guide
   to entertainment and everyday living*

Korbel Champagne Cellars
13250 River Road
Guerneville, CA 95448
Phone (707) 824-7000
Website: www.korbel.com
   *Website offers company history, wedding ideas
   and more*

National Distributing Company, Inc.
441 Southwest 12th Avenue
Deerfield Beach, FL 33442
Phone (954) 421-9990
Facsimile (954) 425-7777
   Distributors of fine wines

Northern Trust Bank of Florida
301 Yamato Road, #1111
Boca Raton, FL 33431
Phone (561) 998-9100
Facsimile (561) 998-0359
Website: www.ntrs.com
   Bank and trust company

Office Depot
2200 Old Germantown Road
Delray Beach, FL 33445
Phone (561) 438-4800
   Low prices every day

Premier Beverage Company
3700 Commerce Parkway
Miramar, FL 33025
Phone (954) 436-9200

Rutherford, Mulhall and Wargo, P.A.
Highwoods Square
4th Floor
2600 North Military Trail
Boca Raton, FL 33431-6348
Phone (800) 741-1600
Facsmile (561) 241-3815
    Attorneys at law

Sun-Sentinel
3333 South Congress Avenue
Delray Beach, FL 33445
Phone (561) 243-6600
Facsimile (561) 243-6547
    (Newspaper) Sun Sentinel—with your area's
    most complete food section every Thursday

Tyco International, Inc.
1 Town Center Road
P.O. Box 5035
Boca Raton, FL 33431-0835
Phone (561) 988-7200
Facsimile (561) 988-3704
    A diversified manufacturing and service
    company

Restaurants

32 East
32 East Atlantic Avenue
Delray Beach, FL 33444
Phone (561) 276-7868
Facsimile (561) 276-7894
    Contemporary American cuisine

Boca Raton Resort & Club
501 East Camino Real
Boca Raton, FL 33432
Phone (561) 447-3000
Facsimile (561) 447-3183
    The elegant place to play

Dakotah 624
270 East Atlantic Avenue
Delray Beach, FL 33444
Phone (561) 243-8177
Facsimile (561) 274-4849
    A new American Bistro

Darrel & Oliver's Café Maxx
2601 East Atlantic Boulevard
Pompano Beach, FL 33062
Phone (954) 782-0606
Facsimile (954) 782-0648
    Regional Floridian cuisine

East City Grill
505 Ft. Lauderdale Blvd.
Fort Lauderdale, FL 33304
Phone (954) 565-5569
Facsimile (954) 565-5582
    "Global American cuisine"—Seafood with an
    Asian, Caribbean and Pacific Rim influence

Gigi's Tavern, Oyster Bar and Café
346 Plaza Real
Boca Raton, FL 33432
Phone (561) 368-4488
Facsimile (561) 368-5118
    French Bistro

Acknowledgments to community members who loaned treasures and talents

Debbie Anderson
Mr. and Mrs. Michael Baker
The Binnie Family
Brian Black
Diane Bliss
Calico Corners
City of Boca Raton
Ecco Restaurant
Linda Dragin
David Feder
Bobby Genovese
Michael Glennie
Alan Goldberg
Health Communications, Inc.
Sydney Heard
The Hillsboro Club
Susan Hodder
Colleen Keeley
The Krebsbach Family
La Tienda
Peg McCall
Rick McManus
Morikami Park, Gardens and Museum
Norma Morrison
Dr. and Mrs. Charles F. Mohaupt
Erica Orloff
Outback Steakhouse
Royal Palm Polo
Joan Reiling
Rick Rochon
Nancy Sergio
Todd Shallan
Chuck Smith
Kathleen Smith
South Inlet Park
Cindy Sprott and Back Bay Hair
Mr. and Mrs. Roger Staley
Sara Jane Sylvia
John Tolbert
Cristina Vazquez
Peter Vegso

Recipe Index

Non-Recipe Index

To order, send or fax to:

Junior League of Boca Raton, Inc.
261 N.W. 13th St.
Boca Raton, Florida 33432

Telephone
561/620-0765

Fax
561/620-0767

Toll free
1-866-574-9229

Website
www.jlbr.org

E-Mail
cookbook@jlbr.org

Please send me:

_____ copies of *Savor the Moment* @ $29.95 each $ _____

_____ copies of *Savor the Moment* CD ROM @14.95 each $ _____

_____ copies of *Savor the Moment* Combo
(Cookbook and CD ROM) @ $36.95 each $ _____

Shipping and Handling (*see below*) $ _____

Florida residents add 6% sales tax $ _____

Total $ _____

Shipping and Handling (*Continental United States*)
   $8.50 for first cookbook or combo ($2.00 for each additional)
   $6.00 for first CD ROM ($1.50 for each additional)

Name   Telephone

Address

City   State   Zip Code

Payment Method: ☐ VISA   ☐ MasterCard   ☐ American Express
       ☐ Check payable to Junior League of Boca Raton, Inc.

Account Number   Expiration Date

Cardholder Name

Signature

Photocopies accepted.

*Proceeds benefit the many projects of the
Junior League of Boca Raton, Inc.*